# NATO in Afghanistan

# NATO in Afghanistan

*Fighting Together, Fighting Alone*

David P. Auerswald and Stephen M. Saideman

PRINCETON UNIVERSITY PRESS

*Princeton and Oxford*

*Library of Congress Cataloging-in-Publication Data*

Auerswald, David P.
  NATO in Afghanistan : fighting together, fighting alone / David P. Auerswald, Stephen M. Saideman.
      pages cm
  Summary: "Modern warfare is almost always multilateral to one degree or another, requiring countries to cooperate as allies or coalition partners. Yet as the war in Afghanistan has made abundantly clear, multilateral cooperation
is neither straightforward nor guaranteed. Countries differ significantly in what they are willing to do and how and
where they are willing to do it. Some refuse to participate in dangerous or offensive missions. Others change tactical
objectives with each new commander. Some countries defer to their commanders while others hold them to strict
account. *NATO in Afghanistan* explores how government structures and party politics in NATO countries shape
how battles are waged in the field. Drawing on more than 250 interviews with senior officials from around the world,
David Auerswald and Stephen Saideman find that domestic constraints in presidential and single-party parliamentary systems—in countries such as the United States and Britain respectively—differ from those in countries with
coalition governments, such as Germany and the Netherlands. As a result, different countries craft different guide-
lines for their forces overseas, most notably in the form of military caveats, the often-controversial limits placed on
deployed troops. Providing critical insights into the realities of alliance and coalition warfare, *NATO in Afghanistan*
also looks at non-NATO partners such as Australia, and assesses NATO's performance in the 2011 Libyan campaign
to show how these domestic political dynamics are by no means unique to Afghanistan" —Provided by publisher.
  Includes bibliographical references and index.
  ISBN 978-0-691-15938-6 (hardback)
  1. Afghan War, 2001– 2. North Atlantic Treaty Organization—Afghanistan. 3. International Security Assistance
Force (Afghanistan) I. Saideman, Stephen M. II. Title.
  DS371.412.A84 2012
  958.104'74—dc23      2013027793

British Library Cataloging-in-Publication Data is available

This book has been composed in Minion Pro and Franklin Gothic

Printed on acid-free paper. ∞

Printed in the United States of America

10 9 8 7 6 5 4 3 2 1

# Dedication

Dave dedicates this book to his partner in crime, Jenny, and Steve dedicates this book to his siblings, Ellen, Larry, and Susan, who have been tremendous yet underthanked allies over the years.

# Contents

# Illustrations

## Tables

## Figures

# Abbreviations

| | |
|---|---|
| AFRICOM | U.S. Africa Command |
| ANA | Afghan National Army |
| AOR | area of responsibility |
| AWACS | Airborne Warning and Control Systems planes |
| CDA | Christen-Democratisch Appèl (Christian Democrats, Netherlands) |
| CDF | chief of the Defence Force (Australia) |
| CDS | chief of defense staff |
| CDU | Christian Democratic Union (Germany) |
| CDV | Christen-Democratisch en Vlaams (Christian Democrats and Flemish party, Belgium) |
| CEFCOM | Canada Expeditionary Forces Command |
| CENTCOM | U.S. Central Command |
| CF | Canadian forces |
| CJCS | chairman of the Joint Chiefs of Staff (United States) |
| CJOC | commander of Joint Operations Command (Australia) |
| CJSOR | Combined Joint Statement of Requirements (NATO) |
| COIN | counterinsurgency |
| COMISAF | commander of the International Security Assistance Force |
| CSU | Christian Social Union (Germany) |
| CU | Christian Union (Netherlands) |
| DCDS | deputy chief of defense staff |
| DFID | Department for International Development (United Kingdom) |
| DND | Department of National Defence (Canada) |
| DPP | Danish People's Party |
| DSACEUR | deputy supreme allied commander for Europe |
| D66 | Democrats-66 (Netherlands) |
| FDP | Free Democratic Party (Germany) |
| FGC | force generation conference |
| ISAF | International Security Assistance Force |
| JDP | Justice and Development Party (Turkey) |

| JSOC | Joint Special Operations Command |
| KFOR | Kosovo force |
| MC | Military Committee of NATO |
| MOD | Ministry of Defense |
| MRTF | Mentoring and Reconstruction Task Force |
| NAC | North Atlantic Council |
| NATO | North Atlantic Treaty Organization |
| NTC | National Transitional Council (Libya) |
| OEF | Operation Enduring Freedom |
| OMLT | observer, mentor, liaison team |
| OpPlan | operations plan |
| OSD | Office of the Secretary of Defense (United States) |
| OUSDP | Office of the Under Secretary of Defense for Policy (United States) |
| PA | principal-agent |
| PJHQ | Permanent Joint Headquarters (United Kingdom) |
| PRT | provincial reconstruction team |
| PvdA | Partij van de Arbeid (Labor Party, Netherlands) |
| PVV | Partij voor de Vrijheid (Party for Freedom, Netherlands) |
| RC | regional command |
| ROE | rules of engagement |
| SACEUR | supreme allied commander for Europe |
| SAS | Special Air Service |
| SDSR | Strategic Defense and Security Review (United Kingdom) |
| SHAPE | Supreme Headquarters Allied Powers Europe |
| SLD | Sojusz Lewicy Demokratycznej (Democratic Left Alliance, Poland) |
| SOF | special operations forces |
| SOTG | Special Operations Task Group (Australia) |
| SPD | Sozialdemokratische Partei Deutschlands (Social Democratic Party, Germany) |
| SV | Sosialistisk Venstreparti (Socialist Left Party, Norway) |
| TCR | theater capabilities review |
| UNSC | United Nations Security Council |
| VTC | video teleconference |
| VVD | Volkspartij voor Vrijheid en Democratie (People's Party, Netherlands) |

# Acknowledgments

The initial, and perhaps unconscious, impetus for this book came out of the U.S. experience in the Balkans. Steve Saideman spent the 2001–2 academic year in the Pentagon's Joint Staff Directorate of Strategic Planning and Policy on the Bosnia desk when the North Atlantic Treaty Organization (NATO) was still engaged in the Bosnian stabilization mission. Dave Auerswald had previously worked on the U.S. Senate Foreign Relations Committee staff during NATO's intervention in Kosovo. These experiences gave us our first exposure to the challenges of NATO interventions, which by no means followed the textbook of how a NATO operation was supposed to work. Thus, our first acknowledgments are to the Council on Foreign Relations and the American Political Science Association for the fellowships that inspired this project.

Our second greatest debt goes to Mike Tierney. Mike's views helped shape our initial approach to NATO as a multilateral institution at the beginning of the project. Then, toward the end, Mike facilitated a book workshop at the College of William and Mary that was incredibly helpful in sharpening our arguments. Everyone there, from faculty to students, provided useful feedback, although Mike, Cullen Hendrix, Amy Oakes, Sue Petersen, and Maurits van der Veen went above and beyond on our behalf. They were very generous with their time, expertise, and insights.

We depended on a variety of funding sources to facilitate this project. Specifically, we are grateful to the Social Science and Humanities Research Council of Canada; the Canada Research Chairs program; the Canadian Department of National Defence's Security and Defence Forum; NATO's Public Diplomacy Division; and the Institute for National Strategic Studies and the National War College, both entities of the U.S. Department of Defense.

We are grateful to a group of very dedicated research assistants: Chris Chhim, Bronwen De Sena, Katarina Germani, Alexia Jablonski, Jenyfer Maisonneuve, Sarah-Myriam Martin-Brûlé, Mark Mattner, Harish Seshagirirao, Scott Shaw, Stephanie Soiffer, Ora Szekely, and Lauren Van Den Berg. All were very sharp, taking our vague instructions (we tend to be delegators rather than micromanagers) and running with them. We are also grateful to Mari Ikeda and Emilia Scogna-miglio for handling the paperwork for our grant spending in Montreal.

In the course of the project, we relied heavily on people in the countries we have been studying to recommend interview subjects. Officials at the Australian, British, Danish, Dutch, French, German, New Zealand, and Polish embassies were very helpful, especially Ambassador Wim Geertz and Commander Frits Stam of the Netherlands, Major General Andrzej Falkowski of Poland, Shaw James of New Zealand, Jakob Henningsen of Denmark, and Jamie Patten-Richens of Aus-tralia. Members of the Canadian Embassy in Berlin were also quite helpful. The U.S. embassies in Copenhagen (Chris McDonald and Tina Rasmussen), Lisbon, London, Paris, The Hague (especially Denny Meredith there), and Warsaw were terrific. James Snyder, Samantha Stockley, and Judith Windsor facilitated our interviews at NATO headquarters in Brussels, Brunssum, and Mons. Thanks go to Rebecca Shrimpton of the Asia-Pacific Centre of Excellence on Civil-Military Relations (now the Australia Civil-Military Centre). She proved to be a fixer extraordinaire who arranged nearly all of the interviews in Canberra and Sydney, provided her own insights along the way, and took care of driving on the "wrong" side of the road.

Many scholars and experts provided useful contacts and guidance. In Ger-many we were helped by David Bosold of the Deutsche Gesellschaft für Auswär-tige Politik e. V. (the German Council on Foreign Relations) and Markus Kaim of the Stiftung Wissenschaft und Politik (German Institute for International and Se-curity Affairs). Sten Rynning and Peter Viggo Jakobsen were most generous as we worked on the Danish case. We are grateful to Theo Brinkel, Martijn Kitzen, and Bas Rietjens of the Royal Dutch Military Academy for organizing interviews and providing their sound advice and views. Rem Korteweg of the Hague Center of Strategic Studies organized an incredibly insightful roundtable. Bastien Irondelle of Sciences Po was most helpful in Paris. Otto Trønnes provided keen insights, along with pieces of his own work, so that we could understand the Norwegian case. He connected us to Per Marius Frost-Nielsen, who helped us with Norway's participation in the Libyan mission. Ilmari Käihkö and Robert Egnell assisted us in understanding the Swedish case. James Yarker arranged a large number of interviews in England and knows a great pub near the Ministry of Defense.

In Canada, we relied heavily on people in two parts of the Department of Na-tional Defence (DND)—the Security and Defence Forum (SDF) and the Public Relations Office—as we were able to talk to nearly every Canadian who com-manded in Afghanistan or in the chain of command back in Ottawa (or both). We are especially grateful to Anne Therienn, Jamie Gibson, and Aaron Hywarren of the SDF, Susan Christopher and Andre Berdais of the Montreal Public Relations division of the DND, and Brian McCarthy of Canada's CEFCOM. We are also indebted to the people who helped facilitate Saideman's trip to Afghanistan in 2007 as part of a NATO/Canada junket: Megan Minnion, Brenna Morrell, and Albert Wong. Similarly, we are grateful to the DND Public Relations office in Montreal, which arranged a trip to the fighter base in Bagotville, Quebec, in June 2011 that allowed us to meet Canadian pilots (and one British officer on exchange) who had flown in the missions over Libya.

We are very thankful to the scholars and practitioners who read drafts of our papers and chapters and gave us very useful criticism and suggestions. These generous people include Victor Assal, Doug Bland, Richard Boucher, Robert Brown, John Carey, Jonathan Caverley, Joseph J. Collins, David Haglund, Peter Viggo Jakobsen, Pat James, Markus Kaim, Christian Leuprecht, Patrice MacMahon, Bill Maley, Mark Mattner, Kathleen McInnis, Frederic Merand, Kim Nossal, Victoria Nuland, Roland Paris, Mikkel Vedby Rasmussen, Brian Rathbun, Stephane Roussel, Anne Sartori, Anthony Seaboyer, Hendrik Spruyt, James Stavridis, Paula Thornhill, David Tretler, Doug Van Belle, Stefanie Von Hlatky, Jon Western, Hugh White, and William Wood. We are especially grateful to the careful insights of Theo Farrell, Sarah Kreps, Philippe Lagassé, Matthew Shugart, and Patricia Weitsman.

We appreciate the comments we received during presentations of various pieces of our work at the Asia-Pacific Civil-Military Relations Centre of Excellence, Bridgewater State University, the Canadian Department of Foreign Affairs and International Trade, the Canadian Political Science Association meeting in Vancouver, the Centre for International Governance and Innovation, the College of William and Mary, the Department of National Defence's Security and Defence Forum, Grove City College, King's College (London), Laval University, Mount Holyoke College, the National Defense University's Afghanistan-Pakistan Hands Program, Northwestern University, Queens University (Kingston, Ontario), the Royal United Services Institute, Stiftung Wissenschaft und Politik, Trinity College Dublin, the University of New Brunswick's Gregg Centre, the University of Ottawa, the University of Southern California, the U.S. Army War College, and multiple meetings of the American Political Science Association and the International Studies Association.

Portions of this research have already appeared in print. We would like to thank the editors of *International Studies Quarterly* for publishing our article on caveats in Afghanistan; Patrice McMahon of the University of Nebraska–Lincoln and Jon Western of Mount Holyoke College for including us in their edited volume *The International Community and Statebuilding* (Routledge, 2012); and Theo Farrell of King's College for including us in his edited volume *Military Adaptation and the War in Afghanistan* (Stanford University Press, 2012).

The anonymous reviewers provided constructive criticism for which we are most appreciative. We are very grateful to Chuck Myers, our first editor at

Princeton University Press, who provided terrific guidance during the earlier stages of the publication process, and to our second editor, Eric Crahan, who shepherded the manuscript the rest of the way. Eric Henney was particularly helpful throughout the publication process, as were Natalie Baan, Brian Bendlin, and Jan Williams.

Last but not least, we owe a huge debt to our families for putting up with all of our travel, both because it was inconvenient to them and because we did not take them with us. Our wives and daughters have been most supportive, and for that we are incredibly indebted.

A final disclaimer is in order. The views expressed in this book are those of the authors and not of the National Defense University, the U.S. Department of Defense, or any other agency of the U.S. government, nor the Canadian Department of National Defence. All remaining errors are the responsibility of the authors, who will blame each other for any lapses.

# NATO in Afghanistan

# 1 NATO at War

## In Afghanistan and at Home?

*I would rather fight a coalition than be part of one.*
—Napoleon Bonaparte

*There is at least one thing worse than fighting with allies—and that is to fight without them.*
—Winston Churchill

In the spring of 2006 a riot took place in Meymana, a city in Faryab Province of northwestern Afghanistan, because of a misunderstanding as to what a nongovernmental organization was doing in the region. The Norwegian provincial reconstruction team (PRT) in the area came under attack and called for help from nearby NATO forces. This was the first time that NATO forces were really tested since they had begun to take responsibility for security in Afghanistan beyond Kabul. The test did not go well. The Norwegians were outgunned, and the International Security Assistance Force (ISAF) command could not send nearby forces to assist because of national caveats on those forces. Essentially, other ISAF forces (the Germans, to name the most significant contingent in this case) were prohibited from leaving their geographic areas of responsibility (AORs). The British, who at the time were moving into southern Helmand Province, eventually sent an emergency relief force to assist the Norwegians, but in the words of one senior U.S. general with direct knowledge, "it was a near thing."[1]

As this example makes clear, war is an inherently dangerous endeavor. At the extreme, war risks the potential survival of the nation. At the least, it translates into soldiers dying on the battlefield with the potential for civilian casualties as well. Domestically, war has the potential to ruin political careers, end the tenure of governments, and risk the political lives of state leaders.[2] The Dutch government fell in 2010 over whether to continue participating in the NATO effort in Afghanistan. A previous Dutch government had fallen in 2002 after the release of a report documenting Dutch failures in Srebrenica, Bosnia, in 1995. More

---

1 Interview with senior U.S. military officer, Brussels, July 2007.
2 See Bueno de Mesquita and Siverson 1995; Bueno de Mesquita et al. 2005; and Chiozza and Goemans 2004.

recently, NATO alliance governments have faced criticism for their treatment of Afghan detainees. Germany faced domestic and international approbation over the Kunduz bombing incident in September 2009 in which more than a hundred civilians were killed. Simply put, war is inherently risky from international and domestic perspectives.

War may be risky, but fighting as a coalition or as an alliance is harder still. Managing the risks of war is complicated when one's troops are under the command of officers from other countries. A book covering the North Atlantic Treaty Organization's (NATO's) effort in and over Kosovo was appropriately titled *Winning Ugly* (Daalder and O'Hanlon 2000). A similar book covering Afghanistan might be titled *Fighting Ugly* to reflect the coordination difficulties that confront the alliance in South Asia. While we cannot blame NATO's Afghanistan performance entirely on the difficulties of multilateral warfare, given the challenges posed by poppies, Pakistan, and President Hamid Karzai,[3] there is no doubt that the complexities of fighting together have hampered the effectiveness of the international effort.

Why is coalition warfare so hard? After all, countries often join military coalitions or an alliance effort because they share common interests. Shared interests, however, do not always equate to agreement as to the best ways to pursue those interests. Too often, individual countries engage in efforts that either distract from or undermine the overall coalition effort. The Americans and Italians disagreed over how to proceed in Somalia in 1993, and the French seemed to confound the Americans in Bosnia in 1998.[4] It has been repeatedly asserted that French officers may have undermined NATO's pursuit of war criminals in Bosnia, including Radovan Karadzic, by passing word of planned operations to the Serbs. Indeed, American officials were so confident of this and so upset that they publically accused France.[5] The French government did not deny that French officers passed on such tips to the Serbs, only that it was not the policy of the French government.[6]

These examples illustrate some of the difficulties facing any coalition operation. NATO operations in Afghanistan are no exception. Despite NATO being the most powerful, institutionalized, interoperable, practiced security institution in

---

3 See, for example, Anderson 2011; Bergen 2011; Blanchard 2009; Brewster 2011; Felbab-Brown 2009; Jones 2009; Qazi 2010; Rashid 2009; Rubin and Rashid 2008; and Rubin, Saikal, and Lindley-French 2009.
4 Alan Cowell, "Italy, in U.N. Rift, Threatens Recall of Somalia Troops," *New York Times*, July 16, 1993, http://www.nytimes.com/1993/07/16/world/italy-in-un-rift-threatens-recall-of-somalia-troops.html, accessed April 5, 2011.
5 Richard J. Newman, "Hunting War Criminals," *U.S. News and World Report*, June 28, 1998, http://www.usnews.com/usnews/news/articles/980706/archive_004280_3.htm, accessed January 7, 2011.
6 Sean M. Maloney, "Radovan Karadzic's Time on the Lam: What Took So Long," *National Post*, July 23, 2008, http://network.nationalpost.com/np/blogs/fullcomment/archive/2008/07/23/sean-m-maloney-on-radovan-karadzic-s-time-on-the-lam-what-took-so-long.aspx, accessed January 7, 2011. This was also the conventional wisdom within the Balkans Branch of the U.S. Joint Staff's Directorate of Strategic Planning and Policy, as observed by Saideman in 2001–2.

existence today and perhaps ever, NATO decisions are made by consensus norms. Reluctant NATO members can opt out of operations altogether, supply capabilities on a purely voluntary basis, and invoke national caveats that specify restrictions on how individual military contingents are used. The effects on NATO operations are profound. The combination of troop limitations, equipment shortages, and caveats in Afghanistan gave insurgents breathing room and forced the United States to nearly double the number of troops deployed to Afghanistan in 2009 (Lafraie 2009) and then surge even more in 2010. "Gen. John Craddock (head of NATO's military at the time) . . . says these caveats 'increase the risk to every service member deployed in Afghanistan and bring increased risk to mission success.' They also are 'a detriment to effective command and control, unity of effort and . . . command.'"[7]

Caveats have produced resentment within the alliance. Some countries are seen as withholding their full effort. The Germans, Spanish, and Turks are frequently criticized. Others believe themselves to be bearing a disproportionate burden. For example, U.S. and British forces have exhausted themselves by deployments in Iraq and Afghanistan and have suffered significant casualties from Afghanistan, as table 1.1 indicates. The Canadians, Danes, and Estonians have paid an even steeper price per capita than most other countries. Such disparities have generated persistent discussion of a two-tier NATO, differentiating "warrior states" from "ration-consumers" (Noetzel and Schreer 2009), leading some to fear for the potential demise of the alliance. These arguments put the burden-sharing debate of the 1980s, focused on defense spending, in sharp relief (Duffield 1995; Hartley and Sandler 1999; Murdoch and Sandler 1991; Olson and Zeckhauser 1966; Palmer 1990). More broadly, understanding operational restrictions and differing conceptions of the ISAF mission is important if we want to comprehend the limits and effects of international cooperation during conflicts (Barnett and Finnemore 2004; Hawkins 2006).

This book seeks to understand both the specific case of NATO in Afghanistan and the broader dynamics involved whenever countries seek to cooperate in combat. To do that, we first present a series of vignettes in this chapter to illustrate the central puzzles confronting multilateral organizations contemplating military interventions. Countries have a variety of means through which they can tailor their participation in multilateral military efforts, and we uncover which countries choose which mechanisms and why they do so in the following chapters. In the remainder of this chapter we introduce our approach to understanding why countries vary in what they do on the ground during multilateral conflicts. We

---

7 Arnaud de Borchave, "Commentary: NATO Caveats," UPI.Com, July 10, 2009, http://www.upi.com /Emerging_Threats/2009/07/10/Commentary-NATO-caveats/UPI-47311247244125/, accessed July 15, 2009.

**Table 1.1.** Casualties, Absolute and Relative, 2001–9

| Country[a] | Killed in Action[b] | Size of Contingent[c] | Population | KIA per Contingent | Rank, KIA/Pop |
|---|---|---|---|---|---|
| Australia | 11 | 1200 | 21,262,641 | 0.92% | 11 |
| Belgium | 1 | 510 | 10,839,905 | 0.20% | 21 |
| Bulgaria | 0 | 460 | 7,563,710 | 0.00% | 30 |
| Canada | 138 | 2830 | 33,487,208 | 4.88% | 3 |
| Croatia | 0 | 290 | 4,425,747 | 0.00% | 29 |
| Czech Republic | 3 | 340 | 10,506,813 | 0.88% | 17 |
| Denmark | 30 | 750 | 5,500,510 | 4.00% | 1 |
| Estonia | 7 | 150 | 1,340,127 | 4.67% | 2 |
| France | 36 | 3070 | 64,420,073 | 1.17% | 9 |
| Germany | 29 | 4245 | 82,329,758 | 0.68% | 14 |
| Greece | 0 | 125 | 11,305,118 | 0.00% | 28 |
| Hungary | 2 | 310 | 10,014,324 | 0.65% | 19 |
| Iceland | 0 | 8 | 317,630 | 0.00% | 27 |
| Italy | 20 | 2795 | 58,126,212 | 0.72% | 15 |
| Latvia | 3 | 165 | 2,248,374 | 1.82% | 7 |
| Lithuania | 1 | 250 | 3,329,039 | 0.40% | 16 |
| Luxembourg | 0 | 8 | 502,066 | 0.00% | 26 |
| Netherlands | 21 | 2160 | 16,715,999 | 0.97% | 8 |
| New Zealand | 0 | 220 | 4,213,418 | 0.00% | 25 |
| Norway | 9 | 600 | 4,660,539 | 1.50% | 6 |
| Poland | 16 | 2025 | 38,482,919 | 0.79% | 13 |
| Portugal | 2 | 105 | 10,637,713 | 1.90% | 20 |
| Romania | 11 | 990 | 22,215,421 | 1.11% | 12 |
| Slovakia | 0 | 240 | 5,424,925 | 0.00% | 24 |
| Slovenia | 0 | 80 | 2,046,976 | 0.00% | 23 |
| Spain | 22 | 1000 | 40,525,002 | 2.20% | 10 |
| Sweden | 2 | 430 | 9,059,651 | 0.47% | 18 |
| Turkey | 2 | 820 | 76,805,524 | 0.24% | 22 |
| United Kingdom | 245 | 9000 | 61,113,205 | 2.72% | 4 |
| United States | 947 | 31855 | 307,212,123 | 2.97% | 5 |
| Average | 52 | 2234 | 30,887,756 | 1.20% | |

*Note*: Entries in shaded rows indicate top five countries in terms of costs paid per contingent, per population.
[a] This includes all NATO countries plus three key non-NATO contributors—Australia, New Zealand, and Sweden.
[b] The figures here are through the end of 2009. To be clear, many countries have paid a very high price since then.
[c] Size of contingent comes from the December 2009 NATO placemat for ISAF, http://www.nato.int/isaf /docu/epub/pdf/placemat_archive/isaf_placemat_091001.pdf, accessed November 29, 2011. As we learned in our interviews at Supreme Headquarters Allied Powers Europe in February 2010, the numbers NATO reports are inexact at best. See chapter 2 for a discussion.

then consider several alternative accounts, demonstrating that none explains well NATO member behavior in Afghanistan and why a new approach is required. Finally, we preview the implications of this study, explain its scope, and conclude by outlining the rest of the book.

# The Challenges of National Control in Coalitional War

To demonstrate some of the distinct and recurring problems inherent in multilateral warfare, we present a series of examples that illustrate how countries have controlled their forces in multilateral operations. National control of military forces in multilateral combat is not a new problem, and it is not unique to NATO in Afghanistan. We group these tasks into four categories: limits on what troops do, oversight of deployed forces, incentives to encourage correct behavior, and selecting appropriate commanders.

## LIMITS ON DEPLOYED TROOPS

### *A Pop Star Prevents World War III with a Red Card*

One key to multilateral military success is knowing that various national contingents in an operation will do their part as ordered. Yet national contingents frequently, if episodically, opt out of multilateral missions. In NATO parlance, national commanders have a metaphorical red card that they can play when they feel they cannot obey an order from their multinational commander.[8] Red cards exist because each national contingent is still essentially beholden to its country, even in a multilateral effort. National commanders often prioritize their country's individual interests over those of the multilateral coalition of which they are a member. For instance, commanders can choose not to obey orders coming down the multinational chain of command if the local commander views the orders as being illegal, contrary to his or her country's national interests, or excessively reckless.

At the end of the Kosovo air campaign on June 12, 1999, a crisis developed over Russian control of Pristina International Airport in Kosovo. A Russian unit that had been part of the international effort in Bosnia moved to control the airport in an attempt to present NATO with a fait accompli. Whatever motivated the Russians, their actions upset NATO plans for setting up its stabilization effort. In the words of U.S. General Wesley Clark, the supreme allied commander for Europe (SACEUR), "The danger was that if the Russians got in first, they would

---

8 The "red card" analogy comes from soccer. To be clear, this is a term used widely among NATO countries and beyond.

claim their sector, and then we would have lost NATO control over the mission."[9] Clark ordered the lead British troops to block the runways at the airport and thus prevent the Russians from reinforcing their unit.

The commander of the leading British unit, James Blunt (now a famous pop singer), questioned the order as being far outside the expected mission.[10] British general Sir Mike Jackson backed up Blunt and told Clark, "I'm not going to start the Third World War for you."[11] Jackson played the red card, telling Clark, "Sir, I'm a three-star general; you can't give me orders like this. . . . I have my judgment" (Clark 2001: 394). Clark understood that "Jackson remained under his national command authority, even though he was serving under me" (Clark 2001: 398). Clark tried to go over Jackson's head to Charles Guthrie, the British chief of defense, to no avail.

This example suggests that contingents can opt out of particular operations in multilateral efforts. In most cases, the most senior member of a nation's contingent is the red card holder, empowered to veto orders from the multilateral chain of command.[12] Clark (2001) reports in his memoir that "red-carding" is a normal practice in multilateral operations. "It was well understood *that nations always retained ultimate authority over their forces and had the right to override orders at any time*, if they chose to do so" (399; emphasis added). When do officers play the red card, and why? As we will see in the pages that follow, red-carding is just one method by which national contingents and concerns often trump multilateral imperatives in coalition military operations.

## Caveat Emptor and Coalitions of the (Un)Willing

The red card situation described above addresses situations that are unanticipated. *Caveats* are restrictions placed upon a contingent anticipating what they will be asked to do and setting rules for those circumstances. The most obvious restriction is geographic: where a unit can serve. Countries can limit not only where a contingent is based but whether and under what conditions it can move outside of its sector to help allies elsewhere. Caveats may also limit the use of force. Some contingents can only engage in defensive operations. Some contingents are

---

9 See Clark 2001: chap. 15.

10 BBC News, "Singer James Blunt 'Prevented World War III,'" November 14, 2010, http://www.bbc.co.uk /news/uk-politics-11753050, accessed January 4, 2011.

11 BBC News, "Confrontation over Pristina Airport." Clark reports this conversation in his book as well, suggesting that the "frank argument" was due to "fatigue and frustration" (2001: 394–95).

12 Pilots usually have this authority, as they must make decisions about whether bombing particular targets falls within their country's rules given possible changing ground circumstances. For example, during the 2011 Libya operation, British planes aborted bombing missions due to the presence of civilians in the area. See BBC News, "RAF Tornadoes Abort Mission in Libya," March 21, 2011, http://www.bbc.co.uk /news/uk-12803217, accessed March 21, 2011.

restricted from operating at night or in the snow.[13] Some contingents are not allowed to operate with certain other participants in the mission. Some caveats restrict the size of units to be deployed so that a battalion or a brigade cannot be dispersed in smaller units to engage in counterinsurgency efforts.[14]

Caveats are perhaps the most prominent means by which countries control their militaries in multilateral operations. They have, as has been documented elsewhere, been a critical point of tension among the countries participating in the mission in Afghanistan.[15] But caveats are not unique to the ISAF mission in Afghanistan. In the aftermath of the invasion of Iraq in 2003, the United States was surprised to find that many of the countries contributing forces to the Operation Iraqi Freedom coalition of the willing significantly constrained what their troops were allowed to do. As Thomas E. Ricks notes, "The Japanese weren't allowed to secure their own perimeter and had to rely on the Dutch to do it. Nor did their rules allow them to come to the aid of others under attack. The Thai battalion's rules didn't even allow them to leave their camp . . ." (2006: 346).[16]

Caveats are not just found in ad hoc coalitions of the willing, but also when an institutionalized alliance goes to war, as observers of NATO know well. In Bosnia, the Canadians stayed within their sector even though they had certain unique capabilities in their Coyote reconnaissance vehicles that could have been useful to other parts of the NATO Stabilization Force.[17]

## National Capabilities as a Key Constraint

Rather than *telling* a military officer what he or she can or cannot do, the people at the top of the chain of command can limit what their contingent can *actually* do by deploying only limited capabilities. Helicopter shortages have been a recurring theme in Afghanistan, but this is not the first place that countries have chosen to deploy less than they could and by doing so critically constrain what their national contingent can accomplish in a multilateral effort.

During NATO's spring 1999 intervention in Kosovo, for example, the Americans refused to use Apache helicopters, the weapon that NATO commanders believed would be most useful against Serb ground forces. The administration

---

13 In interviews with military officers, this was repeated frequently with regard to Afghanistan but with no one country mentioned. A Canadian member of parliament's personal observation during a trip through Afghanistan revealed that the Germans—at least for some stretch of time—did not appear, as a rule, to operate at night. Claude Bachand, interview, Ottawa, March 27, 2007.

14 One could distinguish between legal and technical caveats or between geographic and operational ones, as Trønnes (2012) does. In the chapters that follow, we discuss a variety of restrictions and focus less on typologies.

15 For a few examples, see Jones 2009; Lafraie 2009; and Medcalf 2008.

16 See also Woodward 2006: 292.

17 Interview with Major General Tim Grant, Ottawa, February 7, 2008. Grant served as a commander of the Canadian contingent in Bosnia.

of President Bill Clinton did not want to start a ground war over Kosovo, and from the beginning of the conflict ruled out the use of ground troops. In a March 24, 1999, televised address, Clinton represented a near consensus in Washington when he said, "I do not intend to put our troops in Kosovo to start a war."[18] So while senior officials allowed for the deployment of Task Force Hawk to Albania, the administration was not about to authorize using the task force's Apache helicopters in combat (Clark 2001: 224, 227, 230–33). The administration insisted that the helicopter crews undergo a rigorous training regime in Albania. They further constrained the Apaches by delaying the deployment of supporting units, including the ground spotters necessary for effective operations. The administration maintained these requirements and impediments until early June, ensuring that the task force was never authorized to operate within Kosovo or Serbia.

## Phoning Home during a Bosnian Counterterrorism Mission

The use of red cards or obeying caveats are most likely when a deployed commander believes what is being asked of him by the multinational coalition exceeds his authority or violates common sense, in the former case, or violates his rules of engagement in the latter case. Situations will arise, however, in which the commander will seek advice before acting. A commander's first call is often to his national command authority rather than to his multilateral superiors. In an age of instantaneous telecommunications, we might think that such a phone call home is a relatively trivial exercise. However, as the following tale suggests, calling home is more complicated than it might seem and can seriously hamper multilateral interventions.

In October–November 2001, the Bosnian government arrested six Algerians who had allegedly been planning terrorist activities against American and NATO targets.[19] In January 2002, the government was compelled to release them due to problems with both the evidence (the United States was not releasing the intelligence used to identify these individuals) and Bosnia's laws on conspiracy to commit terrorist acts. American commanders in Bosnia and in Europe needed guidance about how to respond to this event, so they called Washington, D.C., to get approval to send American troops from their base in Tuzla to pick up the six

---

18 Similar statements by the president and other senior administration officials over the next week are reprinted in Auerswald and Auerswald 2000: 755, 781, and 790.

19 This story was covered by local and international media after the fact. See "Bosna u borbi protiv terorizma: Deportacija uprkos zakonima" [Bosnia in the Fight against Terrorism: Deportation Despite Laws], *Dani*, January 25, 2002, http://www.bhdani.com/arhiva/241/t24112.shtml, accessed December 16, 2010; Helen Gibson, "The Algerian Connection," *Time*, February 4, 2002, http://www.time.com/time /magazine/article/0,9171,198990,00.html, accessed December 16, 2010; and Craig Whitlock, "At Guantanamo, Caught in a Legal Trap: 6 Algerians Languish Despite Foreign Rulings, Dropped Charges," *Washington Post*, August 21, 2006, http://www.washingtonpost.com/wp-dyn/content/article/2006/08/20 /AR2006082000660_pf.html, accessed December 16th, 2010.

individuals in Sarajevo and fly them to Guantanamo Bay. Instead of getting a simple yes or no, these commanders had to wait a couple of days for the interagency process to play out.[20] The delays were significant, and they allowed protesters to organize outside the Bosnian prison. This risked turning a potentially quick handover into a possible riot. Ultimately, officials in Washington sent guidance to U.S. forces in Bosnia to pick up the six Algerians and put them on a plane headed to Guantanamo.

The need to get authority from home delayed resolution for a couple of days, which could have had significant political consequences. On the battlefield, as we will see in chapter 4 when discussing the French in Afghanistan, a delay in authorization of only twenty-four hours can be quite significant indeed. For some countries such as the Netherlands, as will be discussed in chapter 6, the phone serves as the primary means of influencing how troops are used.

## THE OVERSIGHT OF DEPLOYED UNITS

Caveats, red cards, and requirements to call home will have their greatest impact if the people on the ground know that they will be caught if they do not follow the rules. Oversight, thus, is a critical part of any delegation process. The intent of those delegating power to subordinates will matter most when the people farther down the chain of command understand that their actions will be monitored. Absent oversight, there is every reason for far-flung commanders to implement policy in ways that they, rather than their superiors back home, believe is best. Oversight is particularly important when deployed commanders and superiors back home have different priorities, beliefs, or pressures facing them.

Belgian colonel Roger Housen's experience illustrates the problem facing many home governments. Colonel Housen commanded the Belgian contingent to ISAF from October 2003 to March 2004. His unit's primary responsibility was to secure Kabul International Airport in conjunction with German forces. He also worked in the ISAF Joint Operations Center, with responsibility for collecting heavy weapons from various subnational Afghan factions. This latter task required that he travel to the dangerous Panjshir Valley north of Kabul. Yet Belgian caveats prevented him from using Belgian troops outside ISAF headquarters or the Kabul airport, and no other coalition partner would provide security forces in the Panjshir Valley. When the Belgian defense minister refused to grant Housen's

---

20 As observed by Steve Saideman from his desk on the U.S. Joint Staff. The key stumbling blocks in this case were the desire of the lawyer representing the Office of the Secretary of Defense (OSD) to make recommendations that were beyond his or her responsibility (the lawyer's job was to rule on the legality of the decision, nothing more) and the unwillingness of the people working in the OSD to bother Secretary of Defense Donald Rumsfeld after 7:00 p.m.

request for an exception to that caveat, Housen went ahead and used his Belgian troops anyway, in large part because Belgian authorities had no oversight procedures with which to monitor his behavior and would not know what he did unless someone died during the mission.[21] In the case studies discussed in subsequent chapters, we find that countries vary in how attentive they are to what their troops are actually doing. Some invest significant time engaging in oversight while others do not.

## INCENTIVES FOR CORRECT BEHAVIOR

Just as caveats and other restrictions only matter if the deployed actors are monitored, oversight works best when those who exceed their authority or break the rules are punished and those who behave appropriately are rewarded. Sanctions for incorrect behavior are both a punishment and a deterrent in that sanctions not only hurt violators but send a clear signal to everyone else. Rewards are a positive incentive for the opposite behavior. The Canadian reaction to the 1993 beating death of a detainee in Somalia serves as clear contrast to the American response to the revelations about Abu Ghraib in 2004. The former sent a clear signal to the Canadian military, while the latter sent ambiguous signals to U.S. forces.

In 1993, Canada was a participant in the United Nations mission in Somalia, and the Canadian Airborne Regiment found itself dealing with Somalis trying to steal supplies. On March 16, members of the regiment captured Shidane Abukar Arone and beat him to death. Once the news got out, it became a significant controversy back in Canada. Not only were a group of soldiers court martialed, but consecutive chiefs of defense staff (John de Chastelain and Jean Boyle) were compelled to resign. The Airborne Regiment was disbanded. The official inquiry into the incident came to very blunt conclusions. According to the official inquiry report, "Somalia represents the nadir of the fortunes of the Canadian Forces. There seems to be little room to slide lower."[22] This incident is tied to a "decade of darkness" during which the Canadian Forces absorbed severe budget cuts and a sharp decline in morale and public confidence.[23] It also meant that years later the Canadian media, politicians, and military paid a great deal of attention to how detainees were treated by the Canadians and the Afghan authorities in Kandahar.

This reaction is quite distinct from the American response to the revelations about Abu Ghraib, when it was found that American soldiers had abused Iraqis at

---

21 Interview with Belgian Army Colonel Roger Housen, Brussels, July 12, 2007.
22 Somalia Commision of Inquiry, "Executive Summary," *Report of the Somalia Commision of Inquiry,* http://www.dnd.ca/somalia/vol0/v0s1e.htm, accessed April 5, 2011. See also Bercuson 1996; Dawson 2007.
23 Hillier 2010: chap. 7 provides a good internal perspective of the bottoming out of the Canadian forces.

the site of one of Saddam Hussein's prisons.[24] Reservists from the 320th Military Police Battalion engaged in torture, taking pictures that eventually appeared in the *New Yorker* and on *60 Minutes* and other news programs.[25] As in Canada, the lowest-level soldiers involved faced courts martial. However, except for a reprimand and demotion for the facility's commanding officer, Brigadier General Janis Karpinksi, no high-level U.S. officials faced any sanctions. The secretary of defense, the chairman of the Joint Chiefs of Staff, the theater commander, and the ground commander received no punishments at all.[26]

The comparison illustrates that accountability varies across countries and conflicts. It should be no surprise, then, if senior officers in different militaries vary in how they respond to restrictions and oversight. Where officers know that they will be held accountable, they are more likely to stay within their lanes. Deployed officers are free to act as they want in the absence of accountability.

## SELECTING MILITARY COMMANDERS

When all else fails, you can fire your commander. Replacing a high-level officer in the middle of a war is always controversial, but it may become the best way to change what the military is doing on the ground. The most famous case is perhaps President Harry S. Truman's firing of General Douglas MacArthur. This is not only a case of a leader sacking an insubordinate general, but also one of removing one's senior military representative in a multilateral effort.

At the time, General MacArthur headed not just the American effort but that of the United Nations force involved in ejecting North Korean forces from South Korea. Always a difficult person, MacArthur repeatedly undermined President Truman, first in the press and then by writing to Republican leaders of Congress to criticize the president's limited strategy in Korea (Pearlman 2008). Truman dismissed MacArthur, provoking a significant controversy at home in which Republicans repeatedly criticized the president in the media. It even provoked a Senate investigation (McCowan 1987). While Truman prevailed and was able to replace MacArthur with Matthew Ridgway, a general more suited to the task, Truman paid a significant political price at home for the incident.

While controversial, this case still stands as an object lesson that civilian officials will usually consider other means to control their troops, as firing commanders

---

24 There is significant literature on this event. For a start, see Gourevitch and Morris 2009; Strasser 2004; and U.S. Department of Defense 2005.

25 Seymour M. Hersh, "Torture at Abu Ghraib," *New Yorker,* May 10, 2004, http://www.newyorker.com /archive/2004/05/10/040510fa_fact?currentPage=1, accessed April 5, 2011.

26 Lt. General Ricardo Sanchez claims that Abu Ghraib cost him a fourth star in his memoir (Sanchez and Phillips 2008), but this is doubtful given that Sanchez was widely viewed as performing quite poorly overall.

is likely to require a significant payment in political capital. Still, in any democracy with civilian control over the military, commanders who do not follow the intent of their civilian overseers can be removed. As we will see in chapter 4, U.S. secretaries of defense have frequently used this tactic to change military behavior.

# Why Study National Control in Multilateral Interventions?

These vignettes illustrate many of the challenges facing the overall commander of a multilateral operation. In most such operations, there is a competition for control between individual states and the multilateral chain of command. Individual countries sign onto multilateral interventions, yet they have a variety of means to influence how their contingents operate within an alliance or coalition effort. The real puzzle is not that NATO commanders (or those of any coalition, alliance, or multinational organization) do not have complete control over the forces assigned to them; it would be surprising if they did. Rather, the crucial question is why there is significant variation in control mechanisms used by countries involved in multilateral interventions and by some countries over time. Why do some countries use particular mechanisms to influence their contingents while other countries rely upon other means? Why do some countries employ caveats while others focus on incentives and sanctions to make promises to or threaten their senior military representatives? Why do some countries more intensively constrain what their contingents do while other nations give their ground commanders more latitude to follow the multilateral chain of command?

The goal of this book is to demonstrate the existence and explicate the sources of such variations. Explaining why some allies are willing to fight and sacrifice while others are not is not a trivial exercise of interest only to scholars closeted in ivory towers. It is certainly not trivial for the outcome of NATO's mission in Afghanistan. Nor was it trivial to the conduct of NATO's 2011 intervention in Libya or in earlier NATO interventions in the Balkans. Differences in the willingness of NATO allies to fight to their fullest extent possible may fracture the alliance as the peacetime burden-sharing debates of the past become much more severe, with blood, the fate of nations, and votes at home in the balance. If recent debates are any guide, burden bearers in Afghanistan will be less enthusiastic about contributing to future missions. Those criticized for doing too little will not want to find themselves in a similar situation. And the United States could easily find itself back where it was after Kosovo: highly frustrated by NATO.

Each partner in an alliance or coalition effort will exert influence over how its military contingents are used. No country willingly surrenders this crucial element of sovereignty. Neither NATO nor any other institution can eliminate these challenges of multilateral warfare. Developing a new *strategic concept*, streamlining command structures so that they look less like spaghetti, approving language to drop caveats in extremis, and hectoring allies will not eliminate caveats, red cards, and the like or give alliance commanders appreciably greater control over individual national contingents deployed under the alliance banner.

Any country interested in acting militarily alongside others will need to be aware of the domestic challenges of multilateral war. Crises and conflicts will continue to emerge in the world, and countries will align together to face them. And they will squabble with each other over how to proceed. The quotes at the start of the chapter indicate that Napoleon and Churchill knew whereof they spoke: fighting alongside other countries is challenging. Napoleon refused to accept those challenges. Churchill, unlike Napoleon, understood that there is often no other choice. For those whose thinking is more akin to that of Churchill's, this book provides some clues about where countries will tend to line up and which mechanisms they will use when operating in multilateral interventions.

## Explaining Variation in National Control

Our argument in this book starts with the observation that explaining ISAF behavior requires a focus on individual ISAF participants and not just a review of what occurs at NATO headquarters. There is simply too much systematic variation in the behavior of ISAF contingents to suggest that the NATO alliance is determining the behavior of its members. Instead, we argue that NATO's procedures allow each member's political processes to shape what it contributes and what its troops do. To gain consensus, the alliance as an institution provides members with the ability to opt out of individual operations and even entire categories of missions. To do otherwise—for example, to require participation in all operations— would lead countries to vote against most, if not all, alliance missions. Getting less enthusiastic alliance members to assent to new missions requires allowing countries to play the red card. Indeed, NATO's procedure for gathering troops to deploy on a mission—the force generation procedure we explain in the next chapter—is entirely voluntary. To get enough contributions, NATO has to offer countries exit options.

The question then becomes why countries vary so much in their behavior both over time and within the alliance. We invoke principal-agent theory to highlight the importance of national decisions and to explain variation in behavior across nations. In terms of the former, we argue in chapter 2 that NATO's structure and processes establish what we call a hybrid principal-agent relationship between the multiple entities delegating authority to deployed military units and those military units themselves. The alliance's structure and processes gives an advantage to the authority of individual contributing states when compared to the alliance as a whole. Members are able to exert more control over their militaries than can the collective alliance.

At the same time, we use lessons from principal-agent theory to understand which types of behavior are most important when we consider control over and direction of deployed military units. Principal-agent theory addresses problems of delegation: how do civilians back home make sure that the authority they give to military commanders in the field will be used as desired? Commanders on the ground will have more information about the conflict situation and their own actions in that conflict. They can potentially take action that their superiors would not approve of and might not have the tools to correct. The stakes are high and the potential power of those commanders is great; after all, the tactical actions of military units in modern war potentially have strategic effects, including the failure of the mission. Principal-agent theory thus tells us what sort of challenges to look for when examining the decisions of individual alliance members.

Though principal-agent theory can tell us what to look for, it is not particularly useful for explaining broad variations in the behavior of different alliance members. For that we turn to theories of domestic institutions in chapter 3. We differentiate between government institutions that decide on questions of war or peace via collective decision making or individual decision makers. Parliamentary coalitions engage in collective decision making. Coalition governments will not be able to respond to international pressures if it means that their governments will collapse. Minority governments face similar pressures, at least if it is relatively easy to replace them with new parliamentary governments. Presidents and prime ministers in single-party governments more often reflect the decisions of individual decision makers. Presidents and parliaments led by single-party majority governments have more domestic leeway to follow the alliance's guidance, but there is no guarantee that they will do so if it does not serve their interests.

Each type of government demonstrates specific behavioral patterns during NATO interventions. For instance, countries governed by parliamentary coalitions tend to place more restrictions upon their deployments in terms of caveats, requirements for phone calls, and limited capabilities than do either presidents or prime ministers leading single-party governments. This trend, we argue, is largely because of internal bargaining within the parliamentary coalition. The less enthusiastic members of a coalition government will demand conditions be placed upon the deployment, and the more enthusiastic coalition partners will have to relent if they want the mission to take place. In general, we find that parties to the left will be less enthusiastic about military interventions than those on the right side of the political spectrum. In government systems with single key decision makers, much will depend on that person's attitude toward risk. Some presidents and prime ministers (and those to whom they delegate) will be more focused on the behavior of their deployed troops, minimizing the risks of the operation either in terms of the danger faced by their contingents or the strategic implications of their military's behavior. Others will focus more on outcomes, such as achieving mission success, even if that is a risky proposition. We find that the former category of individual will impose more restrictions on troops than will the latter.

## Alternative Accounts: Threats, Public Opinion, and Strategic Culture

Surprisingly, few works develop a systematic understanding of why countries manage their roles in multilateral military efforts as they do.[27] Nora Bensahel (1999) develops the trade-off between political cohesion and military efficiency within a coalition, but is more focused on comparing different alliances than understanding variations within a single multilateral effort. Sarah Kreps (2011) and Patricia A. Weitsman (2013) address how coalitions and alliances differ and why the United States chooses various forms of cooperation from unilateralism to multilateral institutions, but they are less concerned with variation among members in coalitions and alliances. There has been a great deal of study about how civil-military relations influences military doctrine and grand strategy,[28] some comparative work that largely omits actual operations (Brooks 2008; Brooks and Stanley 2007; Diamond and Plattner 1996), and a great deal of work on NATO burden-sharing.[29] Work on alliance politics tends to focus on the creation of alliances and their duration rather than their operation during wartime,[30] and how alliances affect decisions to go to war (Pressman 2008; Snyder 2007).

We can distill from the various works in this area at least three alternative arguments that might help explain the patterns we observe within alliances. Specifically, we focus on the implications of realism, the potential constraints of public opinion, and the impact of strategic culture. Each approach is intuitively plausible and based on theories with long traditions in security studies. However, each fails to capture the significant variation either across nations associated with ISAF operations or within individual nations as the mission unfolded over time.

27 Bensahel (2003, 2006) and Weitsman (2004) address key dimensions of multilateral warfare but do not systematically address the varying patterns of the participants' means for controlling their forces within coalitions.
28 For the classics in the field, see Mearsheimer 1983; Posen 1984; and Snyder 1984.
29 See Hartley and Sandler 1999; Lepgold 1998; Olson and Zeckhauser 1966; Oneal and Elrod 1989; Palmer 1990; Sandler and Forbes 1980; and Shimizu and Sandler 2002.
30 See Altfeld 1984; Bennett 1997; Gartzke and Gleditsch 2004; Leeds 2003; Leeds and Savun 2007; and Thies 2009. Bensahel (1999) makes the same point but at greater length—that alliance scholarship essentially never reaches the battlefield.

## REALISM: WARS OF CHOICE
## AND REDUCED COMMITMENTS

One could argue that Afghanistan was a war of necessity for some while for others it was a war of choice.[31] That is, for many participants, they were there to fulfill an alliance obligation but do no more, while others were motivated to do more by the threat posed by terrorism emanating from Afghanistan (and Pakistan). This builds on one of the classic approaches to understanding international relations: realism. A dominant theme in later realist writing asserts that countries respond to threats and little else (Walt 1987; Waltz 1979). Countries facing a greater threat are more likely to balance against that threat by forging alliances, arming themselves, or both. In terms of conflict behavior, a natural extension of balance-of-threat theory is that countries facing threats will allow their military to do what is necessary for success.[32] Other countries that face less of a threat may still choose to participate in a conflict to please an ally or to respect treaty obligations, but will be more likely to restrict their forces from doing anything that endangers those troops or risks drawing the state deeper into the conflict.

The question then is which countries were most threatened by Afghanistan and/or terrorist threats that emanate from that part of the world and, thus, would respond most assertively and with the least restrictions on their troops. Logically, it would be those countries that have been hit hard by terrorists tied to groups formerly based in Afghanistan—al-Qaeda, to be specific.

Table 1.2 illustrates that a country's experience with terrorism is not at all correlated with its behavior in Afghanistan. Spain and Turkey have faced significant violence from terrorists tied to al-Qaeda, yet they continued to limit what their troops could do on the ground. Indeed, as later chapters will show, countries did change how they managed their ISAF contingents in the aftermath of terrorist attacks. Moreover, we see significant variation among those countries that have not paid a high price for al-Qaeda–related terrorism. In short, the notion of threat or national interest in the war in Afghanistan does not help us to understand why countries vary so much in how they approached this war.[33]

---

31 See Brzezinski 2009; and Haass 2009, 2010.
32 Some realists, including Posen (1984), assert that civilians intervene more in military affairs when relative threat is high, as the civilians are better equipped to discern what is necessary to adapt to than military officers who are motivated by bureaucratic politics.
33 If one considers the size of one's Muslim population as an indicator of vulnerability to terrorism emanating out of Pakistan (which is a bit of a stretch), there is no correlation between that and the level of restrictions on the troops, although the case of Turkey may be instructive. We tested this using data from the Pew Forum on Religion and Public Life, "Mapping the Global Muslim Population: A Report on the Size and Distribution of the World's Muslim Population," October 2009, http://pewforum.org /newassets/images/reports/Muslimpopulation/Muslimpopulation.pdf, accessed January 21, 2010.

**Table 1.2.** Terrorism and Caveats

| Country[a] | Fatalities caused by AfPak-based terrorists, 2001–9[b] | Caveats[c] |
|---|---|---|
| Australia | 0[d] | Medium |
| Belgium | 0 | Tight |
| Canada | 0 | Medium, then Loose |
| Denmark | 0 | Loose |
| France | 0[e] | Medium, then Loose |
| Germany | 0 | Tight |
| Italy | 0[f] | Tight |
| Netherlands | 0 | Medium |
| Norway | 0 | Medium |
| Poland | 0 | Loose |
| Romania | 0 | Medium |
| Spain | 3/11/04: 191 | Tight |
| Sweden | 0 | Medium |
| Turkey | 11/15/03: 25<br>11/20/03: 28 | Tight |
| United Kingdom | 7/7/05: 56 | Loose |
| United States | 9/11/01: 3,000 | Loose |

[a] This table and the following include only those countries providing 500 troops or more in 2009.

[b] Center for American Progress, http://www.americanprogress.org/issues/2007/09/alqaeda_map.html, accessed January 21, 2010. Double-checked with the Global Terrorism Database, http://www.start.umd.edu/, accessed January 21, 2010.

[c] While caveats can range quite widely, we focus largely on two for the purposes of coding them here: whether troops could operate in the more dangerous southern and eastern parts of Afghanistan and whether the contingent could engage in offensive operations.

[d] Australia has not been hit directly, but the Bali bombing of October 12, 2002 did kill nearly ninety Australian tourists. In addition, a September 2004 car bomb exploded near the Australian embassy in Jakarta.

[e] This does not include terrorist acts committed by Basque or Corsican separatists.

[f] A Moroccan blew himself up in Italy on March 28, 2004, but it is not clear what his ties were. Global Terrorism Database.

Of course, one could argue that terrorism thus far, even for those that have been hit relatively hard, is just not an existential threat (Mueller 2006, 2009; Mueller and Stewart 2010). Accordingly, countries could restrict their troops (or not) as they saw fit in Afghanistan and conflicts like it because the stakes were actually quite low. Failure in Afghanistan would not lead to the conquest of any country, so even the most interested of countries, such as the United States, could risk doing less than their fullest efforts without posing an existential threat to their homeland. If Afghanistan was so important, say critics, the United States would not have been so quick to put far greater effort into a second war in Iraq. For such critics, our focus on domestic institutions and politics might account for

Afghanistan and situations like it, but not for the big wars and existential threats of the past and future. Balancing against threats should matter more in those circumstances.

There are at least two responses to such a criticism. First, if our approach only applies to multilateral interventions since the end of the Cold War, then our book still has broad applicability and extended relevance, as such interventions continue to take place in Libya, Congo, and Darfur, among other places. Most uses of force since the end of—and even during—the Cold War were in multilateral contexts short of existential conflicts. NATO engaged in three conflicts before Afghanistan (Bosnia, Kosovo, Macedonia) and one since (Libya), along with continuing antipiracy efforts. The United Nations has engaged in over thirty armed interventions since 1990. The European Union and the African Union have recently engaged in military efforts. Iraq is not the only case of an ad hoc coalition military effort. So, even if our argument only applies to conflicts with limited stakes, this is not a rare phenomenon and is one of significance for both academics and policy makers.

Second, when existential threats do arise, allies may differ as to how best to react to them. Countries in the most dire of conflicts may disagree about how to deploy their troops, causing one or more to invoke red cards and other national means of controlling their contingents. During World War II, for example, Japan posed a very significant threat to Australia. Winston Churchill wanted to redeploy the Australian divisions that had been fighting in the Middle East to the Dutch East Indies in early 1942 and gave orders to that effect without seeking permission from Australia. Australia's prime minister John Curtin vehemently disagreed since he wanted the two divisions to protect his country from the approaching Japanese. After heated arguments, Curtin had his way.[34] So, even in the most destructive conflict in recent human history, one ally asserted national control despite the wishes of other allies.

The Soviet existential threat during the Cold War also produced its share of alliance friction. For example, there was extensive debate in the 1980s about how best to defend western Europe, and specifically West Germany, from a Soviet invasion (Mearsheimer 1983). NATO planning had to deal with two key conflicting imperatives driven by West German interests and domestic politics. For Germans, defense started at the border of West and East Germany. For the West Germans it was not politically possible to have a serious defense-in-depth strategy through which NATO forces would allow the Soviet Union and the Warsaw Pact countries to cross the border easily but then face NATO forces where the alliance chose.

---

34 The story of Curtin confronting Churchill is still highlighted in Australia's War Museum, as well as the John Curtin Prime Ministerial Library; see http://john.curtin.edu.au/manofpeace/crisis.html, accessed November 29, 2011.

West Germany would not surrender territory to buy the alliance time since that territory was inhabited by West Germans. At the same time, NATO could not build significant defensive structures at the inter-German frontier. Obstacles such as walls, fences, minefields, trenches, and the like would not only be reminiscent of the Berlin Wall but also make quite real and lasting the division of Germany.[35] While there may have been a military logic to forward defense (Mearsheimer 1981), it made little sense if NATO would not build significant defenses at the border. The contrast between the inter-German border during the Cold War and that between North and South Korea is quite instructive as West German domestic politics played a heavy role in what NATO could and could not do.

The point here is simply that domestic political imperatives will cause some alliance partners to impose restrictions on their forces, influencing alliance strategy and effectiveness even when the threat is actually quite high. To sum up, then: realism cannot account for the cross-national variation in how countries operated in Afghanistan. Realists would argue that the ISAF experience has limited generalizability because it is no longer a war of necessity. We would respond that such has been the case with nearly all of the major military activities countries have engaged in for the past twenty years. We would also point out that realists are not even right about that, given the frictions among allies even in the gravest of circumstances. Consequently, we believe that one need look beyond realism to understand why countries vary in how they operate in the midst of a multilateral effort.

## PUBLIC OPINION AND HALF-HEARTED EFFORTS

It may be the case that countries are more likely to impose restrictions upon a mission if it is unpopular at home. Politicians seeking to maintain their positions may be less willing to pay the domestic costs of a distant and unpopular mission (Aldrich et al. 2006; Chan and Safran 2006; Holsti 2004). Instead, politicians may impose restrictions on their troops to keep deployments off the domestic radar. Limits on where troops can operate, restrictions on offensive operations, requirements to call home for permission, intensive oversight, and harsh penalties for commanders' less successful decisions can mitigate the political risks of an unpopular military effort because these strictures reduce the probability of casualties or military atrocities. Some of the countries widely reputed to have the most significant restrictions—Germany, to be specific—were precisely those where public support seemed to be the lowest.

---

35 For typical articles that mostly assumed that there would be no barrier building due to West German objections, see Cross 1985.

**Table 1.3.** Public Opinion and Caveats

| Country | Public Opinion[a] | Caveats | Country | Public Opinion | Caveats |
|---------|-------------------|---------|---------|----------------|---------|
| Turkey | 18% | Tight | Canada | 41% | Reduced |
| Poland | 21% | Loose | Sweden | 43% | Medium |
| Spain | 32% | Tight | Australia | 47% | Medium |
| United Kingdom | 35% | Loose | Netherlands | 48% | Medium |
| France | 37% | Reduced | Denmark | 48%[b] | Loose |
| Italy | 37%[c] | Tight | Norway | 49% | Medium |
| Germany | 38% | Tight | United States | 57% | Loose |

[a] Mean public support from August 2006 to December 2008, from Kreps 2010, unless otherwise noted. Belgium and Romania are omitted here, as we could not find comparable surveys.

[b] Angus Reid Public Opinion, "Danish Split on Ending Afghanistan Mission," February 27, 2009, http://www.angus-reid.com/polls/view/danish_split_on_ending_afghanistan_mission/, accessed January 18, 2010.

[c] The Italian number is based on a poll asking whether one supports a withdrawal (gradual or immediate) or opposes a withdrawal—the number here is the percentage opposing a withdrawal, which we take to mean support of the mission. Angus Reid Public Opinion, "Italians Want Troops out of Afghanistan," August 3, 2009, http://www.angus-reid.com/polls/view/33924, accessed January 18, 2010.

The problem is that public support does not covary with caveats and other mechanisms used to manage risky troop deployments.[36] Table 1.3 lists major coalition contributors, ranked by levels of public support for the ISAF operation, from least to most supportive. The data show that hostile publics are a poor predictor of their countries' policy decisions. Both Turkey and Poland had very unhappy publics, but their behavior on the ground varied tremendously. Polish troops were sent to some of the more dangerous parts of Afghanistan with few restrictions. Turkish troops faced significant geographic restrictions on their movements and could not engage in offensive operations. The ISAF mission had slightly less public support on average in Great Britain than in Germany, yet British troops were far less restricted than were their German counterparts. It would appear that general patterns of public opinion tell us very little about how countries manage their troops.

If there is a pattern, it is one of increased delegation to battlefield commanders as the ISAF mission lost popularity. France changed how it operated in Afghanistan quite significantly in 2007 (see chapter 4 for details), deploying troops into harm's way at a time when the mission was declining in public support. Canada

---

36 Kreps (2010) finds that public opinion does not correlate with ISAF troop levels deployed to Afghanistan either.

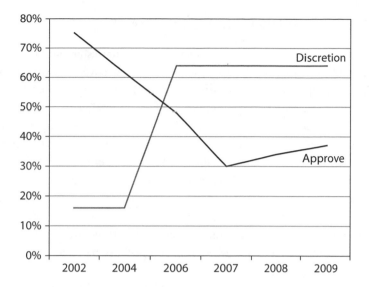

**Figure 1.1** ◆ Trends in Canadian Public Opinion and Discretion
*Note:* The approval numbers come from Angus Reid Public Opinion,
*Issue: Afghanistan,* http://www.angus-reid.com/issue/afghanistan/page
/9/, accessed December 2, 2011. We use Canada here simply because
we have more public opinion data on this case.

is an even clearer case, as figure 1.1 illustrates. The decrease in the ISAF deployment's popularity did not cause Canadian politicians or military officers to impose restrictions on their troops. Instead, the shift to Kandahar and to more war-fighting coincided with changes in how the Canadian forces operated, and these changes then produced a decrease in support for the mission, as we will see in chapter 5. While Canada ultimately pulled out of Kandahar in 2011 and shifted into a highly restricted training effort, the timing was not due to a collapse in public support but instead to how public opinion played out through domestic political processes—elections that produced minority governments.

The cases of Canada and France are not unique. Other countries gave their troops more latitude as public support declined. In short, public opinion almost certainly matters, but not as systematically as one might think. Instead, political institutions mediate the responses of politicians to unpopular missions, leading to varying responses to public pressure in different domestic institutional settings.[37]

---

37 See Auerswald 2004 for a discussion and application to Kosovo.

## STRATEGIC CULTURE AS A CONSTRAINT

The third alternative is that countries and their militaries are bound by shared cultural understandings of the appropriate ways to behave, developing military doctrines and capabilities that constrain choices (Farrell 1998, 2005; Glenn 2009; Katzenstein 1996; Kier 1997; Legro 1995).[38] It is impossible to discuss German behavior in Afghanistan, for instance, without considering the weight of the past upon the present day: the pacifism produced by the World War II experience, the reluctance to kill or suffer casualties, and that the German military may have rules and procedures that are directly derived from these experiences. Certainly one could argue that German police and army units are restricted from operating together because of their post–World War II desire for strict separation of the military and police in Germany (see chapter 6). As a result, the fact that German training of Afghan police had to take place on military bases significantly hampered the training effort.[39]

Despite its insights, there are three problems with applying cultural arguments to the question of military behavior in Afghanistan. First, some cultural approaches imply or explicitly assert that change is quite difficult, as cultural norms and mutual understandings take significant time to alter, especially if they are based on key historical moments or geography (Berger 1998; Johnston 1995; Katzenstein 1996; Meyer 2006), unless some sort of factor outside of the culture provides a significant shock (Farrell 2005). Yet as we will show in this book, countries have sometimes quickly changed how they operate. Second, some cultural approaches suggest convergence upon a particular way of doing things, especially in highly institutionalized settings such as NATO (Eyre and Suchman 1996; Farrell 2001; Terriff, Osinga, and Farrell 2010), yet we see significant variation in ISAF, even among democracies with extensive interaction and shared histories. We see value in the strategic culture approach and in focusing on organizational norms, but the patterns of variation we find in Afghanistan point elsewhere—to politics at the highest levels within each country that contributed troops. Third, our approach is more efficient for cross-national comparative analyses.

We address some of these alternative arguments as they arise in the chapters that follow. Ultimately, we find that neither security threats nor public opinion systematically covary with how countries manage their militaries in Afghanistan. Nor do we find strategic culture accounting for the changes countries make over the course of the ISAF mission.

---

38 Again, the literature is extensive, but space constraints limit a fuller discussion.
39 Interview with senior German Ministry of Interior official, June 2009.

# The Plan of the Book

Chapter 2 considers NATO itself: how the organization works, how its origins give its members latitude to influence their contingents, and how the commanders of its multilateral efforts cope with the challenges of multilateral contingents. As caveats, red cards, phone calls, and other techniques for managing individual contingents have proven to be problematic, NATO has worked hard to mitigate those techniques' impact upon ISAF's effectiveness. Despite these efforts, we demonstrate that the alliance cannot hope to compete with national command chains. We demonstrate this empirically by briefly reviewing the alliance's force generation and command processes. We then compare the intervention venues states can use from a theoretical perspective, to include unilateralism, coalitions of the willing, and alliance actions. We find that NATO interventions provide individual alliance members with the benefits of multilateralism while maintaining ultimate national controls on deployed troops. In NATO interventions, national commands have authority over choosing their nation's commanders, delegating authority to those commanders, conducting oversight, and providing incentives for appropriate military behavior—authority that the alliance cannot match. In sum, chapter 2 assesses why NATO functions as it does, and why we must look inside individual alliance members if we are to explain their behavior in Afghanistan.

Chapter 3 presents one way of understanding how and why politicians delegate to their military commanders. We use domestic institutional analysis to highlight key differences between alliance members that operate under collective decision making, as exemplified by coalition governments, and individual decision making, as in the case of presidential political systems and those parliaments governed by single parties. We argue that institutional distinctions between governments can explain much and point to when and where additional information is needed, particularly with regard to the ideology and size of governing coalitions (in coalition governments) and the preferences of individual decision makers (in presidential and single-party parliamentary governments).

Chapter 4 focuses primarily on two presidential systems, those of the United States and France. In each country, an individual is empowered to make significant military decisions or delegate those decisions to subordinates. While we could write a book on the U.S. experience (as many have and will), we focus on two particular elements that distinguish how the Americans ran their war compared to many of the other countries: agent selection and incentives. Because the United States led an ad hoc effort (Operation Enduring Freedom) and only later became the leader of the NATO effort, the primary means of control was leadership selection and termination. The United States famously cycled through a variety of generals. We then turn to the French case, where we see a significant change in behavior on the ground that followed the presidential transition from Jacques Chirac to Nicolas Sarkozy. Chirac placed significant restrictions on where the French were deployed and with what capabilities. Sarkozy lifted those restrictions but still answered the phone when questions arose in the field. We then briefly address the case of Poland.

Chapter 5 focuses on a second type of political system where individual leaders are empowered: parliamentary systems with a single party controlling the government. Great Britain and Canada have been important players in Afghanistan, with both showing significant variation in what they were willing to do over time. One key difference is that Canada was led by a minority government for nearly all of its time in Afghanistan. Thus, we have two countries with very similar institutions, similar political cultures, and large variations in how they have performed in Afghanistan and how they have been governed at home. These differences allow us to tease out the key forces shaping decision making when prime ministers are unencumbered by the requirements of maintaining a domestic political coalition. This chapter then touches on two other countries in this category: Spain and Turkey.

Chapter 6 examines parliamentary coalition governments. Leaders in coalition governments face great challenges, not least because members of the coalition will vary in their enthusiasm for the mission. As a result, most countries in this category have tended to place more significant restrictions upon their forces in Afghanistan. We consider three key cases in detail. Germany has been the poster child or exemplar of a country viewed as being far more capable in theory than in practice due to the restrictions imposed by a series of coalition governments. The Netherlands illustrates the domestic consequences of a coalition government fighting a war, as the Dutch government collapsed over Afghanistan. Denmark, the third case in this chapter, is quite exceptional: the Danes fought with few restrictions in the most dangerous part of the most dangerous province in Afghanistan. Comparing these three countries allows us to consider how variations in the kinds of coalition governments may help to explain why some in this category are more flexible on the ground than others. We conclude this chapter by briefly examining other coalition governments in ISAF: Belgium, Italy, and Norway.

Chapter 7 considers two countries, Australia and New Zealand, that are partners with but not members of NATO. Australia and New Zealand have British-style political institutions, with the key decisions made by the prime minister and his or her minister of defense. We consider these two cases to see if membership in NATO makes a difference. We find that nonmembership can actually be a shield that countries use to deflect harder choices and more responsibilities. Otherwise, the domestic dynamics work like they do in Great Britain or Canada, demonstrating that the military constraints imposed by nations are driven far more by domestic politics than by NATO institutions.

Chapter 8 applies our model to the 2011 intervention in Libya, a conflict begun as a coalition of the willing that later evolved into a NATO intervention. We find that many of the same dynamics appeared in Libya as occurred in Afghanistan. Presidential and majoritarian parliamentary governments had wide discretion to act as they saw fit. Coalition governments were constrained by their need to maintain parliamentary confidence. Two other interesting findings were apparent in Libya. First, the intervention was a dramatic example of multilateral forum shopping, with the main participants trying two alternative organizational arrangements during the intervention. The fact that they settled on the NATO mechanism holds promise for the alliance's future. Second, the Libya case highlights some of the nuances required when explaining parliamentary coalition behavior, particularly with regard to the coalition's ideology and the viability of alternative governing coalitions.

In chapter 9 we assess the key factors shaping how countries manage their participation in multilateral military operations and develop implications for policy makers and academics. We develop suggestions for policy makers on anticipating and responding to challenges arising from the dynamics that we have found. Caveats and other means used to control national military contingents are inherent in modern democracies. Rather than publicly blasting recalcitrant allies, alliance leaders will need to understand which allies can do more and how to get them to do so. This has implications for the choice of coalitions versus alliance interventions, for the transition out of Afghanistan, and for NATO's recent Smart Defence Initiative. For scholars, we discuss the implications of our findings for the literature on forum shopping between alliances versus coalitions of the willing, principal-agent approaches to civil-military relations, and the broader role of domestic politics in foreign policy. We conclude with final thoughts on the future of the NATO alliance.

## The Scope of the Project

Before moving on, we need to clarify what this book is and is not. This book is an effort to understand how countries manage their militaries in multilateral operations. Our study focuses almost entirely on the NATO effort in Afghanistan. We initially planned to compare ISAF to the NATO efforts in Bosnia and Kosovo and to the ad hoc effort in Iraq, but the Afghanistan story became sufficiently complex, with enough variation to warrant an entire book.[40] Our contention is that

---

40 Davidson (2011) compares allies of the United States in how they responded to Kosovo, Afghanistan, and Iraq, but his Afghanistan chapter only touches upon three countries: the United Kingdom, France,

the problems NATO has experienced in Afghanistan are not unique to that one intervention. Indeed, our vignettes at the start of this chapter come from a variety of multilateral military efforts, and, as we show in chapter 8, are applicable to the Libyan effort of 2011. These additional cases demonstrate that the challenges we identify and explain in the Afghan case are relevant elsewhere.

We focus most of our attention on the major contributions to ISAF: those countries that consistently provided five hundred or more troops to the mission between 2003 and early 2010. This size restriction allows us to compare relatively serious commitments of forces. Countries deploying only very small contingents (i.e., Estonia's deployment of approximately 150 soldiers) do not face the same choices about the kinds of operations and deployments in the field as those having at least something that approximates a battalion. Studying New Zealand in chapter 7 allows us to get at the effect of size. While sending a small force is one way to limit risk, as Greece has ably demonstrated, our focus is more on variation among relatively capable contingents.

Sixteen countries provided five hundred or more troops to ISAF in Afghanistan. Of these, we focus detailed attention on eight key states: Australia, Canada, Denmark, France, Germany, the Netherlands, the United Kingdom, and the United States. Why these cases? First, because our approach focuses on domestic institutions, we sought to study at least two cases in each category of presidential, single-party parliamentary, and coalition parliamentary governments. We explore two presidential or quasi-presidential systems in detail: those of France and the United States;[41] two single-party parliamentary systems in the United Kingdom and Canada; and three coalition parliamentary systems: Denmark, Germany, and the Netherlands. This allows us to assess variations between and within the domestic categories to assess the constraints of the domestic institutional design but also how actors within each institutional type have some room for making decisions. Second, we chose to place more attention on the countries that operated in Regional Command South (RC-South), which included Australia, Canada, Denmark, the Netherlands, the United Kingdom, and the United States.[42] RC-South was the most multilateral sector in ISAF, with command rotating among the British, Canadians, and Dutch during the 2003–10 time frame, and it has been one of the most dangerous parts of the country. Together these two realities allow us to see how different countries react to similar stresses. Third, most of these

---

and Italy. Baltrusaitis (2010) examines allies and their contributions to Iraq. Neither presents an argument like ours that applies institutional analyses to modern democracies.

41 France is a premier-presidential system and, thus, not a purely presidential government, but the president reigns supreme in the realm of defense policy and military operations with parliament taking a very small role. Consequently, we include France with the other presidential systems.

42 The other significant contingent deployed to this area was Romania, but we were unable to do extensive fieldwork on the Romanian contribution to RC-S.

countries varied over time in terms of civilian leadership, and in some cases in terms of the command structure of their militaries, which provides variation in the causal mechanisms in which we are most interested. Fourth, we chose to study Australia because it was both a participant in RC-South and was not a member of NATO. We examined Australia's and New Zealand's contributions to ISAF to assess what effect variations in alliance membership might have on how countries operate in Afghanistan. Fifth, and finally, we address the contributions made by Italy, Poland, Turkey, and others in shorter discussions, and include them in our tables throughout the book.

Data for this project came from more than 250 interviews with senior civilian officials, military officers, and experts from ISAF-contributing nations as well as partner nations operating in Afghanistan. Civilians included a president, a former prime minister, three former defense ministers, and a variety of lesser but still senior policy officials. Military officers included two overall ISAF commanders, two overall commanders of U.S. Operation Enduring Freedom forces, dozens of flag officers, many colonel equivalents, and many officers who served as their country's senior military representative on the ground, often those empowered to play the red card. We also interviewed those who were on the other end of the phone back in the national capitals: the military and civilian officials in charge of international operations abroad.

In all, we conducted extensive and concentrated interviews with American, Australian, Belgian, British, Canadian, Danish, Dutch, German, French, New Zealand, Polish, Portuguese, Spanish, and Turkish officials, as well as the heads of eight ISAF delegations serving at U.S. Central Command. We interviewed members of the international staff at NATO headquarters, Supreme Headquarters Allied Powers Europe, and Joint Forces Command Brunssum. Some interview subjects agreed to be cited by name. The majority, however, shared their views on the condition that we protect their anonymity. Interview subjects were asked to keep their comments to the unclassified level. We also gained some insights when Steve Saideman toured Kabul and Kandahar as part of a Canadian and NATO effort to inform "opinion leaders" about the mission in December 2007. Whenever possible, we verified claims with multiple sources, public record documents, or press reports before including information in the narrative.

Such interview-intensive research required us to limit the project's scope in two ways. The first limitation was one of time. We focus largely on the period from 2003, when NATO started to play a role in Afghanistan, up to the beginning of 2010. Studying an event that is ongoing is always difficult, and something that we repeatedly warn our students not to do. The fall of the Dutch government over Afghanistan and the start of the troop surge in early 2010 served as a key point in the history of the international effort in Afghanistan and as a natural cutoff for a study on NATO in Afghanistan. We also chose the start of 2010 for practical reasons. Much of our research was conducted from 2007 through 2010. We realize that choosing any end date for this study is inherently problematic precisely because we do not know when the NATO effort in Afghanistan will end. The Lisbon Summit in November 2010 and the Chicago Summit in May 2012 suggest the transition will be well underway, if not completed, in 2014. We think this book will provide some insights into how NATO gets out of this conflict, as the dynamics discussed here will complicate the transition strategies developed by NATO, which we address in chapter 9.

The second limit is that we rarely address the management of special operations units. The information, including rules of engagement, for conventional units is often classified, but we have been able to get relatively good, publicly accessible information via interviews and media coverage. We have not been able to get comparable information consistently for the more secretive special operations units operating in Afghanistan. This is a problem since our interviews suggest that more than a few countries with relatively restricted conventional units have employed special operations units more freely. Indeed, using such units is one way to evade the limits placed on conventional forces. We try to address these dynamics in the case studies, but admit that we simply do not have the information to rigorously cover the special operations efforts.

# The Bottom Line, Up Front

This book demonstrates that operating in a multilateral military effort is challenging, to say the least. NATO would be more effective if every contingent had no politically imposed restrictions, but that is not to say that the alliance or any multilateral effort is utterly ineffective and doomed to fail. Caveats, red cards, intrusive oversight, selection of officers, and incentives all matter in shaping how the contingents operate. These are political impediments to countries operating together on the battlefield, and they are not just about caveats.[43] It might seem like that at times because the public debates about caveats have been more extensive than discussions about red cards, phone calls home, oversight, incentives, or—with the United States as a notable exception—selection of commanders. As our cases illustrate, countries have varied in their reliance on caveats, sometimes using other means to manage their troops, sometimes using caveats in conjunction with alternative means of influence. To be sure, if our book only helps to clarify caveats, this would be a significant contribution given the paucity of systematic

---

43 This book will not focus on the technical interoperability that NATO achieves on a regular basis: multinational medical teams, air support from several countries helping out yet another, logistical support for NATO and non-NATO countries in a very harsh and distant land, and the like.

study of such restrictions. However, we aim to do more than that. We hope this book provides a relatively comprehensive understanding of the means by which countries manage their participation in multilateral operations and the choices they make.

Restrictions driven by domestic political processes that emanate out of particular institutions cannot be wished away. Countries will vary systematically in how much they can contribute to the fight, wherever the fight happens to be. These dynamics will become increasingly problematic over the next several years, as most NATO countries (and many others) will be cutting defense spending due to various fiscal crises and associated budget constraints. For example, the processes discussed in this book have the potential to undermine one means by which countries could seek to alleviate their fiscal problems: via specialization— NATO's Smart Defence Initiative. Alliance members are already tempted to cut their defense budgets. To cope, the alliance has encouraged its smaller members to produce niche capacities and rely on allies to provide the various capabilities that the country will no longer be able to procure. In theory, this makes a great deal of sense, but in alliance warfare, allies sometimes do not always show up on the battlefield when needed. The restrictions imposed on some allies will mean that other countries with specialized militaries will be at great risk should firing start, hoping that political restrictions do not impede the support they expect and need from their domestically constrained allies.

These political restrictions have a dual-edged impact on the possibility of future NATO and other multilateral efforts. On the one hand, those who bear greater burdens (such as the Canadians from 2005 to 2011, the Danes, the British, and the Americans) because their allies are domestically constrained from doing the same will face more criticism at home for "carrying" the alliance, making it harder to maintain the mission. Indeed, the claim that Canada was alone in Kandahar made it harder for Canada to keep its combat mission going. The apparent unfairness within the alliance undercuts public and political support at home. On the other hand, the ability for countries to control their contingents while engaged in multilateral operations makes possible any participation at all. Countries would simply not hand over troops to another country's commanders without some way to influence how they are used. Modern democracies must maintain civilian control of their militaries even as or especially when they are formally under the command of a multinational institution. Countries will simply not contribute troops without retaining some influence. It is abundantly clear that the dynamics addressed in the pages ahead are going to remain relevant despite the hopes of the less restricted members of the NATO alliance.

# 2 NATO and the Primacy of National Decisions in Multilateral Interventions

*Force generation is begging.*
— Official at Supreme Headquarters Allied Powers Europe, February 2011

In the early years of the twenty-first century, pundits were suggesting that NATO was becoming the world's primary means by which order would be kept (Daalder and Goldgeier 2006). Now global NATO seems unrealistic given the alliance's uneven performance in Afghanistan and, more recently, Libya. These interventions made obvious what was always true—that participation in any NATO out-of-area military operation is not required and does not guarantee maximum effort by each member of the alliance.[1] Countries that participate are volunteers, varying in how willing they are to do what alliance commanders ask. We saw this in the alliance's two major military interventions in Kosovo and Afghanistan. There and in Libya, the alliance's behavior reflected more a series of decisions by individual member states and less a coordinated design by a multilateral organization.

Still, NATO remains the most interoperable and effective multilateral security organization in the world, one that provides a degree of legitimacy and convenience when a crisis arises. Indeed, if we were to expect multilateralism to affect a military intervention, it would be when a strong and institutionalized military alliance engages in hostilities. NATO is the modern era's most formal and enduring alliance. It should be a most-likely case for multilateralism's positive effects on a military intervention.

This chapter reviews how the organization works, how alliance members can exacerbate the alliance's inherent, structural limitations, and what has been done in response. The chapter provides both empirical and theoretical rationales for why national decisions often trump the needs and potential efficiencies of the

---

1 Participation within the North Atlantic can be optional as well: Great Britain opted out of its turn in the rotation of countries temporarily deploying fighter planes to Iceland (Hoyle 2008).

NATO alliance's efforts in Afghanistan and elsewhere. The empirical case rests on a reexamination of alliance procedures and short tests of expected versus actual behavior when it comes to the alliance's capabilities and internal coordination. The theoretical argument is that the alliance's procedures create a particular type of principal-agent relationship that dramatically advantages national chains of command over the alliance chain of command. We begin by going back to first principles and exploring how the alliance makes decisions.

# Evolution under Fire: NATO's Introduction to Afghanistan

In late 2001, the United States led a small coalition of countries under the banner of Operation Enduring Freedom (OEF) to overthrow the Taliban government and hunt down al-Qaeda operatives. After the fall of the Taliban, OEF remained an ongoing operation. A parallel and often complementary approach was taken by the international community. At the end of 2001 in Bonn, Germany, an international agreement was negotiated to develop a force, called the International Security Assistance Force (ISAF), under the auspices of the United Nations. ISAF began with a limited mandate: it would provide security in and around Kabul, and help the new Afghan government increase its governing capacity. So while ISAF initially focused its attention on the capital, OEF forces spread throughout the country, with particular concentrations in the south and east.

ISAF eventually became a NATO mission with military contributions from a wide range of alliance members as well as other partner countries. The original UN mandate allowed for the possibility of ISAF spreading its coverage beyond Kabul, and the mission expanded in a series of steps between 2004 and 2006. ISAF divided Afghan territory into five regional commands (RCs), as pictured in figure 2.1. ISAF deployments beyond Kabul began in the north, considered at the time the least dangerous of the four regions outside the capital, and extended its reach in a series of counterclockwise steps around the country. American OEF forces turned over the majority of responsibilities for a region as ISAF moved in, though elements of the U.S. military continued to operate across the country in parallel to ISAF forces. As the rollout proceeded, the alliance named a different lead nation for each regional command. The United States remained the lead nation in Regional Command East (RC-East).

ISAF and OEF continued to coexist through 2010, the end of this study, with ISAF focused predominately on peacekeeping, stability operations, and counterinsurgency, and OEF focused predominantly on counterterrorism and training the Afghan National Army. Yet that distinction often blurred, sometimes very quickly. Countries might have operated under different chains of command (ISAF or OEF)

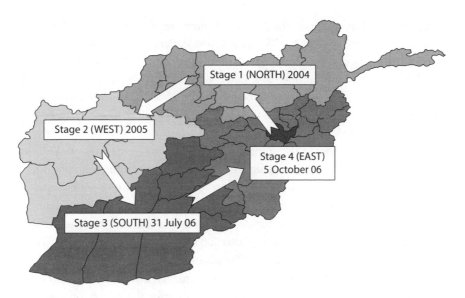

**Figure 2.1** ◆ NATO Expansion of ISAF

but largely engaged in the same enterprise. Regardless of the command, operations in Afghanistan required that foreign forces work in a difficult environment against serious opposition. Indeed, ISAF countries that had signed up for what they envisioned as peacekeeping duties often found themselves in an increasingly hostile environment beginning in late 2005. Their reactions to that environment varied tremendously, leading to the question of why that should be the case in a multilateral intervention by a strongly institutionalized alliance.

# The Empirical Case for National Primacy

## NATO DECISION MAKING AND UNANIMITY

The NATO alliance has two main organizational entities above and outside its military chain of command. The North Atlantic Council (NAC) is the supreme decision-making body of the alliance, overseeing its political and military policies. Each member state has a seat on the NAC. The NATO secretary general chairs the NAC; he has always been a European civilian appointed by the alliance's member states.[2] NAC meetings can be called by any member state representative

2 North Atlantic Treaty Organization, *Final Communique of the Ninth Session of the North Atlantic Council (The Lisbon Decisions)*, February 25, 1952, http://www.nato.int/cps/en/natolive/official_texts_17303.htm, accessed April 23, 2013.

or by the secretary general. The Military Committee (MC) provides advice on military policy and strategy to NATO's political leaders but is not in the alliance's operational chain of command. That chain of command runs from the supreme allied commander for Europe (SACEUR; an American by tradition) through NATO's regional commands and down to deployed forces. Each country has a military representative at the MC, with the MC also chaired by a European or a Canadian. The MC is subordinate to the NAC.

The common wisdom specifies that NAC decisions are based on the unanimity principle; as Beer notes, "The unanimity rule was implicit, with each nation preserving a possible veto over decisions" and it "prevented decisions which individual nations chose strongly to oppose" (1969: 13, 52). As a result of the unanimity rule, NAC decisions either devolve down to the lowest common denominator, suffer severe delays, or never occur (Gallis 2003).

To take two examples, consider NATO actions with regard to Kosovo in 1998 and the defense of Turkey in early 2003. In the former case, one reason the administration of President Bill Clinton did not push for the use of force against Serbia in 1998 was over concerns that the alliance could not reach consensus. Alliance members with troops in Bosnia would object, other allies believed an intervention would advantage the Kosovo Liberation Army, and some believed that UN authorization was required before NATO could intervene (Daalder and O'Hanlon 2000). In the words of then U.S. national security advisor Sandy Berger, "moving that alliance to act is a Herculean undertaking which would happen only in the most egregious circumstances" (Berger, quoted in Daalder and O'Hanlon 2000: 31). In the latter case, Turkey was concerned for its security in the 2003 buildup to the Iraq War and asked the alliance to reinforce Turkish defenses. Belgium, France, and Germany all objected, in large part because of their opposition to the Iraq War, and by their votes temporarily blocked the assistance from reaching Turkey (Lindstrom 2003). These examples would seem to point to a hugely important effect on the ends, ways, and means associated with intervention by a multilateral alliance like NATO, and are one reason that some senior U.S. officials disparaged NATO during the administration of President George W. Bush.

Yet the need for unanimous decisions—and the need for a lowest common denominator policy—is true only in the loosest sense of the word. Nothing in the original North Atlantic Treaty requires unanimous NAC decisions, with the exception of decisions that expand NATO's membership.[3] Instead, the unanimity "rule," as it has become known, is in fact a behavioral norm that has been

---

3 North Atlantic Treaty Organization, *North Atlantic Treaty*, April 4, 1949, http://www.nato.int/cps/en/natolive/official_texts_17120.htm, accessed April 23, 2013. The procedures for new membership are described in Article 10 of the treaty.

creatively defined to accommodate divergent opinions among member states and to ensure the alliance's continued viability. Specifically, decisions by the NAC "are agreed upon on the basis of unanimity and common accord." At the same time, "There is no voting or decision by majority."[4] Instead, member states consult until they can reach a "consensus," even if that means agreeing to disagree.[5] Contentious proposals are debated for a particular period and then considered agreed to—absent objection, which is called "breaking silence" (Michel 2003). States who object to a proposal's contents can break silence privately or (rarely) publicly if they so choose. States who object privately, or who acquiesce even if they disagree with the proposal, usually have their anonymity secured by a related practice of the secretary general: only releasing summary statements of NAC deliberations rather than transcripts of the full NAC debate (Michel 2003: 3).[6]

A modification to popular characterizations of the alliance as ruled by unanimity might be that NATO decision processes reinforce the primacy of national decisions over the needs of the alliance. NATO decisions are "unanimous" only in the sense that no state is strongly enough opposed to voice opposition. The ability to object or acquiesce to a policy outside public scrutiny facilitates the alliance as a whole, making decisions consistent with the desires of the more powerful member states and/or those states that care deeply about the specific issue at hand. NAC decisions, then, may diverge from the ideal policy of any one member state and get no public objection from that state. They can opt out or be bought off by more powerful member states. In the words of an alliance ambassador to NATO headquarters, NAC decisions are made by consensus with special weight given to those who do the most.[7] Rather than requiring unanimity, *the alliance's decision rules would seem to encourage deal making by powerful and/or passionate members who want to get their way.*

Greece's quiet acquiescence to NATO's air campaign in Kosovo is a prime example of both phenomena. The Greek government was deeply opposed to NATO involvement in Kosovo for domestic political reasons, yet Greece did not choose to oppose publicly the United States and other important NATO members in NAC decisions related to the war (Michel 2003: 2). NATO sweetened the bitter pill of the air war through concrete actions that enhanced Greek security and formed a buffer between the violence in Kosovo and Greek territory. NATO provided:

---

4 North Atlantic Treaty Organization, *The North Atlantic Council*, http://www.nato.int/cps/en/natolive/topics_49763.htm, accessed April 23, 2013.
5 North Atlantic Treaty Organization, *Consensus Decision-Making at NATO*, http://www.nato.int/cps/en/natolive/topics_49178.htm, accessed April 23, 2013.
6 An example is "Statement by NATO Secretary General Solana on Behalf of the North Atlantic Council, February 19, 1999," reprinted in Auerswald and Auerswald 2000: 515.
7 Interview with alliance ambassador to NATO headquarters, Brussels, February 2011.

- explicit NAC support for UN preventative deployment forces in neighboring Macedonia
- enhancements to Partnership for Peace activities with Macedonia
- deployment of an armed extraction force in Macedonia
- deployment of resources and troops into Macedonia and Albania to absorb and contain refugees leaving Kosovo before they reached Greece
- threats of NATO reprisals had Serbian forces attacked neighboring states

Moreover, the Greeks were cognizant that NATO membership was their only security guarantee against Turkey.[8] All this is to say that the alliance may need to accommodate reluctant members' concerns on the margins, but that does not necessarily translate into a lowest common denominator alliance policy.[9] Instead, it points to the role of individual national preferences and the pulling and hauling of political deals within the alliance.

Our argument is that the crucial locus of power remains with the individual nation-states that make up the NATO alliance. The text of the North Atlantic Treaty supports this perspective, especially when it comes to the use of force, in that *nothing in the North Atlantic Treaty obligates member states to contribute to NATO missions.* Acquiescing to an alliance intervention does not obligate members to help implement that policy in any particular way, even in cases where allies are subject to direct attack. Article V of the treaty requires that if a member is attacked then each member "will assist the Party or Parties so attacked by taking forthwith, individually and in concert with the other Parties, *such action as it deems necessary.*"[10] By this language, an individual member takes action as it deems necessary, not as the alliance deems necessary. Even when member states participate in NATO missions, they can choose to set their own ground rules for their national contingents in the field. If other states do not like those rules, the national contingent can always be brought home. It is our contention, then, that in interventions such as Afghanistan, individual national decisions trump NATO decisions.

---

8 See North Atlantic Council Statement, May 28, 1998, reprinted in Auerswald and Auerswald 2000: 170; Statement by the North Atlantic Council on Kosovo, December 8, 1998, reprinted in Auerswald and Auerswald 2000: 351–53; Statement by the North Atlantic Council, April 4, 1999, reprinted in Auerswald and Auerswald 2000: 788–89; Statement by the North Atlantic Council, April 12, 1999, reprinted in Auerswald and Auerswald 2000: 818–20; and North Atlantic Council Statement on Kosovo, April 23, 1999, reprinted in Auerswald and Auerswald 2000: 887–90.

9 In the aforementioned 2003 case of Turkey, the United States was able to push the alliance into providing enhanced defenses for Turkey by taking the decision to the alliance's Defense Planning Committee, which excluded France, and putting significant political pressure on the German and Belgian governments until they acquiesced. See Gallis 2003: 1–2; and Michel 2003: 4.

10 The invocation of Article V after September 11, 2001, did not require specific actions by any member to support the United States, and some countries refrained from participating in the most visible manifestation of that effort—the NATO airborne warning and control planes sent to fly over American cities during major events in 2002. NATO, *The North Atlantic Treaty*, emphasis added.

# NATO's Force Generation Process

A review of NATO's force generation process makes our point.[11] Whenever NATO military assets deploy, they create an operations plan (OpPlan) that describes the forces needed; the deployment requirements and scheduling; logistical needs; rules of engagement; and the sequencing, scope, and type of foreseen military operations. For our purposes, this section will focus on the force generation process associated with NATO OpPlans.

NATO commanders on the ground send their force capabilities requests up through the alliance's military chain of command. Ultimately, those requests reach the Supreme Headquarters Allied Powers Europe (SHAPE) outside of Mons, Belgium. The force generation team at SHAPE, under the command of the deputy supreme allied commander for Europe (DSACEUR), translates those requests into a standardized NATO format, which is then fed into the NATO Combined Joint Statement of Requirements (CJSOR)—a spreadsheet listing each military unit that is viewed as necessary for the effort. The CJSOR is transmitted to all NATO member states with a request that members contribute toward its fulfillment. The force generation staff at SHAPE follows up on the CJSOR by contacting representatives from each member state on a nearly daily basis, hoping to secure informal commitments as to who will be providing what capabilities for the NATO commanders in the field. National commitments are made informally from the respective Ministry of Defense to the SHAPE team, via that country's national contingent stationed at SHAPE.

Informal promises are translated into formal commitments at NATO force generation conferences (FGCs), where representatives from all member states meet to discuss the CJSOR. There is an annual FGC dealing with NATO requirements worldwide. For the period of our study, there usually were two ISAF-specific FGCs each year, in the early summer and in November, depending on the need. Member nations formally announce what they will contribute at each FGC. These commitments take the form of "force preparation" messages and are followed by formal "transfer of authority" messages (transferring command of the national contingent over to NATO) about a month before the actual deployment. In a perfect world in which alliance concerns trumped national concerns, requested forces would be forthcoming at the FGCs, the deployed commanders would get on with the business of implementing the NATO OpPlan, and the force generation process would end until the next set of requests was sent from the field commanders. The whole process would take between six and nine months from an initial request to a transfer of authority message and deployment.

---

11 This section is largely based on interviews with officials at SHAPE on February 1, 2011.

Unfortunately, the force generation process rarely, if ever, works this way according to several senior NATO officials we interviewed in Mons.[12] Again and again we were told that national concerns routinely trumped alliance needs. For example, in late 2010 and into early 2011, ISAF commanders had identified roughly 8,000 unfilled in-country positions. More than 750 of those shortfalls were in the area of military and police trainers, one of the most critical missions for ISAF and one of the specific skill sets that is very difficult to resource.[13] Shortfalls can occur for a plethora of reasons. Ministers make promises at a series of different NATO meetings, often creating confusion as it is not clear whether a new commitment is being made or an old one is being reiterated.[14] It is also not uncommon for members to rescind their initial offers of support between their informal commitment and an FGC, or between the conclusion of an FGC and an actual deployment, often for political reasons within the individual member state. NATO Airborne Warning and Control Systems planes (AWACS) could not fly over Afghanistan with German crews, for instance, because one of the minor parties in the German coalition government refused to allow it. When pressured by the government of German chancellor Angela Merkel in June 2009, the party relented but then refused to allow German-piloted AWACS to be based in the Persian Gulf, rendering them effectively useless. As a result, the German AWACS teams were not deployed, despite being needed by the alliance.[15]

For two reasons, NATO is faced with a dilemma when such shortfalls arise. First, remember that there is nothing in the North Atlantic Treaty requiring member states to contribute to alliance military operations. Second, the common understanding at NATO is to keep those rescissions out of the public eye so as not to upset certain member states and perhaps jeopardize current or future commitments. The dilemma, then, is what to do when faced with a shortfall. Absent sufficient capabilities, the deployed commanders can change the OpPlan to reflect diminished or unfulfilled capabilities. That, of course, is politically risky, particularly if changing the OpPlan calls into question the alliance's ability to achieve alliance goals, to say nothing of contradicting those goals outright. Alternately, the DSACEUR and his staff can get to work twisting arms. It is this latter option that is most often pursued.

---

12 One of the authors, Steve Saideman, observed force generation from the other end of the process when he served on the Bosnia desk of the U.S. Joint Staff in 2001–2. Even six years after NATO got involved in Bosnia, force generation was an ongoing concern with significant parts of the CJSOR left unfilled.

13 Interviews with a NATO lieutenant general, major general, and supporting staff officers in Belgium, February 2011.

14 Kathleen McInnis, who used to head the ISAF desk at the office of the U.S. Secretary of Defense, pointed this out to us.

15 This may have changed in the summer of 2011 as Germany sought to compensate for pulling people out of NATO AWACS planes engaged in the Libyan mission.

The force generation team is the first responder when the alliance faces a capabilities shortfall. The team mines its contacts in each member state, asking for additional forces via a number of strategies. Solutions are sometimes as simple as ensuring that the alliance asks a country to fill a role it is comfortable filling with a targeted request, such as base security versus counternarcotics, to use one example. The team can work deals in which country A can delay deploying a particular capability that country B can deploy immediately, in exchange for deploying a different needed capability now. For example, the Dutch offered to send twenty trainers into Afghanistan to perform a job already being undertaken by a German contingent. The force generation team asked the Germans to take on another task. The Germans complied, and ISAF was able to employ usefully both nations' contingents. A country also can be asked to deploy now in exchange for a promise of relief in the future. Or finally, the force generation team can negotiate with other nations to help country A with logistics, force protection, transportation, and the like if that is what is needed to get a deployment commitment. This is frequently the case with the less capable newer and smaller allies and partners.[16]

If none of this works, the process moves steadily higher up the military and political chains of command. The DSACEUR is next in line should his force generation team be unable to get needed results. According to officials at Mons, the DSACEUR frequently, if not regularly, contacts the chiefs of defense of individual member states to request additional forces from them. Should that not work, the SACEUR has been known to call defense ministers directly. The president of the United States has even become involved in specific instances should the SACEUR be unable to get results for critically needed capabilities.

Officials at Mons are sensitive to the domestic political constraints facing individual member states, and tailor the information available to the public with those constraints in mind. As an example, consider that NATO maintains what is known as a "placemat" of deployed forces, as represented in figure 2.2.

The placemat provides a picture of who is deployed where, with what capabilities, and in what numbers.[17] It is a political document for public consumption that essentially papers over the primacy of national decisions vis-à-vis the needs of the alliance. Specifically, the placemat reproduced in table 2.1 only displays the national contingents that fulfill the CJSOR requirements. It does not represent the reality on the ground, in that the placemat does not reflect any additional support elements (i.e., base security, logistics, communications, etc.) or special

---

16 A partner is a country outside of NATO that seeks to participate in the NATO mission. These countries can prove to be quite useful and willing, as we show in chapter 7.

17 NATO's archived placemats can be found at http://www.isaf.nato.int/isaf-placemat-archives.html, accessed September 5, 2011. NATO was much less consistent about providing any kind of placemat for the Libyan effort in 2011—see chapter 8.

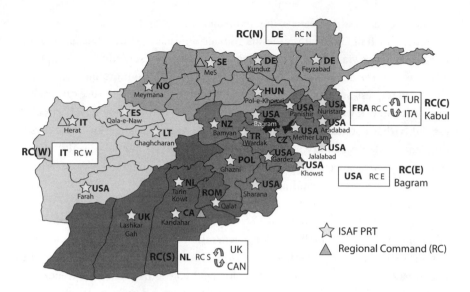

**Figure 2.2** ◆ NATO Placemat, December 2009

operations units not under ISAF command that an individual nation may demand or require but that NATO did not request in the CJSOR. At the same time,
SHAPE leadership sometimes asks member states to exceed temporarily and
privately their deployment caps to enhance a military operation. In some cases,
keeping that information private is necessary because revealing those additional
elements would publicize that the member state is exceeding a domestically imposed cap on deployed troops. Several nations, for instance, could not deploy
more than a specific number of troops to Afghanistan, a number specified in
legislation. In other cases, publicizing those additional deployments would have
embarrassed partner nations who either should have provided those additional
capabilities but were not, or were providing those capabilities but in a way that
instilled no confidence among alliance partners. And finally, keeping additional
deployments secret is justified for operational reasons. In short, the deployment
placemat is a political document that does not necessarily represent reality on
the ground, for both operational and domestic political reasons of individual
member states.

The above argument supports our contention that national concerns rather
than the alliance's overall needs dominate the force generation process. The
CJSOR is never completely filled, and the ISAF placemat is a useful fiction, due
both to domestic political factors and the alliance's permissive rules.

**Table 2.1.** NATO Placemat Data, December 2009

| Country | Size of Contingent |
|---|---|
| Albania | 250 |
| Australia | 1200 |
| Austria | 4 |
| Azerbaijan | 90 |
| Belgium | 510 |
| Bosnia and Herzegovina | 2 |
| Bulgaria | 460 |
| Canada | 2830 |
| Croatia | 290 |
| Czech Republic | 340 |
| Denmark | 700 |
| Estonia | 150 |
| Finland | 130 |
| France | 3070 |
| Georgia | 1 |
| Germany | 4245 |
| Greece | 125 |
| Hungary | 310 |
| Iceland | 8 |
| Ireland | 7 |
| Italy | 2795 |
| Jordan | 7 |
| Latvia | 165 |
| Lithuania | 250 |
| Luxembourg | 8 |
| Former Yugoslav Republic of Macedonia | 185 |
| Netherlands | 2160 |
| New Zealand | 220 |
| Norway | 600 |
| Poland | 2025 |
| Portugal | 105 |
| Romania | 990 |
| Singapore | 2 |
| Slovakia | 240 |
| Slovenia | 80 |
| Spain | 1000 |
| Sweden | 430 |
| Turkey | 820 |
| Ukraine | 10 |
| United Arab Emirates | 25 |
| United Kingdom | 9000 |
| United States | 31855 |
| Total | 67700 |

## CHAIN OF COMMAND

Force generation is only one means through which to measure the degree of national primacy in the ISAF effort. Examining the chain of command is another such measure. In theory, according to senior military officials in NATO, SHAPE headquarters translated the political guidance it received from the NAC into strategic level military plans. NATO's Allied Joint Forces Command in Brunssum, Netherlands, provided additional guidance and detail for (in this case) the overall ISAF commander (COMISAF), who operated out of ISAF headquarters in Kabul. The COMISAF crafted the detailed operational plans that supported the strategic military plan. Each regional command used that operational plan as the basis for its regional courses of action. And finally, localized supporting plans were devised by individual country contingents operating within Afghanistan, consistent with the direction given by the regional command and the overall operational plan crafted by the COMISAF. In theory, then, the overall political guidance devised by the NAC flowed seamlessly from NATO headquarters to Mons, then to Brunssum, to the COMISAF, to ISAF regional commands, and on down to the individual national contingents for implementation.

Much of the time this system worked. Countries identified what they were willing to do and what they refused to do when they signed transfer of authority agreements with the ISAF command. The COMISAF's task was to select the right countries for the right missions, and thereby utilize those national forces to the maximum extent possible to achieve ISAF goals.

To better understand this process, consider a line that represents the spectrum of military effort exerted in Afghanistan, as can be seen in figure 2.3. The left margin represents zero effort. Moving to the right along the line is representative of a country exerting more military effort. Now imagine two countries, and the overall NAC, placed along this line, with the placement on the line representing these entities' maximum desired military effort. Country A is located somewhere to the right of zero effort. The NAC's maximum desired effort is to the right of country A. Country B is to the right of the NAC. This translates into the following narrative: The alliance has come to a collective agreement on some level of military effort. For whatever reason, country A is unwilling to do as much the alliance wants to do. In the Afghan context, examples of country A might be Germany, Spain, or Turkey; country B, on the other hand, has incentives to provide more

**Figure 2.3** ◆ Maximum Effort by NATO Members and the NAC

effort than the alliance can agree to. The obvious example in the case of Afghanistan might be the United States.

The overall ISAF commander must get the maximum effort possible out of each country. Assuming that COMISAF can deduce or is told of the maximum effort country A is willing and able to sustain, the trick is to assign country A to missions that do not exceed its maximum effort. In other words, assign missions to country A that are equal to or to the left of A on the line. Country A cannot reasonably shirk its responsibility because it is not being asked to exceed what it has already agreed to do. In this example, country A fulfills its commitment, and the COMISAF gets some military value from that nation, however small that contribution might be (this is in addition to any political value to the alliance from country A's participation in the alliance endeavor).

In the above example, the military commander from country A will behave consistent with both the ISAF chain of command and his home government's chain of command. The two chains of command are in agreement. In theory, a military commander in that situation is relatively free to execute the mission in his preferred manner as long as he stays within the overlapping range of acceptable policies from his country and the NAC. In short, we should not see commanders from country A engaging in what either their home government or the NAC believes is inappropriate behavior.

Problems arise when (1) the COMISAF asks the country A commander to exceed his country's maximum effort, (2) the COMISAF has imperfect information as to where country A's maximum effort level lies, or (3) country A decides unexpectedly to restrict its military's behavior, moving country A's maximum effort level to the left on the line. In those cases the commander from country A is faced with conflicting orders. Should he listen to his home chain of command or the ISAF chain? If he prioritizes his home chain of command, country A's military commander will appear to be violating or ignoring the ISAF chain of command. If he prioritizes the ISAF chain, he violates his own military chain of command.

The situation with regard to country B is perhaps more interesting. The COMISAF can assign country B to any mission within the NAC's acceptability range, represented by points equal to or to the left of the NAC on the line. Country B will not shirk its responsibility for the same reasons given for country A. As country B's maximum effort exceeds the NAC's maximum effort, there is less chance of the COMISAF inadvertently forcing country B's commander to choose between the two chains of command. Assuming that the COMISAF gets clear guidance from the NAC, he cannot ask more of country B than the NAC's maximum effort; such a request would exceed the limits agreed upon by the NAC. In theory, then, the COMISAF will not ask more of country B than the NAC maximum even though country B is willing to exceed the NAC's maximum effort.

This confronts country B with a dilemma. It can order its military commander to follow the COMISAF's orders if it is not concerned with accelerating the pace or scale of alliance operations. In this case, there is no conflict between the ISAF and home chains of command, and country B's military commander will behave consistent with both chains of command. Yet what if country B wants its military contingent to do more? In such cases the country's military commander must choose whether to follow the ISAF or home chain of command. Country B's military commander will appear to be ignoring the COMISAF's orders if he chooses the home chain of command, but in the opposite direction than might country A. To avoid that situation, country B can deploy troops solely or partially under its home chain of command rather than as part of ISAF. Certain types of special operations forces from the United States, France, and other nations have done just that, operating under the OEF umbrella rather than as part of ISAF. Those troops can exceed the NAC maximum military effort without violating the alliance's agreement. Absent such arrangements, country B's commander must chose between ISAF and his home government.

This discussion suggests instances in which ISAF and home governments can pull national contingent commanders in two different directions. Our interviews with senior ISAF officials suggest that there have been significant disconnects between what is given to ISAF and what often is implemented by the national contingents operating within Afghanistan.[18] It is this disconnect that reinforces the notion that national decisions take primacy of place over alliance decisions. Misperception of or imperfect information with regard to caveats are one cause of these disconnects. The need for coordination across and within ISAF components is another major source of disconnects between ISAF and national contingents. We next turn to those coordination challenges.

## U.S.-ISAF Relations

One of the major points of contention within ISAF, and a continual cause of concern for many ISAF nations during the period of this study, was poor coordination between U.S. forces and other national contingents. The United States operated in both the OEF and ISAF chains of command. We review this relationship in more detail in chapter 4, but some U.S. military assets operated as part of OEF throughout the country, with most concentrated in RC-East. The United States also had forces that operated as part of ISAF, and, finally, it had special operations forces that answered to their own chain of command rather than through either OEF or ISAF commands. For much of the conflict, OEF and ISAF forces

---

18 Interviews with a NATO lieutenant general and major general, Brussels, February 2011.

had very different missions, to say nothing of very different interpretations of events and assessments of progress. OEF forces were focused primarily on counterterrorism missions, with a large kinetic component.[19] ISAF forces, in contrast, had a counterinsurgency and peacekeeping mission, which often but not always put less emphasis on kinetic operations.

Coordination between American OEF units and their allied counterparts varied by country and by mission. Some allied contingents operated as part of the OEF coalition, particularly though not exclusively before ISAF took over the regional commands in 2006. There was tight coordination between coalition and U.S. forces when all were operating within OEF. For example, Polish forces found it easy to coordinate with the United States in RC-East.[20] French forces operating in RC-East as part of Task Force Warrior reported excellent coordination between their battalion and the United States in Combined Joint Task Force 101. Indeed, French and U.S. OEF forces operated side by side all through 2008 and into 2009 with no major problems.[21] Coordination also was relatively easy among NATO forces that had significant experience with American operations and relatively advanced military capabilities. Almost none of the British senior officers we interviewed, for example, complained of coordination problems with the Americans. Canadian brigadier general David Fraser characterized working with OEF as akin to being "essentially a family member."[22]

Other national contingents were not as sanguine about coordinating with U.S. forces. Spanish officers, for example, complained about U.S. OEF operations being conducted in their area of responsibility (AOR) without the approval of or coordination with the Spanish commander.[23] Countries with significant geographic caveats had difficulties coordinating with more mobile OEF forces. Such complaints were particularly vocal when it came to U.S. special operations forces (SOF). We were repeatedly told by allied military officers of months of patient outreach to local populations being undermined by a night raid by U.S. special operations troops. Even the otherwise tight U.S.-French military relationship on the ground suffered when it came to SOF units due to different conceptions as to how those units should be used, leading the French to withdraw some two hundred SOF personnel from OEF in mid-2007.[24]

19 In military parlance, *kinetic* refers to using force. Nonkinetic operations are those in which no force is used.
20 Interviews with Polish officials, Brussels, February 2011, and Krakow and Warsaw, May 2012.
21 Interview with senior French officers, Paris, February 2009.
22 Interview with Brigadier General David Fraser, Edmonton, Alberta, January 29, 2007.
23 Interview with Spanish officials, Brussels, February 2011.
24 Interview with senior French officer, Paris, February 2009. Other French officials suggested that SOF were withdrawn because they had completed their mission. The two perspectives are not necessarily in conflict.

Some of that friction came from a lack of intelligence sharing. Indeed, intelligence sharing has been a huge impediment to coordination across national contingents, particularly between the United States and other ISAF nations. From the perspective of some partner nations, U.S. forces on counterterrorism missions did not share intelligence or mission planning. In the absence of robust intelligence sharing, two neighboring national contingents may have a different picture of reality, and be much less willing to support one another's operations across the boundaries between their AORs. The less complete a picture of their circumstances that a particular national contingent has, the more reluctant that contingent might be to take action beyond its narrow area of responsibility, and the more caveats that country might place on its forces.[25] To be clear, this went both ways, as some countries were quite reluctant to share with the United States biometric data (fingerprints, DNA, etc.) that they had collected from detainees.

## Regional Commands

The OEF-ISAF relationship was the most visible example of a problem endemic to ISAF operations in the regional command structure.[26] It was by no means the only problem, however. As noted above, ISAF operated four distinct regional commands in addition to that of the capital (RC-Capital), starting with Regional Command North (RC-North), all the way around the country to Regional Command East (RC-East). A different lead nation ran each regional command, as is shown in table 2.2. For the six years that we are concerned with (2004–10), Germany served as lead nation in RC-North; the Italians led RC-West; the British, Canadians, and the Dutch rotated leadership in RC-South; and the United States controlled RC-East.[27]

Three problems have been evident over time with this arrangement. The first was inherent in the designation of lead nations in each regional command. Splitting Afghanistan into ISAF regional commands run by different countries established the conditions for coordination problems across commands. Having the same country lead a regional command for long periods of time may have exacerbated such problems, and presented ISAF's adversaries with opportunities to exploit the seams among the RCs. A second challenge was due to the geography of the regional commands, which caused disconnects between national contingents. Parts of RC-West, for example, were inaccessible from other parts of the regional

---

25 Interview with a NATO lieutenant general, Brussels, February 2011. Conflicts over intelligence sharing are an old NATO story; Steve Saideman heard these complaints regarding Bosnia in 2001.
26 The Afghans have a different regional command map than does ISAF. Thanks to Kathleen McInnis for pointing this out.
27 In the summer of 2010, Helmand was split off of RC-S, calling it RC-SW, when U.S. Marines were sent in as part of the surge, and put under American command.

**Table 2.2.** ISAF Regional Commands

|  | RC-North | RC-West | RC-South | RC-East | RC-Capital |
|---|---|---|---|---|---|
| Feb 2006– Nov 2006 | Germany | Italy | Canada | United States | France |
| Nov 2006– May 2007 | Germany | Italy | Netherlands | United States | France |
| May 2007– Feb 2008 | Germany | Italy | United Kingdom | United States | Turkey |
| Feb 2008– Nov 2008 | Germany | Italy | Canada | United States | Italy |
| Nov 2008– May 2009 | Germany | Italy | Netherlands | United States | France |
| May 2009– Feb 2010 | Germany | Italy | United Kingdom | United States | France |

command for much of the year, but were accessible from RC-North. The problem was that the Germans, in the lead in RC-North, did not want to take responsibility for additional territory in RC-West.[28] This posed a particular problem for the Norwegians since their provincial reconstruction team (PRT) was in RC-North but quite close to RC-West. A third glitch was that the RC headquarters often lacked the capability or the authority to serve truly as operational headquarters. RC-South, for instance, was not very directive until British major general Nick Carter took command in late 2009, bringing with him the personnel and structures of a divisional headquarters. Until then, the various RC-South commanders served to coordinate the operations within the provinces but did not serve as the operational commanders of the theater. Only with the appointment of Carter and with the backing of the COMISAF, General Stanley McChrystal, did RC-South start to command operations. Until then, each contributing country did most of the operational planning for their sector within RC-South.[29] As a result, for most of the mission and for nearly the entirety of the scope of our book, each country managed its own battle space with relatively little regard for how others were running their AORs—*each country was fighting its own war*, as we highlight in the title of this book.

The coordination challenges evident across regional commands also existed *within* regional commands because national contingents were given responsibility for specific geographic territory in the region. The Balkanization of ISAF

---

28 Interview with NATO senior military officer, Brunssum, Netherlands, February 2011.

29 Interview with Lieutenant General Marc Lessard, Ottawa, January 8, 2008. Lessard had commanded RC-South in 2008 and then led the Canada Expeditionary Forces Command (CEFCOM) starting in August 2011. As we detail in chapter 5, CEFCOM provided operational planning for Kandahar through 2009.

contingents sometimes worked well, or at least did no harm. In mid-2006, for example, the RC-South commander, Canadian lieutenant general David Frasier and the commander of British forces in the region, brigadier general Ed Butler, agreed to "let the UK get on with their plan while the Canadians got on with their plan."[30] This somewhat Balkanized approach did not produce tremendous coordination, but neither did it lead to friction.

Too often, however, differing national perspectives did lead to friction. Neighboring national contingents did not always agree on their goals in Afghanistan, to say nothing of the wisdom of specific operations. For example, later in 2006 the Dutch and British contingents in RC-South disagreed as to the operation of Task Force Helmand.[31] The Dutch commander of RC-South wanted the task force to operate throughout the province. The British objected, arguing that Dutch troops were not mobile and could not help the British, forcing the British to operate alone, which would be too risky given the limited assets available. The dispute eventually went all the way up to the ISAF commander at the time, UK general David Richards, who sided with the British commander and told him to disregard the Dutch orders. In short, a difference of opinion between national contingents yielded very little coordination within RC-South, and contributed to the belief among some commanders that multinational coordination in ISAF was dysfunctional.

Provincial reconstruction teams were another key indicator of national parochialism. An innovation from the Iraq experience, each PRT focused on governance and reconstruction efforts to facilitate Afghanistan's development into a functional, self-sustaining government. Most PRTs were led by a single country. Many, but not all, NATO countries led PRTs, as table 2.3 illustrates. The PRTs varied in how large they were, how many civilians they had, and even whether they were led by civilians, military officers, or both. They represented the shared intent to engage in a "comprehensive approach" in which the three main efforts of governance, security, and development were supposed to be integrated. Countries each engaged in this effort in various ways, so that some "whole of government" efforts really did involve individuals from aid agencies, foreign affairs, police, and the military, but others relied much more on just the military.[32]

Coordinating across PRTs became a core problem for ISAF command. In the words of a high-ranking officer at NATO's Joint Force Command–Brunssum, "PRTs have huge problems because they are nationally run" rather than being standardized and coordinated by ISAF.[33] A senior British Ministry of Defense official agreed, characterizing ISAF PRTs as a number of national task forces in their

---

30 Interview with Brigadier General Ed Butler (retired), London, October 21, 2009.
31 Interviews with senior British officers, Washington, D.C., and Tampa, Florida, February 2009.
32 For comparative analyses of the various efforts, see Maley (forthcoming).
33 Interview with NATO senior military officer, Brunssum, Netherlands, February 2011.

**Table 2.3.** National Control of PRTs, 2005–9

| RC-North | |
|---|---|
| Feyzabad | Germany |
| Kunduz | Germany |
| Meymana | Norway |
| Mazar-e-Sharif | Sweden |
| Baglan | Netherlands → Hungary |
| **RC-West** | |
| Qala-e-Naw | Spain |
| Chaghcharan | Lithuania |
| Farah | United States |
| Herat | Italy |
| **RC-South** | |
| Kandahar | Canada |
| Qalat | United States |
| Tarin Kowt | Netherlands |
| Helmand | United Kingdom |
| **RC-East** | |
| Bamyan | New Zealand |
| Ghazni | United States |
| Kapisa | United States |
| Khowst | United States |
| Logar | United States → Czech |
| Parwan | United States |
| Wardak | Turkey |
| Asadabad | United States |
| Gardez | United States |
| Jalalabad | United States |
| Mether Lam | United States |
| Sharana | United States |

*Note*: There are no PRTs in RC-Capital.

own areas rather than a coordinated effort.[34] Afghan officials complained that the PRTs neither coordinated their efforts with the government plans nor shared information about what they were doing.[35] Problems arose when a PRT run by one

---

34 Interview with senior UK Defense Ministry official, London, September 2009.
35 Roundtable at the Afghan Ministry of Rural Reconstruction and Development, Kabul, December 2007.

country did not often coordinate with neighboring PRTs run by other countries. One PRT might be focused on protecting infrastructure while a neighboring team to the west would be engaged in offensive kinetic operations while another to the east would be focused on population protection. The French military objected to creating their own PRT for these very reasons. In their view, it was too difficult to coordinate between PRTs because no one in the ISAF chain of command was empowered to enforce order among national contingents.[36]

Observer, mentor, liaison teams (OMLTs, or "omelets") are a second NATO construct that can be compared across the contingents.[37] OMLTs were small numbers of soldiers and officers embedded in Afghan National Army units, especially the basic fighting unit known as a *kandak*, which is roughly similar to a battalion. As their name suggests, the OMLTs were a crucial part of the training and war effort, as they trained key elements within Afghan units and served critical functions such as communicating with artillery, air support, logistics, and other NATO assets in the field. This was one of the most important efforts of the entire NATO mission since the eventual NATO transition (departure) depended on Afghan forces becoming capable enough on their own. OMLTs were a key part of the process for making the kandaks functional and independent.

During a tour of Afghanistan in 2007, we often heard "We need more omelets in Afghanistan." Given the shortfalls, there were significant consequences associated with the variance in country's willingness to provide OMLTs and in restrictions on what they could do. Countries could opt out of providing OMLTs because of various risks involved in having small units operating at all and particularly operating with the Afghans, who might be viewed as more reckless, less competent, and more likely to engage in atrocities. If they did opt in, countries could restrict where their OMLTs could go. Again, national priorities would appear to trump alliance priorities on the training front, just as they have done on the PRT, regional command, and (for the United States) national levels.

## The Theoretical Case for National Primacy on NATO Decisions

The previous section provided evidence from those on the ground that national decisions, rather than alliance decisions, were the primary drivers of ISAF behavior in Afghanistan. This section will make the *theoretical* case for national primacy

---

36 Interview with senior French officer, Paris, February 2009. Other French officers (interviews, Paris, June 2009) suggested that the lack of a PRT was a result of President Jacques Chirac's reluctance to make a lasting commitment to NATO's effort in Afghanistan or to support NATO in doing work that should be left to civilians.

37 The units focusing on Afghan police are known as POMLTs. In French, OMLT is spelled ELMO.

during NATO operations, exploring dynamics that apply beyond NATO to other multilateral institutions. Here we argue that NATO procedures, coupled with the institutional disadvantages of the alliance compared to national command authorities, advantages each separate NATO member when it comes to determining the behavior of its troops on the ground. National governments have more power than does the alliance to select military commanders, determine their rules of engagement, oversee their behavior, and provide them incentives for appropriate behavior. There are logical reasons, then, why national decisions drive military behavior during multilateral interventions.

Military interventions are in large part an exercise in large-scale delegated authority. Civilian officials and/or national military leaders delegate to their deployed military forces the authority and the means to act on behalf of their nation. The discretion of military commanders during operations is central to the civil-military relations literature.[38] How much room do officers have to operate in, and—as important—how does the choice of unilateral, coalition, or alliance intervention affect national control over any nation-state's military?

## FORUM SHOPPING FOR INTERVENTION PARTNERS

A nation's control of its military's behavior when deployed depends both on *how* the intervention is conducted and on the underlying civil-military relationship within that country. A wide variety of frameworks are available when deciding how to intervene militarily in some distant locale. In Afghanistan, for example, the United States cycled through an initial unilateral intervention, transformed that effort into a coalition of the willing, and finally settled on military operations as part of a formal alliance effort (with certain exceptions, particularly with regard to special operations forces).[39] There were obviously policy reasons behind the United States' shift from one institutional setting to another, to include international political legitimacy, the resources required for the 2003 U.S. intervention in Iraq, the continued viability of the NATO alliance, and the limits of American military power. But, that said, there were important advantages to the United States to be gained by ultimately choosing an alliance effort over a coalition intervention or unilateralism. The alliance effort allowed the United States to maintain control over its own military forces, exert significant influence over the ISAF effort, and reap the benefits of multilateral legitimacy. The same was not

---

38 The literature starts with Huntington (1957) and Janowitz (1961). Feaver (1999) provides an excellent review of the work on civil-military relations. For more recent work on civil-military relations, see also Cohen 2002; Feaver and Gelpi 2004; Krebs 2004; and Mahnken and FitzSimonds 2003.

39 The same pattern held true for the French in Libya, as will be discussed in chapter 8.

the case with other institutional arrangements (i.e., unilateralism or coalitions of the willing).

The emerging literature on political forum shopping can help explain why the United States might choose to utilize NATO as opposed to intervening unilaterally or using a coalition of the willing. Forum shopping is a concept whose origins lie in the legal community. In its original legal context, *forum shopping* refers to the practice of a litigant searching for a judge or court that will be sympathetic to the litigant's case. The concept recently has been applied to international affairs, principally but not exclusively to international legal, financial, and trade regimes (Busch 2007; Drezner 2007). As Karen Alter and Sophie Meunier succinctly note, forum shopping in this context involves "strategies where actors select international venues based on where they are best able to promote specific policy preferences, with the goal of eliciting a decision that favors their interests" (2009: 16).

Each intervention forum—unilateralism, multilateral coalitions of the willing, and NATO efforts—had advantages and disadvantages from the U.S. perspective. To really appreciate the merits of each forum, however, to say nothing of why the United States ultimately selected the forum it did, requires a brief review of principal-agent relations.

## Principal-Agent Relations

In its simplest form, principal-agent theory focuses on the problem of delegated authority and compliance with orders. *Delegation* occurs when an actor X (or actors X, Y, and Z), authorized to make a decision or take some action, conditionally designate(s) some other actor (or actors) to make that decision or take that action.[40] When one actor delegates authority to another actor, the former is acting as a *principal* and the latter becomes her *agent*.[41] Principals are the actors within a hierarchical relationship in whom authority ultimately rests (Lyne and Tierney 2003).[42] Agents are the actors who are hired (and potentially fired) by principals. Agents are conditionally designated to perform tasks in the principals' name and have the requisite authority to do so. In the case of military interventions by democracies, military commanders are the agents of civilian principals.[43]

---

40 This definition is developed in Hawkins (2006).
41 For a good review of principal-agent models, see Miller 2005.
42 This definition is similar to those found in Bergman, Müller, and Strøm 2000; Grossman and Hart 1983; Kiewiet and McCubbins 1991; and Mirrlees 1976.
43 For examples, see Avant 1994; Desch 1999; Diamond and Plattner 1996; Feaver 1998, 1999, 2003; Stulberg 2005; and Zegart 1999. For an application of principal-agent theory to other organizations involved in international intervention, see Cooley and Ron 2002; and for an application to U.S. intelligence agencies, see Zegart 2007.

Many commonly (if subconsciously) default to this model when thinking of the U.S. president acting as commander in chief.

Anytime a principal delegates authority to an agent, authorizing the agent to act on her behalf, there will be some agency costs, in that a principal who delegates to an agent no longer has complete control over that agent's behavior.[44] The question confronting the principal is how much power to delegate to an agent who rarely has preferences that are identical to those of the principal (Williamson 1975). This is known in the principal-agent literature as *Madison's Dilemma*, referring to James Madison's argument during the Constitutional Convention against concentrating power in any one government branch. Delegating too much power creates a risk to civilian governance. Delegating too little creates an impotent military. Overdelegation might be a trivial problem except that agents become privy to information that principals do not possess. In the principal-agent literature this is the problem of *hidden information*. Moreover, agents can often take actions of which the principal is unaware: the problem of *hidden action* (Moe 1984).

These concepts take on real meaning when we consider military interventions and try to determine how much discretion to give military commanders who have better information than do their civilian counterparts and can keep actions hidden from civilian officials. In the realm of military operations, these gaps can be quite significant because of differences in civilian and military ideology, the expertise military officers possess compared to civilians, the necessity for action by the military agent in far-flung locales, and, often, the requirement for secrecy so that the adversary does not learn of the military plans. And lest we forget, there are potentially dire consequences whenever military force is used. Which intervention forum is chosen has the potential to dramatically change the principal-agent (PA) relationship between civilian leaders and their deployed military forces, with implications for the primacy of national decisions.[45]

## Unilateral Interventions

The United States initially tried going it alone in the very early days in Afghanistan. Unilateral intervention would establish a *single-principal* relationship along the lines just discussed. The advantages here revolve around the relatively simple relationship between the principal and agent, with the potential for robust control of national military forces. The downsides here are well known, if admittedly

---

44 This conceptualization is similar to those found in Bergman et al. 2000; Grossman and Hart 1983; and Kiewiet and McCubbins 1991.

45 Kreps (2011) argues that the choices between coalitions and alliances is not so much about principal-agent relationships but due to time horizons with alliances more attractive when countries care more about the future.

outside of the core tenets of PA theory, to include the lack of political legitimacy associated with unilateralism, the high costs of unilateral intervention, the atrophy to the NATO alliance, and so on. From the U.S. perspective, those disadvantages soon outweighed the simplicity of going it alone.

## Coalitions of the Willing

The United States had tried a coalition of the willing in Iraq and as part of OEF operations. Such a coalition could embody two different types of PA relations, depending on the chain of command structure used by the coalition.[46] First, a coalition of the willing could be organized under a unified military command taking direction from the collective decisions of coalition members. The coalition principals would establish a contract with a single military agent, akin to the *collective principal-agent* relationship displayed in figure 2.4.

Here multiple principals share a single delegation contract with an agent. The most familiar delegation relationships in politics and government involve collective principals. Voters delegate to politicians, legislators delegate to party leaders, and nation-states delegate to international organizations (Kiewiet and McCubbins 1991). In all of these situations, a group of actors comes to a decision among its members and then the group negotiates a contract with an agent. *There is a single contract between the agent and his collective principal.* If the group cannot come to a decision a priori, it cannot change the status quo. This goes for initial hiring decisions, renegotiating the agent's employment contract, or giving the agent new instructions.

Collective PA relationships exacerbate the problems of Madison's Dilemma, hidden information, and hidden action. A collective principal may have difficulty reaching agreement on how much power to delegate to its military agents. An initial delegation contract, once established, may be hard to revisit unless the members of the collective principal can reach consensus. Problems of hidden information may afflict members differently in that some members may have more expertise and/or information than do others. An uneven distribution of information obviously advantages some collective members more than others, with the potential of making it harder for the collective principal to arrive at consensus decisions. The same is true for hidden action, in that some members will be better able to discern just what their agent is doing. This may make it harder for the agent to hide its actions, but only if members of the collective principal share that knowledge with each other and can decide what to do about

---

46 Weitsman (2013) contrasts coalitions with alliances, but focuses more on effectiveness and less on the implications of civilian control.

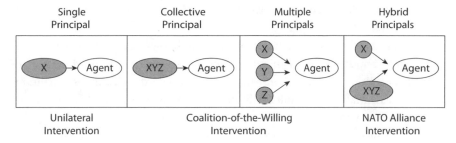

**Figure 2.4** ◆ Intervention Forums and Principal-Agent Relations
*Note*: Thanks to Michael Tierney for help in conceptualizing this figure.

it. Finally, collective principals create a problem associated with *signaling* their shared agent in that a collective principal may have significant difficulties presenting a unified message to that agent. In such cases, an agent may face tremendous difficulties correctly divining the preferences of each principal or the collective principal as a whole. In essence, a collective principal is more likely to send confusing messages (or no authoritative messages in a timely manner) to its agent than is a unitary principal.

Applied to Afghanistan, the problems associated with such an arrangement focus on the coordination problems associated with generating an agreed-upon set of orders for the military agent. From the U.S. perspective, this dilutes U.S. control over the overall military effort, something the United States has been opposed to in the past.

Second, the coalition members could establish individual contracts with a unified military agent, akin to the *multiple principal* model in figure 2.4. Many more complications arise in such a situation. Individual actors each form their own delegation contract with the same agent. No single principal can be assured of the agent's complete loyalty, because of the inherent problems associated with PA relationships, the agent's need to respond to orders that might directly contradict each other, and/or the agent's inability to anticipate the preferences of very different principals. Such institutional structures can lead to incoherent policy implementation, additional shirking on the part of the agent, or one of the two principals not getting its preferred policy (Calvert, McCubbins, and Weingast 1989; Lyne and Tierney 2003; Maltzman 1998). A relevant example is when a national military is beholden over the long term to the legislative and executive branches, as is the case in the United States (Avant 1994). Opportunism is yet another possible by-product of delegation via multiple principals. Agents may attempt to advance their own agendas, either irrespective of their principals' desire or by playing one principal off against the other. The U.S. military is often accused of such tactics when it comes to procurement, playing the U.S. Congress against the president.

As applied to Afghanistan, the problems with this arrangement are obvious. A coalition had no formal mechanism to reach a consensus position, which meant that the coalition's military could receive conflicting orders from each coalition member. Essentially, this would establish a large number of *individual* principal-agent contracts within the coalition. While this simplifies the PA problems from the perspective of any one nation vis-à-vis its own military, it establishes the conditions for the various militaries to work at complete cross-purposes to each other. In short, the United States could maintain robust control over its own military, but the multilateral effort would suffer unless other nations agreed to subordinate their forces to U.S. commanders.

## Alliance Interventions

The ISAF model that was eventually arrived at represents a hybrid principal-agent relationship, as pictured in figure 2.4. In a hybrid relationship, there are at least two principals, as is the case in the multiple-principal forum, each with its own delegation contract to the agent. Yet at least one of the principals is a collective entity, giving the hybrid form some of the same characteristics as the collective principal relationship.

An example of a hybrid relationship was the command relationship confronting U.S. General Wesley Clark during the Kosovo War. As SACEUR, his authority ran from both the U.S. president and NATO. Thus, Clark faced a *hybrid* principal: one principal was the U.S. president and the other was a collective entity (the NAC). Each had some authority over his actions. Every NATO commander in Afghanistan is faced with the same hybrid principal dilemma. Commanders are expected to follow orders from the ISAF chain of command once their home country signs over a transfer of authority, as discussed earlier in this chapter. The ISAF chain acts on behalf of a collective principal. At the same time, field commanders never truly stop serving their national chain of command. Commanders thus face a hybrid situation with a collective principal (NATO) and a single principal (their national command authority) both giving them orders. And to complicate matters, the single principal is part of the collective principal's decision-making apparatus, via the NAC, but has an individual delegation contract with the military agent. Figure 2.5 depicts the delegation path for a deployed ISAF commander.

From a U.S. perspective, the hybrid PA relationship works to U.S. advantage. The nature of the NATO alliance provides the United States with tools to overcome any remaining coordination problems associated with a hybrid PA intervention

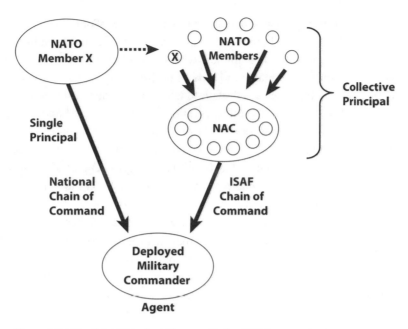

**Figure 2.5** ◆ The Hybrid Principal Structure Facing ISAF Commanders

model. Most important is control over the crucial military commands associated with a NATO alliance intervention. For example, before the United States transferred control over the majority of U.S. troops operating in RC-East to NATO, the flag officer in charge of OEF forces answered only through the U.S. national chain of command. The United States only put the majority of its forces under ISAF command when it was assured that the COMISAF would always be a U.S. flag officer. In addition, the alliance's commanding officer (the SACEUR) has always been an American. In each of these ways, the United States has maintained unique influence over the direction of military operations in Afghanistan, influence that more than outweighs the problems associated with a hybrid PA relationship and that was not possible to the same degree with a coalition of the willing. So even if the alliance was at an impasse, the United States could direct military efforts on the ground through its national chain of command.[47] From the U.S. perspective, then, the ISAF format had significant political advantages and few PA disadvantages when it came to national control over U.S. forces.

At the same time, other NATO alliance members had a mechanism with which to coordinate on common concerns and pass that guidance through the NATO

---

47 The tale in chapter 1 about counterterrorism in Bosnia is an example of the United States taking the NATO hat off American troops and having them operate solely under U.S. command.

chain of command (represented by the right side of fig. 2.5). For the vast majority of issues, the NATO chain should work with a little forethought. Remember from figure 2.3 that country A will gladly follow ISAF orders as long as those orders do not exceed country A's maximum level of desired effort. When those orders conflict, country A has its national chain to fall back on (the left side of fig. 2.5). Country B will not blink at ISAF orders; after all, Country B is happy to exert even more effort than is being asked for by the NAC. It was no surprise, then, that when the United States eventually advocated for and subsequently supported the alliance taking over the military effort in Afghanistan, NATO partners agreed to that institutional design. The alliance served as a coordination mechanism, with individual nations retaining control of their own militaries.

At times, however, the two competing delegation contracts inherent in a hybrid PA relationship will come into conflict. At that point, a deployed agent should be biased toward following the directives of the single-principal delegation path. The agent is likely to get clearer signals from the single principal. The single principal can implement incentives far more easily than can the collective principal. And finally, the single principal can more easily select agents that closely match the principal's preferences than can a collective principal, and can do so more expeditiously as well. These advantages provide theoretic justification for our earlier empirical argument that national priorities should trump alliance priorities during the ISAF operation. We discuss each of these mechanisms in the next section.

## NATIONAL CONTROL IN ALLIANCE INTERVENTIONS

National control is reinforced via a number of mechanisms. The first is in trying to choose agents who are closest to the principal in terms of attitudes and likely actions. If the principal could clone itself and then put that clone in command, there would be no problems of agency slippage. Unfortunately for the hybrid principal, it may have to rely on an agent provided by others (through institutionalized promotion schemes, decisions of a predecessor, etc.). Those agents may not share the same preferences as the current principals, and replacing an agent can be politically costly, as we know from the case of President Harry Truman and General Douglas MacArthur.

In the case of Afghanistan, individual member states (the single principal in fig. 2.5) have more control over which officer will lead their national contingent—that is, agent selection—than does the alliance as a whole. Indeed, many national principals carefully select their agents in an attempt to minimize agency losses from their individual national perspectives. The alliance as a whole has no comparable mechanism. Indeed, the default in ISAF operations is that the alliance has no formal voice in terms of which general officers command which national unit.

The decision rests solely with the national command authorities of the individual nation that deploys that unit (or is put in charge of that unit, for operations that involve personnel from more than one country).[48] While the United States is supposed to consult when it selects the COMISAF or even the SACEUR, it has been known to make a decision and then inform the allies after the fact.

A second management tool used by principals to influence their agents is through restricting the agent's *discretion*. When a principal decides to delegate authority to an agent, part of that decision involves the scope of the authority, ranging from giving the agent carte blanche to micromanagement that requires the agent to contact the principal for every major and minor decision in the field. If the principal either does not trust the agent or is concerned that even a well-intentioned agent may cause significant problems, then the principal will limit what the agent can do. Another indirect way to influence the discretion of the agent is to limit its capabilities. Agents will be less able to exceed their authority if they are given limited means.

Significant restrictions on agent behavior, of one form or another, were enacted by virtually every national contingent operating in Afghanistan.[49] Commanders going into the field were usually given a set of instructions from their home government informing them of the limits of their authority: when they could act on their own judgment, when they must say no to multilateral commanders, and when they needed to call home for authorization of specific operations. National command authorities also limited deployed capabilities on occasion as an indirect means of limiting military discretion. For instance, deploying few helicopters to a modern military campaign will restrict the size and frequency of operations, especially if there are already standard operating procedures that require the availability of helicopters before an operation can commence. Some countries used such tactics to curtail what their troops could do, despite pleas to the contrary from the ISAF leadership.

A third issue in delegating authority is *oversight*. If large disparities in the information possessed by an agent and a principal will equate to that agent having greater freedom of action, then one means of redressing this problem is for the principal to devise appropriate means of monitoring agent behavior. Matthew McCubbins and Thomas Schwartz (1984) illustrate this problem with analogies to "police patrols" and "fire alarms" as two different systems of oversight, with the former being more active and costly to maintain than the latter. Both types of oversight have been attempted in Afghanistan. Individual nation-states have more frequently engaged in active police patrol oversight than has the alliance

---

48 NATO allots command positions to alliance members in a process called *flags to post*. Countries providing more troops and more flexible troops gain more of these positions, but the individuals filling each slot are chosen by the country given the billet.

49 NATO put in place selected protocols that cover ISAF operations as a whole, particularly when it comes to treatment of detainees.

as a whole. Individual states build in more frequent, if still irregular, reporting requirements, given the individual country's justified desire to avoid military or political disaster should hostilities occur. If both a singular and collective principal have some ability to sanction errant agent behavior, then the principal with a relative information advantage will be better served by the shared agent. The advantage again should go to the national command authority of the individual military contingent operating in Afghanistan.

A final tool is *incentives* associated with agent behavior. The principal-agent literature argues that agents attend to principals who have the ability to sanction the agent for poor performance or reward the agent for stellar behavior. Incentives can take any number of forms, but for our purposes a principal's control over the agent's tenure in office, promotion, portfolio of responsibilities, and budget are vital means of ensuring that the agent's behavior will match the preferences of its principals. Control over tenure in office and promotion deal directly with an agent's livelihood—its personal employment and advancement. Control over an agent's portfolio and budget affects that agent's power to achieve desired outcomes. Either or both may be sufficient to ensure some degree of agent compliance with the will of the principal.

The challenge for NATO on this front is that the alliance does not have any real ability to reward or sanction officers. NATO officials can get a contingent commander sent home, but this happens rarely and can be controversial. As a result, commanders on the ground have incentives to focus on the more likely path of punishment—the chain of command going back to their capital and not the chain of command going back to Brunssum, Mons, and Brussels.

To review: the NATO intervention in Afghanistan represented a hybrid principal-agent model. A hybrid relationship involves a state having an independent delegation contract with a military agent but also sharing a second delegation contract with the same agent as part of a collective principal. Hybrid relationships establish the conditions for a two-stage process of providing guidance to the deployed military agent. The first stage involves a game between the singular principal (the individual NATO member) and the other members of the collective principal (the NAC) over what will constitute the collective principal's ideal policy. The collective principal reaches a decision according to its internal procedures and forwards that decision to the shared military agent. In the NATO case, decisions are codified in activation orders that give the alliance commander instructions as to the conduct of the war.

The subsequent actions of the single principal form the second stage. If the individual NATO member is satisfied with the collective alliance decision, it will reinforce that decision via its own independent delegation contract with the agent. Alternately, the alliance member could be dissatisfied with the collective

NATO decision. If that is the case, the member can either attempt to renegotiate the collective direction of the alliance or it can utilize its independent delegation contract with the military agent to alter or countermand the collective alliance decision. The alliance member's choice may depend on whether reopening the negotiation within the collective principal will make the unitary principal better or worse off than the current policy. But, as implied earlier in this chapter, NATO decision-making procedures bias the alliance toward the status quo. Once a decision has been taken by the NAC, it becomes difficult to change the alliance position, as changes would require consensus. Instead of changing the position, countries can always opt out during implementation.

That leaves the singular principal with the independent path, given that reopening the dialogue within the collective will likely result either in no change or in a worse outcome than the status quo policy. Moreover, in most if not all cases, *the individual NATO member will have greater influence over the deployed military agent than does the collective alliance* because national command authorities have more discretion than does the alliance as a whole when it comes to *selecting military commanders, deciding on their discretion* when in the field, *overseeing their actions,* and linking *incentives* to behavior. For these reasons, the deployed military agent is going to be heavily biased in favor of its national master when weighing the guidance of the collective and singular principal and choosing which principal's orders to follow. National demands should trump the alliance's demands.

In a world of perfect information, the primacy of national decision making should pose few problems for alliance coordination. The alliance can anticipate the limits of each country's contribution and design utilization schemes that maximize individual contributions. NATO has made significant efforts to do just that, and has become more efficient over time as a result. Alliance members who want to do more can establish parallel deployments. Individual members have also done exactly that, particularly with special operations forces working with the United States. Unfortunately, however, information is never perfect, and misunderstandings can result between the alliance and national chains of command. Even with perfect information, alliance members would still disagree as to who is and should be bearing the greater burden. The chapters that follow document why these differences might occur and how alliance members have tried to maintain control over their military agents in anticipation of those differences.

# Conclusions

Thus far we have detailed how NATO operates in reality and how we understand it via agency theory. Both history and theory tell us that to understand NATO's effort in Afghanistan we need to understand that ISAF nations were fighting many different wars rather than one big war. As such, we need to leave the alliance's headquarters in Brussels, Mons, Brunssum, and Kabul and go to individual national capitals such as Washington, London, Paris, Berlin, Ottawa, Copenhagen, the Hague, and those of other NATO members and partners. Before doing so, we develop a framework in the next chapter focused on how democratic institutions shape individual delegation contracts. That theoretic framework will guide our national comparisons across the alliance and beyond.

# 3 Explaining National Behavior in Multilateral Interventions

*We need more omelets in Afghanistan.*
— International Security Assistance Force officers, referring to observer, mentor, liaison teams (OMLTs), Kabul and Kandahar, December 2007

In chapter 2 we pointed to the important role of national decisions in International Security Assistance Force (ISAF) operations because national positions trump those of the NATO alliance as a whole when the two conflict. This is not necessarily because of realist concerns regarding national power. Instead, national policies trump multilateralism when the two are in conflict because of the specific procedures and the escape clauses that hold even in the most formal and interoperable of alliances.

Chapter 2's discussion did not address how and why individual NATO members make the choices they do. To explain those choices, we need to consider the institutional structures and decision processes *within* individual NATO member states, the political context within which decisions are made, and the resulting principal-agent (PA) relationships that flow from those processes and priorities. In so doing we will combine institutional analysis, models of party ideology and individual decision making, and PA models to explore systematic variations in national chains of command across ISAF and over time.

We first use a domestic institutional lens to uncover who the primary decision makers are on questions of war and peace in each ISAF nation and what motivates those key decision makers. Specifically, we focus on how the structure of domestic governmental institutions, as modified by specific constitutional and statutory rules in each country, can help predict specific patterns of behavior by that country. We add political considerations to this institutional argument in the form of the political ideology of each country's main political parties. Our premise here is that a party or coalition's ideological leanings can affect broad foreign policy behavior. We also explore the policy preferences of key individual decision makers, particularly how their personal histories affect their priorities during military interventions. We believe this combination of institutional, political, and personal factors goes a long way toward explaining ISAF member behavior in Afghanistan.

Our first task in this chapter is to uncover who is empowered with security decisions in each ISAF country. Who acts as the principal in each country's PA relationship? If the key decision maker in a particular country is a group—like a parliamentary coalition, for example—we argue that this leads to different dynamics than if a single individual is empowered with authority over security decisions in that state. In the former case, bargaining within a parliamentary coalition requires compromises on defining military missions and restrictions on the behavior of that state's deployed troops, compromises whose general direction depends on the coalition's ideological leanings. If an individual is empowered with authority over security decisions within a state (i.e., an individual is that country's principal in its civil-military PA relationship), then we need to consider whether that person prioritizes achieving political-military outcomes or acceptable military behavior. A principal's choice to focus on outcomes versus behavior can have a large effect on military operations.

We develop hypotheses about how countries will influence the operations of their troops in a multilateral operation using this methodology. Our hypotheses focus on four methods used by principals to shape the conduct of their military agents: the selection of top military commanders, the amount of authority delegated to each nation's deployed forces, the oversight of those forces by authorities back home, and the positive and negative incentives linked to those forces' behavior or achievements. The internal decision processes and politics of individual NATO members help explain why they choose and empower particular commanders, monitor them, and reward or sanction their behavior, all of which help determine that nation's behavior in Afghanistan and beyond.

## Unpacking National Decisions during Military Interventions

Democracies vary in how power is distributed across government: to a single individual elected by the people, to a single person elected by a legislative body, or to a group of individuals beholden to different parties (Shugart and Carey 1992). We expect foreign policy behavior will vary as power varies across government institutions. Two types of principals, or ultimate decision units (Hermann and Hermann 1989), are important for our purposes: individual and collective decision makers. The former is a case in which one individual is empowered to make decisions that direct those below in the military chain of command. The latter is one in which a group must come to a decision among themselves before deciding how to direct their subordinates. The institutions of a political system determine whether specific nations are directed by an individual or collective decision maker, and as we shall see, that makes a huge difference for delegation contracts imposed on military agents.

Presidential and single-party parliamentary governments empower individual decision makers. Presidential systems empower individual presidents with fixed terms to make decisions on *when* to use force and *how* to deploy force, even if decisions to send troops abroad are sometimes subject to legislative consent. The important point is that presidents are usually empowered to make the key decisions about what the troops can and cannot do on a day-to-day basis, or choose to delegate that decision to somebody lower in the chain of command.[1] Parliamentary systems ruled by a single governing party can also empower individuals leading that party, at least if the party maintains a modicum of internal discipline and the party leader accurately represents her party's interests. Often parliaments with British-style electoral laws, such as first-past-the-post electoral systems, result in a single party having a majority of legislative seats, empowering the prime minister to make the key decisions or to delegate decision making to subordinates (Kaarbo and Hermann 1998). Indeed, prime ministers in such situations may have more foreign policy power than presidents, since opposition parties have few avenues to block policy (Auerswald 1999, 2000, 2004), at least assuming the prime minister can maintain party discipline regarding the military intervention.[2]

Coalition parliamentary governments generate collective decision making and are best represented vis-à-vis their militaries by collective PA models. Coalition government requires internal bargaining (Hagan et al. 2001), and bargaining usually involves compromise. In coalition governments, the need to bargain among members of different parties can greatly complicate foreign policy making (Beasley et al. 2001; Kaarbo 2008, 2012; Kaarbo and Beasley 2008; Kaarbo and Lantis 2003). In the pulling and hauling among parties, it is likely that there will be differences of opinion about the merits of any military mission, the depth of the commitment to be made, levels of risk acceptance or aversion, and so on. The less enthusiastic members of a coalition can demand conditions for acquiescing to the deployment of forces. The more committed members will have to relent to some

---

1 In this sense we are departing from Avant's (1994) characterization of the United States as a country with two principals: the president and the U.S. Congress. For our purposes, the U.S. president controls three of the four levers of agent control commonly used in PA relationships. The exception is inducements for appropriate behavior, particularly when it comes to congressional control over budgetary inducements. In theory, Congress can influence other PA tools—agent selection, restrictions on delegated authority, and detailed oversight—but more often than not only does so in extreme cases such as the Vietnam War, an issue that the public was deeply divided over and actively engaged in.

2 The prime minister risks being removed from office for poor decisions without that backing. Presidents do not face the same threat, absent extraordinary circumstances, and can potentially garner support from across the partisan aisle without risking tenure in office. Thanks to Matthew Shugart for this clarification. See also Samuels and Shugart 2010.

degree. Otherwise, their country will not deploy forces or its government may collapse, as the Dutch experience in Afghanistan in 2009–10 illustrates (see chapter 6). Our argument is consistent with that of Arend Lijphart (1999), who argues that consensual democracies make decisions based on inclusiveness and compromise, whereas decisions in majoritarian democracies are much less inclusive. Coalition parliaments are more consensual than presidential or majoritarian parliamentary governments. Further, once bargains are struck in consensual systems, they become hard to change since one is likely to need the consent of more than one actor to change policy (Tsebelis 2002). Getting such consent is particularly difficult when the collective decision maker is heterogeneous in some fashion, whether ideologically, culturally, or economically (Lijphart 1999). So policies, once imposed by coalition governments, are likely to stick, at least as long as the coalition holds.

## PREFERENCES OF DECISION MAKERS

If domestic institutional analysis can tell us who the key decision makers on questions of war and peace are in any particular country (i.e., the ones with the formal authority to delegate), that analysis tells us little about the preference of decision makers in those countries. This section considers the preferences of decision makers by disaggregating preference considerations into those of individuals and collectives operating within particular government institutional schemes.

### Individual Decision Makers

We expect individual decision makers to have significant influence in presidential and single-party parliamentary governments. But to comprehend those effects requires a fuller understanding of what motivates key individuals (Kaarbo 1997; Peterson 1996). The next element of our approach, therefore, focuses on how individual officials make choices. Unfortunately, the vast literatures on cognition and personality do not point to a single way to theorize about individuals (Jervis 1976; Khong 1992; Levy 1997), and we have no a priori reason to believe that one theoretical approach to individual decision making is best.

The result is that we used inductive research at this level. Interview data with our first subjects, Canadian politicians and officers involved in Bosnia and Afghanistan, suggested that a key factor driving attitudes toward the conflict was prior personal experience in other military interventions. Specifically, as individuals went through their careers they observed and experienced the effect of specific patterns of military behavior. When these individuals rose to positions of authority, they made decisions based on those experiences.[3] We then applied what we learned from the Canadian case to the rest of the cases.

To simplify for the purposes of generalization, we distinguish between decision makers who, because of prior experience, now focus their behavior toward achieving particular political-military *outcomes* on the ground and those who focus instead on the *behavior* of the military, irrespective of outcomes (Fassina 2004). The former individuals focus on helping the military achieve its mission by whatever means are necessary. These decision makers impose few restrictions on their military, conduct less oversight of those forces, and tailor their incentives to whether the military achieves desired outcomes. Either these officials trust their military's professionalism, or the ends for these officials justify the means used to achieve those ends. Conversely, decision makers concerned with their military's behavior more than with outcomes should impose restrictive rules of engagement, conduct more oversight, and sanction or reward particular behavior rather than outcomes. For these officials, the success of the actual mission is less important than is military conduct during that mission. The ends never justify the means. These categories of outcome- or behavior-oriented decisions allow us to code individuals based on interviews with them and/or people who work with them. Our focus on prior experience simplifies what would otherwise be a difficult job of coding and helps us avoid tautology (Schafer 2000).

## Collective Decision Makers

We expect that collective decision making will be the rule in coalition parliamentary governments. The logic of veto players (Tsebelis 2002) applies quite well as coalition governments, by definition, involve more than one actor with the ability to block a decision. To use PA parlance, coalition governments are examples of collective principals vis-à-vis their national military.

Interest in and enthusiasm for a policy option is likely to vary among the actors whenever more than one is involved in a decision. In a coalition government, the more enthusiastic actor, assumed to be the prime minister for our purposes,[4] is likely to have to give up something to gain the assent of the less enthusiastic actor. The less enthusiastic actor, when it comes to military deployments, is likely to ask

---

3 Since the question of delegation to agents on a dangerous mission inherently involves questions of risk acceptance, another approach would focus on political vulnerability rather than focus on prior experience. Politicians in more vulnerable situations ought to delegate less. Thus, we ought to expect leaders might be more willing to take risks earlier in their election cycle and delegate less as an election approaches (Gaubatz 1999). The problem with this expectation is that there are two ways to manage potentially risky situations: micromanage them to take control and make sure nothing bad happens, or delegate all responsibility so that the blame falls elsewhere.

4 If the prime minister is less interested, then the deployment is unlikely to occur at all or the proposal to deploy will already contain significant restrictions.

for conditions to be placed upon the deployment to mitigate the risks involved. If such demands go unmet, then the prime minister will fail to gain enough support to have the authority to deploy troops and the government may even collapse.

This is essentially what happened to the coalition government in the Netherlands in early 2010. In February 2010, Prime Minister Jan Peter Balkenende tried to extend the Dutch participation in ISAF that was due to end. His coalition partners, the Dutch Labour Party and the Christian Union, disagreed, causing the government to collapse and prompting new elections. The Dutch essentially were gone from Afghanistan by August 2010, turning over Uruzgan Province to the Americans and Australians.[5]

So the threat of a government falling apart over a foreign deployment is a real one for a coalition government. Conversely, single-party parliamentary governments do not face this threat as often (at least with a modicum of party discipline, as noted above), and a government collapsing before the end of its term because of a foreign military intervention is unheard of in presidential systems. The threat of government dissolution forces parliamentary coalition leaders to compromise and attach conditions to the deployment when demanded by coalition partners. These conditions frequently become restrictions on the authority of military commanders. Restrictions can range from specific to quite broad, but their focus is almost always on making sure the troops on the ground *behave* in ways that have fewer ramifications back home rather than on *achieving success* on the ground (Fassina 2004).

How do we account for variation among coalition governments? First, the logic of veto players suggests that "differences in the number, ideological distances, and cohesion" (Tsebelis 2002, 67) of the parliamentary coalition will matter. Regarding the number of parties, it would make sense that with more players there will be a greater chance of ambivalence and concern about the risks involved with a deployment. That translates into a greater likelihood that one or more coalition players will insist on significant restrictions on the behavior of deployed troops and more onerous reporting requirements associated with those deployments. Further, if each of the many coalition players has to support the effort for it to pass muster in parliament, then the actor proposing the intervention has less power to impose his will on a recalcitrant coalition party. Compromises may occur in terms of agent selection, with more competent or expert commanders skipped over in the interest of choosing someone acceptable to or representative of all coalition parties. Moreover, the various parties may make significantly different demands for their support, perhaps leading to contradictory mandates for the deployment over time and divergent signals to the military as to the incentives for acceptable behavior.

---

5 Chapter 7 touches on the story of Australian reluctance to take over for the Dutch.

Second, a coalition of ideologically opposing parties is likely to suffer many of the same pathologies as a coalition of many parties. For example, they are likely to impose greater restrictions on the deployment than a coalition of largely convergent parties. A parliamentary coalition with wide differences in outlook is often a fragile coalition, so there will be a greater desire to minimize the risks of a crucial coalition partner defecting and bringing down the government. Ideologically similar parties are more likely to have a shared level of interest in the deployment, so there will be less need to compromise. An ideologically cohesive coalition should be better able to select agents and arrive at agreed incentive structures for those agents, less sensitive to deviations in agent behavior, and better able to conduct robust oversight if it so chooses.

Third, we should expect that a political party's ideological position on domestic issues translates into predictable foreign policy positions. There is certainly evidence of a relationship between the ideology of extreme parties and their positions on trade policy (Camyar 2011; Chryssogelos 2010). Evidence also suggests a relationship between party ideology and the use of force. For example, Brian Rathbun (2004) explored differences between left- and right-leaning parties on three dimensions that might predict their attitudes toward humanitarian interventions. He found that left-leaning parties were more concerned with promoting the welfare of citizens in other countries than were right-leaning parties, which would rather advance their own national welfare. Leftist parties also were more dovish than their rightist counterparts. And finally, left-leaning parties more readily embraced multilateral solutions to international problems, while right-leaning ones believed more in unilateralism (Rathbun 2004: 19–23). Combined, these factors reinforce the intuition of others, that while parties on the left may not have a monopoly on pacifism, they are likely to have more members that are reticent about the use of force (Roets and Van Hiel 2009). Moreover, that reluctance to use force is most easily expressed in parliamentary systems. In Rathbun's words, "Parties can more easily implement their will in parliamentary systems as these institutions give party members a voice in foreign policy" (2004: 206). The result is that we would expect that parties on the left would be more ambivalent when using force than those on the right. Left-leaning coalitions will be more likely to try to impose significant restraints on how operations are conducted than will conservative coalition governments.

# Hypotheses on National Decisions in Multilateral Interventions

The vignettes in chapter 1 and the discussion in chapter 2 suggest four ways that countries influence their military contingents when operating as part of multilateral military interventions: choosing the commander (agent selection); determining the scope of authority delegated to each nation's deployed forces (discretion); monitoring those forces by authorities back home (oversight), and devising the sanctions or inducements linked to those forces' good or bad behavior (incentives). In this section, we define each of these terms in the context of the ISAF mission and then discuss a variety of hypotheses that could explain why particular countries act the way they do regarding these four behaviors.

## Agent Selection

The principal-agent literature argues that the careful choice of an agent can alleviate many of the problems associated with delegating power. In the ISAF context, we are particularly concerned with the choice of each country's overall military commander for their deployed national contingent. The commander is the individual that provides day-to-day direction for the troops, responds to crises and unusual circumstances, interacts with other ISAF contingents and local Afghan officials, and leads the national force into battle. It is also the individual that can decide on the overall focus of the military mission for their nation, absent direction from home (discussed below), and is the person that usually has the authority to invoke the *red card* discussed in the first chapter. To highlight the importance of choosing a commander, imagine two commanders. One believes the mission in Afghanistan should focus on kinetic counterterrorism operations (night raids, kicking in doors, etc.). The other believes that the military should focus on classic counterinsurgency methods (providing security for and interacting with the local population, etc.). Regardless of the merits of either approach in Afghanistan, a country's choice of one or the other commander can have tremendous effects on military behavior on the ground, all else being equal.

The selected agent that we focus on in subsequent chapters is not necessarily a country's most senior military commander deployed to Afghanistan. Sometimes a senior officer from country X will serve in ISAF headquarters, while a more junior officer will command the national contingent in the field. For example, British general Sir David Richards served as the overall ISAF commander in 2006, while the British contingent in RC-South was led by a British brigadier general. Similarly, Canadian major general Marc Lessard was the commander of RC-South for NATO, but a brigadier general commanded the Canadian contingent in Afghanistan in 2008. We focus on the selection of the national contingent commander because that is the individual who will have more influence on the day-to-day operations of his nation's troops than will most officers at ISAF headquarters, particularly as it relates to deploying red cards, calling home, and interpreting caveats.[6] The exception to that rule is in the case of the overall U.S.

---

6 Indeed, individuals serving in NATO billets, such as Lessard, were given far less direction from home.

commander, who has often been double-hatted as the commander of ISAF (since 2007) *and* commander of in-country U.S. troops.

## Discretion

Caveats are examples of contingent delegation. During conflicts, officials delegate authority over military missions to their deployed forces. Caveats restrict the scope of the military's delegated authority—that is, their discretion—by limiting what the military can do on behalf of the nation. The question is why some national principals delegate significant authority to their military agents while others do not.

As was illustrated in chapter 1, there are a number of ways to constrain a commander's discretion. In subsequent chapters, we consider a variety of restrictions to the discretion of the commanders and contingents on the ground, including formally stated caveats, the requirements and procedures to call home for authorization before taking action, and selective deployments of capabilities. Because the full list of any country's formal restrictions (not to mention the informal, unstated ones) are classified, we code each country's caveats as comparatively loose or tight. A contingent coded as loose can perform most, if not all, of the operations authorized by NATO's rules of engagement and is allowed to operate in the more dangerous parts of Afghanistan. A contingent under tight reign is obviously more limited in what it can do and where it can do it.

Figure 3.1 provides an illustration of a country with relatively few restrictions: In 2007, Canadian troops could operate outside of Kandahar, the province in which its forces were mostly based, without asking permission from Ottawa. They could and did engage in offensive operations. The Canadians participated in training missions with the Afghan National Army (via OMLTs). The one significant restriction placed on Canadian forces by the national command authority in Ottawa was that they could not do crowd control (in chapter 5 we discuss why this changed). Finally, the Canadians, like all other countries operating in the ISAF chain of command, were not authorized to cross the border into Pakistan. All told, however, the Canadian military was relatively unconstrained in what it could do in Afghanistan from 2006 to 2011.

This was not the case for the German contingent. Figure 3.2 illustrates the more restricted delegation that German forces operated under for most of their mission in Afghanistan, despite having the third largest ISAF contingent for much of the relevant period. German troops could not move out of their assigned sector, RC-North, without the expressed consent of the German minister of defense, who, in turn, was only authorized to give consent if the move was temporary, needed for the success of ISAF, and no one else could fulfill the requirement (see chapter 6). These conditions were never satisfied between 2004

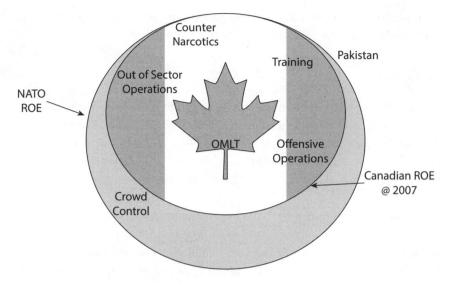

**Figure 3.1** ✦ Canada's Restrictions in 2007

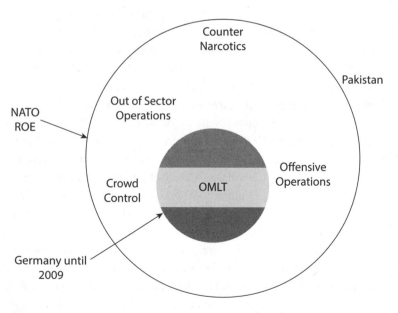

**Figure 3.2** ✦ Germany's Restrictions, 2004–9

and 2009;[7] German troops could not engage in offensive operations until that restriction was loosened in 2009. And like the Canadians, the Germans could not engage in crowd control or operate across the Afghan border.

Most countries operating in Afghanistan ranged between these two extremes, although the United States had even fewer restrictions than Canada (for example, the United States could deploy drones and apparently special operations forces into Pakistan[8]) and several were more restricted than the Germans. In subsequent chapters we focus on several key caveats, such as the rules governing participation in OMLTs, out-of-sector operations, and offensive operations, as bases of comparison across countries. These categories of effort were applicable to most contingents in ISAF, and have been some of the more visible and consequential efforts by the alliance.

## Oversight

Oversight matters for the conduct of specific military operations and for broader debates over civil-military relations. Stringent civilian oversight makes caveats efficacious, which enables home governments to protect their interests but limits the discretion of deployed military commanders. Conversely, lax oversight permits military agents to act against the interests of their civilian bosses. Such "agency slack" can take the form of foot-dragging,[9] personal aggrandizement, or military behavior that is inconsistent with the strategic goals of the civilian leaders.[10] In short, caveats are only as good as the oversight used by civilian officials. Absent oversight, deployed troops are free to follow their professional or personal beliefs rather than their government's (potentially restrictive) rules of engagement.

We expect that the various types of civilian oversight of the military will have predictable consequences for military operations in a combat zone. Passive oversight allows military commanders to be more "forward leaning," able and willing to employ a greater variety of means and engage in a greater variety of operations, even if operations involve risk or are highly politically salient.[11] These commanders can act first and avoid subsequent sanctions from

---

7 The German special forces apparently were not so limited. See Maloney 2009: 105–6.

8 See Ambinder and Grady 2012.

9 Abraham Lincoln famously excoriated General George McClelland for being overly cautious with the army under his command. See Goodwin 2005.

10 General Douglas MacArthur's overextension of American military forces in the Korean War is the quintessential case. His refusal to heed warnings from Washington, D.C., and President Harry S. Truman's inability to monitor decision making on the ground led directly to a U.S. land war with China (and indirectly to MacArthur's firing); see chapter 1.

11 See Snyder 1984 for a historical discussion. The Weinberger/Powell Doctrine is a more recent incarnation of this bias.

their national principals if they have stayed within the broad boundaries of the delegation contract, have been successful in the military operation, or have been successful in hiding operational failures so that the principals never get the bad news. Even though officers in these situations will likely try to anticipate their principals' reactions and stay within the established parameters of the delegation contract, we should still expect much more agent flexibility and creativity in these situations.

Active oversight, on the other hand, often requires that commanders receive approval from their civilian superiors—whether in the field or in the home country—to gain authority to engage in a particular operation.[12] Though we live in an age of instant communications, receiving civilian approval can take time, as we saw in chapter 1. Officers who need such permission are likely to be slower to act and more constrained in the means that they can use in pursuit of their military objectives. Indeed, because the process of asking for permission by its very nature raises the political stakes, commanders may refuse to engage in operations that require permission, even if the likely answer is yes.[13]

We examine the type of oversight used by decision makers at home to control their military contingents deployed as part of coalition operations in Afghanistan. Indicators of active oversight include attempts by principals to gather information about the behavior of their agents and the results produced by those agents. It also includes the construction of new institutions to alter how oversight is conducted or the reform of existing institutions designed to provide such information. For example, the German Bundestag's defense committee meets with the minister of defense once a week to be briefed about operations around the world. This requires the defense minister to receive regular updates from the field at least once a week.[14] This qualifies as active oversight. Another example of active oversight, discussed in chapter 4, was the weekly video teleconference between Secretary of Defense Donald Rumsfeld and Lieutenant General David Barno that started in June of 2004, in which Barno was grilled on all aspects of his operations for hours at a time.[15] Passive oversight is less intrusive, as indicated by irregular or nonexistent attempts to gather information on agent behavior or unwillingness on the part of the principal to adapt existing institutional arrangements to increase information on agent behavior.

---

12 Commissars in the Soviet past were a particularly active form of oversight. President Hamid Karzai apparently replicated this tactic by inserting spies into Afghan army units to cut down on the number of incidents of Afghan troops firing upon members of ISAF (Hodge 2012).

13 Interviews with officers from a variety of NATO countries, 2007.

14 Interview with Mathias Martin, foreign and security policy adviser, Office of the Vice-Chairman of the Sozialdemokratische Partei Deutschlands Parliamentary Group, Berlin, June 18, 2009.

15 Interviews in 2007–8 with several participants in the 2004 VTCs, observing from the Afghan theater.

*Incentives*

Just as limiting discretion only works if there is oversight, oversight only functions well if the agent knows that there will be rewards for doing the right thing and punishment if monitoring catches poor behavior. Oversight sets the preconditions for sanctioning or rewarding one's agent, but it serves little purpose unless coupled with some means of correcting an agent's behavior. Incentives can take many forms, to include restrictions on the agent's authority or issue portfolio, its rank or promotion prospects, its budgets or nonmonetary resources, or even its tenure.[16] Incentives can be used directly to stop inappropriate agent behavior, as in the case when a Canadian contingent commander, Brigadier General Daniel Menard, was sent home in the middle of his tour for inappropriate relations with a subordinate. The principal uses a raw execution of power to rescind the delegation contract. Incentives can also be used as a deterrent, a threat to hopefully prevent inappropriate agent use of the principal's delegated authority. As with any sort of coercion, an incentive's effectiveness at deterring inappropriate agent actions depends on the principal's willingness and ability to implement its promised threats or pay for sufficiently powerful inducements (Miller and Whitford 2007).

Incentives include rewards as well. Prospects of promotion can be a very important carrot with which to ensure compliance. Just as officers can be punished by reducing their authority, officers can be rewarded by an increase in the scope of their authority. In the case study chapters that follow, we track, whenever possible, whether there are particular patterns of promotion and punishment for national contingent commanders to assess which countries have used these kinds of incentives to influence the conduct of their missions.

## HYPOTHESES

Our earlier domestic institutional analysis pointed to an important distinction between two sets of institutions: those with individuals making conflict decisions and those in which intragovernmental coalitions develop policy. In cases where institutions empower individual decision makers, we need to distinguish between individuals focused on the behavior of their military agents and those more concerned with outcomes produced by their agents on the battlefield. In cases in which coalition governments serve as their country's collective principal, we need to uncover the number of parties in the coalition, their ideological spread, and their overall ideological bent to develop expectations as to their

---

16 Overreliance on negative incentives may actually undermine the principal-agent relationship by weakening trust (Miller and Whitford 2002).

conflict policies. The aforementioned domestic institutional analysis, coupled with data on the preferences of key decision makers within those institutions, yields the following PA hypotheses on agent selection, delegation/discretion, incentives, and oversight.

## Agent Selection

Figure 3.3 diagrams the agent selection process. Agent selection is an attractive tool for decision makers operating in single-principal institutional structures, such as leaders of presidential or single-party parliamentary governments. In theory, the principal has all the authority needed to select an optimal military agent. Who gets selected should depend on whether the principal values battlefield outcomes or the behavior of their troops, which in turn is based on the principal's past experiences or historical lessons. Principals valuing outcomes will select very different types of commanders than will principals valuing "correct" or "appropriate" behavior in the field. The former will likely choose commanders that have a more kinetic focus, whether the overall goal of the operation is counterterrorism, counterinsurgency (COIN), or conventional war. The latter will likely choose commanders that are more restrained when it comes to kinetic operations for fear of creating greater risk of failure.[17] At the same time, these decision makers have the ability to replace commanders as they learn more about the fit between the agent's preferences and their own.

Agent selection is a more difficult tool for collective principals. The collective principal would have to agree on a commander, which is particularly difficult with groups that are large in size or contain ideologically disparate parties. Replacing military commanders will be similarly difficult for coalition governments, both in terms of deciding to replace a serving commander and in terms of choosing a replacement. Given those difficulties, coalition governments are more likely to rely on other means to influence the decisions made in the theater.

*Hypothesis 1:* Presidential and single-party parliamentary governments will be more likely to rely on the selection of commanders to achieve their desired results than will parliamentary coalition governments.

*Hypothesis 1a:* Outcome-oriented presidents and prime ministers in single-party systems will choose commanders that prioritize kinetic operations, while behavior-focused leaders in such systems will select commanders that emphasize nonkinetic operations.

---

17 The exception would be where troops are assessed based on a metric like body counts (as was the U.S. Army in Vietnam), which could lead to a greater focus on kinetic operations.

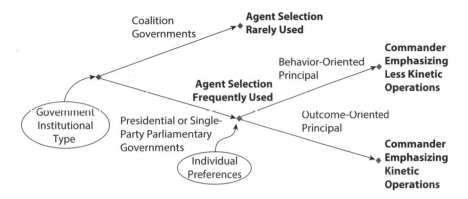

**Figure 3.3** ◆ Selection of Military Agents

## Agent Discretion

Figure 3.4 diagrams the relationship between domestic institutional and individual levels of analysis with regard to the degree of authority delegated to military agents in the field. Collective principals are likely to resort to contingent delegation with caveats, largely for three reasons. First, the actors within the decision-making group will have to compromise to get any set of instructions agreed to by the governing coalition, and compromise produces caveats. To get an agreement past all of the potential veto players (usually the representatives of the parties in the coalition), restrictive delegation may be the only way for the nation to participate in the military intervention. As we have noted, the broader the ideological spectrum represented in the coalition, or the larger the number of coalition parties, the more compromises may be required (Tsebelis 2002). Second, as we have already discussed, agent selection will be particularly problematic as it is difficult to choose an agent who shares the preferences of all members of the collective principal. As a result, there is likely to be less trust between the principal and the agent, with a correspondingly restrictive delegation contract. Third, left-leaning coalitions will be more likely to be dovish, value multilateralism rather than unilateralism, and value the well-being of the population in the target country (Rathbun 2004), all of which implies that they will engage in restrictive delegation.

Single principals are under less institutional pressure to impose restrictive delegation contracts on their military agents. The degree to which a single principal will delegate authority should depend on whether the principal values outcomes or appropriate military behavior. Single principals who prioritize outcomes, regardless of their military's behavior, should grant broad discretion to their troops. Principals who prioritize their troops' behavior, regardless of whether they accomplish

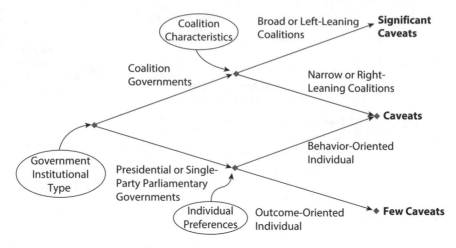

**Figure 3.4** ◆ Discretion of Military Agents

their stated mission, should impose more restrictive delegation contracts.[18] We must, therefore, explore the preferences of those individuals, which takes us to the individual level of analysis and the lower pathways in figure 3.4.

*Hypothesis 2:* Coalition governments are likely to impose more significant caveats, on average, compared to presidential or single-party parliamentary governments.

*Hypothesis 2a:* Coalition governments with more parties and/or parties of widely diverging ideologies will be more likely to impose caveats than those with fewer parties and narrower ideological spreads.

*Hypothesis 2b:* Coalition governments led by left-wing parties will be more likely to impose caveats than those led by right-wing parties.

*Hypothesis 2c:* In presidential or single-party parliamentary governments, leaders focused on outcomes will impose fewer caveats than those focused on the behavior of the military contingent.

## Oversight

Figure 3.5 diagrams the relationship between domestic institutional and individual levels of analysis with regard to oversight of military agents in the field.

18 Single-party minority governments may act like either coalition or single-party parliamentary systems, depending on whether the opposing parties both have the opportunity to affect decisions and can co-operate with each other. If a policy is well within the authority of the prime minister or if the opposing parties cannot cooperate, then the situation will be more like a majority parliamentary government. If the government requires significant support from the opposition, then the situation is more like a coalition government. The Canadian case in chapter 5 will be instructive on this score.

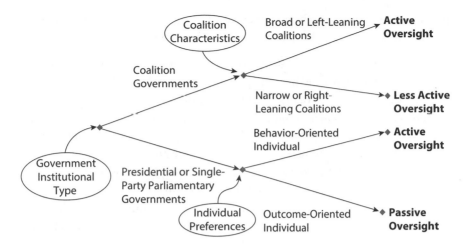

**Figure 3.5** ◆ Oversight of Military Agents

Collective principals in coalition governments have incentive to engage in active oversight. Indeed, the various coalition partners have incentive to do so to avoid being drawn into a situation of which they do not approve, particularly given that collective principals are likely to prohibit their military agent from engaging in specific actions via a restrictive delegation contract. Oversight is likely to focus on the degree to which the military agent is abiding by those restrictions.[19] Broad or left-leaning coalitions have more incentive to engage in active oversight than do narrow or right-leaning coalitions, for the reasons discussed above with regard to restricted delegation. The narrowest "coalition" government—a minority government—should fit the latter category. That government's tenure is more vulnerable than are presidents or prime ministers who have majorities, which provides an incentive to engage in active oversight if only to avoid a parliamentary confidence vote. The degree to which minority governments exhibit more or less relative oversight should depend on their left- or right-leaning ideology.

Single principals in presidential or majority parliamentary governments will engage in active oversight if they care about the behavior of their troops. When single principals care about clearly defined outcomes, they will engage in less active oversight than their behaviorally oriented counterparts.[20] After all, military outcomes are easier to monitor with less-intrusive oversight. As we will discuss in chapter 4, former U.S. defense secretary Rumsfeld appears to have engaged in relatively passive oversight in Afghanistan until he discovered that his commanding

---

19 Coordinating that oversight, however, may be problematic across members of the collective principal.
20 There are institutional impediments to legislative oversight in some single-principal nations. British-style parliaments, for example, tend to give their parliaments very weak oversight authorities over military affairs, to the point that parliamentarians even lack security clearances.

general was focusing on behavior-oriented COIN activities when what Rumsfeld wanted was to get out of Afghanistan at the earliest opportunity.

*Hypothesis 3:* Coalition governments are likely to engage in active oversight, while for presidents and majority parliaments, oversight will depend on whether the principal values military behavior or outcomes.

*Hypothesis 3a:* Coalition governments with more parties and/or parties of widely diverging ideologies will be more likely to engage in oversight than those with fewer parties and narrower ideological spreads.

*Hypothesis 3b:* Coalition governments led by left-wing parties will be more likely to engage in oversight than those led by right-wing parties.

*Hypothesis 3c:* Outcome-oriented presidents and prime ministers in single-party governments will engage in less oversight than will behavior-oriented leaders in similar government systems.

## Incentives

Figure 3.6 displays the relationships among governance institutions, individual preferences, and the ability of a national principal to provide tailored incentives to its military agent.

It is hard for collective principals to arrive at decisions regarding incentives for their agents, due to the potential of any actor to block those decisions. Coalition parliamentary governments have a harder time deciding upon sanctions for incorrect behavior or outcomes, or rewards for good behavior or positive outcomes, than single-principal governments. Once sanctions are devised, they may be hard to enforce by a collective principal, as the agent may attempt to play one principal off against another in an attempt to divide the collective principal.

A single principal can easily reach a decision to reward or impose sanctions on its agent for inappropriate actions since cooperation is not required. Single principals can impose sanctions or rewards contingent on whether the principal values good outcomes or behavior. For instance, behavior-oriented principals will likely sanction inappropriate behavior by deployed troops, regardless of whether those troops accomplished their mission. After the sour experience in Somalia, President Bill Clinton apparently told commanders headed into Bosnia that the key metric of success would be zero American casualties.[21] Outcome-oriented principals sanction troops for substandard outcomes, with less concern for how the troops behave. Here the distinction between minority and majority government is unlikely to matter since the power to punish officers will be in the hands

---

21 This was the conventional wisdom among Joint Staff officers that Steve Saideman observed in 2001–2.

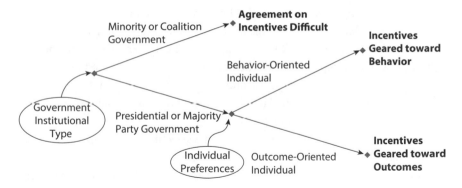

**Figure 3.6** ◆ Incentives for Military Agents

of the government in either case, and, in a system with a minority government, it would require the opposition parties to cooperate with each other to reverse such decisions. In either case, the agent will have no recourse given that there are no other principals to whom to appeal. In short, the agent in these circumstances is subject to the whims of the principal.

*Hypothesis 4:* Coalition governments are less likely to tailor incentives than are presidential and single-party parliamentary systems.

*Hypothesis 4a:* Presidential and single-party systems with outcome-oriented leaders are more likely to punish officers who fail to make sufficient progress, while behavior-focused leaders are more likely to punish officers who misbehave.

Combined, the four sets of action paths in figures 3.3–3.6 yield complex and interesting relationships across leadership selection, delegation, oversight, and incentives. Each country committing to a multilateral operation has a variety of tools to manage their contingents, and these tools can reinforce or contradict each other. Significantly, the tactics national capitals use may vary not just over time, perhaps in response to events on the ground and back home, but also depending on the type of government and the preferences of its decision makers.

Variations across governments are more than just a difference between coalition parliamentary governments and governments that have single leaders, though that is an important difference. Variations on significant civil-military issues exist within presidential and single-party parliamentary governments. Remember, we would expect behaviorally oriented principals in such systems to select less kinetically oriented commanders, restrict those commanders' discretion, engage in more active oversight, and utilize a different set of incentives than should leaders focused on battlefield outcomes.

More specifically, in governments led by a single decision maker, that decision maker has wide latitude to select his ideal agent. Whether that agent is subject to restricted delegation and caveats depends on the experiences of the principal. Oversight will vary depending on whether the principal is focused on military behavior or outcomes. If oversight is conducted, the military agent had best walk very carefully, as a single principal has the undisputed ability to sanction the agent for incorrect behavior or bad outcomes.

A collective principal will have a harder time selecting an ideal military agent, and is likely to limit the discretion of the commanders in the field, particularly if the collective principal represents a large, diverse, or left-leaning parliamentary coalition. The collective principal has the potential for very active oversight. Coordinating the data produced via oversight, however, and then acting upon it in the form of sanctions for incorrect behavior or botched outcomes, or rewards for appropriate behavior and achieved milestones, is likely to be difficult. Violations of the rules of engagement could very well be commonplace. Coordination of incentives becomes even more of a challenge.

## Summary

This chapter drew on a variety of literatures to model the national determinants of military behavior during multilateral interventions. Theories of principal-agent relations point to the importance of knowing who are the ultimate decision units having the power to determine how military forces behave when deployed. One cannot know who those ultimate decision makers are—those principals—without first understanding the domestic political institutions of the relevant nations. Domestic political institutions can either empower a single individual, as is the case with presidential or single-party parliamentary governments, or they can empower a collective body to make decisions, as is the case in parliamentary coalition governments. But to understand the preferences of various principals requires understanding either their political ideology (in the case of collective principals) or how their previous experiences shape their current and future behaviors (in the case of single principals).

There is no single best or most likely way to control a military contingent involved in a multilateral military operation. The combination of government institutions, political ideologies, and individual personal experiences together determine why governments rely on different mechanisms to control their deployed military agents. No government system combines all four mechanisms into a seamless whole. Countries may also vary which mechanisms they use over time, as politicians learn or are replaced or as those parties inside the collective principal change.

In the next four chapters, we focus in turn on presidential systems, single-party parliamentary governments, coalition parliamentary governments, and then non–NATO members. Each category is particularly suited to use one or more key means to influence its military agents in the field. Presidential states are adept at using agent selection, for example, to control their deployed military forces. Coalition governments tend to use restricted delegation (i.e., caveats). More generally, chapters 4–7 will demonstrate why this particular conflict has been fought according to national priorities, often at the expense of the alliance as a multilateral institution, and with highly uneven national contributions. Thus, it has often seemed as if there was not just one war between NATO and the Taliban but twenty-seven or more different wars against the Taliban. The approach sketched out in this chapter will help focus our attention on the key dynamics that account for the similarities and differences among the various contingents that operated in Afghanistan throughout the first decade of the twenty-first century.

# 4 Presidents in Charge
## The United States, France, and Poland

In chapter 3 we argued that presidential systems should exhibit specific patterns of behavior when it comes to their deployed military agents. The president is the principal in the principal-agent relationship because the president usually serves as the commander-in-chief of the military in presidential systems. In the parlance of chapter 2, presidential systems most closely resemble the single-principal model when we look inside the state. Presidents can delegate their authority over military decisions to a subordinate unless such delegation is specifically prohibited by statute or constitution. Civilian defense ministers, military chiefs of defense, or even regional commanders could serve in this manner. These "proximate" principals wield as much or as little authority as the president grants them.[1] Regardless, in these cases the basic principal-agent relationship remains one of a single principal delegating to a military agent, just subordinated one level down the chain of command from the president.

Our expectation for single principals is that, on average, they will focus on agent selection and incentives to direct their agents. Both tools are well suited to single principals. It is easier for a single principal to decide on an agent, for example, than it would be if decided upon by a governing coalition, all else being equal. Given that fact, a president's choice of military agents and the incentives provided to those agents should depend on the president's priorities—in our case, whether they prioritize their troops' behavior or military outcomes (see figures 3.3 and 3.6). Little prevents a president from utilizing contingent delegation contracts or oversight, of course, but a president's use of either should depend on the degree to which he prioritizes the behavior of the military contingents or the battlefield outcomes reached by those troops. Behavior-oriented presidents are likely to impose some degree of caveats on their troops and utilize more active oversight, while outcome-oriented presidents are likely to forgo caveats and utilize passive (i.e., fire alarm) oversight (see figures 3.4 and 3.5).

---

1 The term *proximate principal* denotes that the principal is one step closer to the military agent than is the ultimate principal.

This chapter reviews the actions in Afghanistan of three presidential governments: the United States, France, and Poland. The United States is a classic presidential institutional system with an executive possessing authorities not shared with the legislature and who is not beholden to the legislature for tenure in office. France has a premier-presidential system, containing both a president and a prime minister. The French president, however, controls the national security policy levers in the Fifth Republic, which makes it essentially similar to the United States. Poland also has a premier-presidential system in which the president possesses significant foreign policy powers. We focus most of our attention on the United States given its crucial role in Afghan operations, its aggregate national power, and its central role in the NATO alliance. We then provide shorter analyses of the other two presidential systems' use of a mix of tools. The French varied in the use of contingent delegation (i.e., caveats), with President Nicolas Sarkozy reducing quite significantly the restrictions imposed by his predecessor—President Jacques Chirac. The Poles focused on caveats, agent selection, and oversight to control their deployed national contingent. In each case we observed changes in national principal-agent contracts as new decision makers took the reins of power. In the U.S. case that corresponded to the switch in proximate principals from Secretary of Defense Donald Rumsfeld to Secretary of Defense Robert Gates. In the French and Polish cases, presidential transitions led to changes in their country's principal-agent contract.

## The United States in Afghanistan: Rumsfeld versus Gates

The administration of George W. Bush established its Afghanistan stance soon after the September 11, 2001, attacks. President Bush's public message was that "there will be a campaign against terrorist activity, a worldwide campaign. . . . Clearly, one of our focuses is to get people out of their caves, smoke them out, get them moving and get them. [That] is about as plainly as I can put it."[2] Privately, the administration established a clear counterterrorism goal for Afghanistan: "Our goal in Afghanistan is simple: eradicate the terrorism that led to the strikes that killed the citizens of 78 countries on September 11."[3]

At the same time, the Bush administration was clearly opposed to nation building and suspicious of multilateral interventions (Jones 2009: 109–13). Paul

---

2 White House Office of the Press Secretary, *Remarks by President Bush*, September 19, 2001, http://george wbush-whitehouse.archives.gov/news/releases/2001/09/print/20010919-1.html, accessed August 30, 2011.
3 Condoleeza Rice, *Declaratory Policy on Afghanistan*, September 27, 2001, http://library.rumsfeld.com /doclib/sp/1502/2001-09-27%20from%20Condoleezza%20Rice%20re%20Declaratory%20Policy%20 on%20Afghanistan-%20Memo%20Attachment.pdf, accessed February 25, 2012.

Wolfowitz was known for his preference for ad hoc coalitions and unilateralism long before he was nominated deputy secretary of defense.[4] One of Rumsfeld's first reactions to 9/11 was an opinion piece in which he stated, "This war will not be waged by a grand alliance united for the single purpose of defeating an axis of hostile powers. Instead, it will involve floating coalitions of countries, which may change and evolve. In this war, the mission will define the coalition—not the other way around."[5] For the first five years of the Bush administration, the complexities and impediments of alliance warfare far outweighed its benefits.[6] The next section discusses how the administration's aversion to nation building translated into Afghan policy.

## THE RUMSFELD YEARS: OUTCOMES, AGENT SELECTION, AND OVERSIGHT

President Bush chose Secretary of Defense Donald Rumsfeld as his surrogate to prosecute the U.S. war in Afghanistan.[7] Such delegation was not surprising given Bush's leadership style and that Rumsfeld was perhaps the most experienced secretary of defense in U.S. history. In addition to over twenty years in the U.S. Navy and Naval Reserve, Rumsfeld had previously served as a member of Congress, U.S. ambassador to NATO, White House chief of staff, and then secretary of defense in the administration of President Gerald Ford, and as the chairman of two government commissions dealing with defense and security matters in the 1990s. Rumsfeld's operating style was to utilize careful agent selection and, at times, intensive micromanagement of subordinates (Herspring 2009: 678–79).

Rumsfeld had very particular views as to overall defense policy and the appropriate end state for the war in Afghanistan,[8] views focused on outcomes, not military behavior. He believed firmly that the United States needed to extricate itself from Afghanistan as soon as possible, with the minimal commitment of troops or resources (Jones 2009: 112). In his words, "I do agree that there is a perception that the problem in Afghanistan is security. However, if we responded to the perception, our efforts would be concentrated on increasing the U.S. and foreign security forces in Afghanistan. The result would be that U.S. and coalition

---

4 Patrick Tyler, "U.S. Strategy Plan Calls for Insuring No Rivals Develop," New York Times, March 8, 1992.

5 Donald Rumsfeld, "A New Kind of War," New York Times, September 27, 2001.

6 For an example, see Woodward 2006: 91.

7 Donald Rumsfeld, "Subject: Delegation of Authority" (memo), October 19, 2001, http://library.rumsfeld .com/doclib/sp/1548/2001-10-19%20re%20Delegation%20of%20Authority.pdf#search=%22Snowflake %20on%20Delegation%20of%20Authority%202001-10-19%22, accessed February 25, 2012.

8 On the former point, see Michael O'Hanlon, "A Reality Check for the Rumsfeld Doctrine," Financial Times, April 29, 2003; Greg Jaffe, "Rumsfeld Details Big Military Shift in New Document," Wall Street Journal, March 11, 2005; Carl Robichaud, "Failings of the Rumsfeld Doctrine," Christian Science Monitor, September 21, 2006; and Michael Gordon, "Rumsfeld, a Force for Change, Did Not Change with the Times amid Iraq Tumult," New York Times, November 9, 2006.

forces would grow in number and we could run the risk of ending up being as hated as the Soviets were."[9]

Rumsfeld's solution was to focus on kinetic counterterrorism operations and training the newly formed Afghan National Army (ANA). He vehemently opposed initiatives that would more deeply enmesh the United States in Afghanistan, such as an early 2002 State Department plan to pay for 20 percent of the ANA's costs into the future.[10] In his view, funding the Afghan government was the job of America's European partners, who should take the lead in training ANA forces, the Afghan National Police (ANP), and the judiciary in counternarcotics operations and in the demobilization of militias.[11] He tasked then Brigadier General Karl Eikenberry with coordinating the non-U.S. international effort on these fronts.[12] He also called for the development of a set of metrics by which to measure progress on these fronts, something that an outcome-oriented principal would use.[13]

At the same time, U.S. commanders in 2001–2 were told by Secretary Rumsfeld that they could not deploy large numbers of troops in Afghanistan (Ricks 2006: 41, 70–71). This was consistent with Rumsfeld's view that the military had to be faster, lighter, and more lethal, and that a small footprint would help prevent the United States from making the Soviet mistake of being seen as occupiers. It also allowed the United States to free up troops for operations in other theaters. Deployments increased only to between seven thousand and eight thousand personnel by early 2002, and were based on an unusually large number of individual, rather than unit, deployments. This was against established military practice but consistent with Rumsfeld's desire to ensure as small a U.S. footprint in Afghanistan as possible.

## Franks

General Tommy Franks, the combatant commander for the U.S. Central Command (CENTCOM), was Rumsfeld's key military agent during the first eighteen months of the operation.[14] Franks was given two key missions by Secretary Rumsfeld: to

---

9 Donald Rumsfeld, "Memo to President Bush on Afghanistan," August 20, 2002, http://www.rumsfeld .com, accessed February 25, 2012.

10 See Donald Rumsfeld, "Memo to Colin Powell on U.S. Financial Commitment," April 8, 2002, http:// www.rumsfeld.com, accessed February 25, 2012; and Colin Powell, "Memo to Donald Rumsfeld," April 16, 2002, http://www.rumsfeld.com, accessed February 25, 2012.

11 The White House, *Fact Sheet: Afghanistan Security and Reconstruction*, May 2, 2002, http://georgewbush -whitehouse.archives.gov/news/releases/2002/05/print/20020502-18.html, accessed February 25, 2012.

12 Donald Rumsfeld, "Memo to President Bush on Afghanistan," August 20, 2002, http://www.rumsfeld .com, accessed February 25, 2012.

13 Donald Rumsfeld, "Snowflake to Doug Feith," June 20, 2002, http://www.rumsfeld.com, accessed February 25, 2012. Rumsfeld employed the term *snowflake* for short memos.

14 Interview with Dr. Joseph J. Collins, Washington, D.C., September 2008. Collins held three positions during the first term of the George W. Bush administration: special assistant to Paul Wolfowitz; deputy assistant secretary of defense (DASD) for humanitarian assistance; and deputy assistant secretary of defense for stability operations.

capture or kill the Taliban and al-Qaeda and later to build the ANA so that the United States could withdraw its forces as soon as possible (Barno 2007). These were outcome-oriented goals to which Franks agreed (Jones 2009: 117). Rumsfeld gave Franks full authority to achieve these goals in whatever means possible "without second-guessing."[15]

Rumsfeld relied on Franks to conduct oversight on his behalf during the early part of the war,[16] and limited his own oversight to weekly staff meetings on Afghanistan—even those only starting in early April 2002.[17] The result was that it was unclear what information was being passed to Franks, and through him to Rumsfeld, and whether either person was engaged in any active oversight of Operation Enduring Freedom (OEF) forces during 2002 and into 2003. This was a critical period for the United States in the lead-up to and the conduct of the war in Iraq, which left little time for either Rumsfeld or Franks to focus on Afghanistan.[18] So even assuming that active, comprehensive oversight was possible given the convoluted OEF chain of command in 2002, oversight during this first period was sporadic at best.

Rumsfeld's views on the proper conduct of the war evolved only slightly during Franks's command. Rumsfeld remained committed to counterterrorism operations in 2003, using special operations forces whenever possible, but gradually came to believe that the best way out of Afghanistan was to train the ANA as quickly as possible.[19] Building the ANA was an important facet of the overall U.S. counterterrorism strategy because a large ANA would allow the Afghans to take responsibility for their own country. A joint statement by Presidents George W. Bush and Hamid Karzai in late February 2003 noted that "The United States military will continue with its primary mission to prevent terrorist elements from undermining the security environment, while also building the Afghan national army."[20] By May of

---

15 Donald Rumsfeld, "Important Accomplishments" (memo), October 16, 2002, http://www.rumsfeld.com, accessed February 25, 2012.

16 Some believe that Franks failed at that oversight because of the command structure that emerged in early 2002, based on a series of relatively small contingents, each operating along separate lines of effort. To further complicate the picture, some deployed special operations forces reported solely to Franks rather than to the Combined Forces Special Operations Command. For reviews, see Barno 2007: 33; Ricks 2006: 107; and Elaine Grossman, "Was Operation Anaconda Ill-Fated from the Start?" *Inside the Pentagon*, July 29, 2004, 1. Information also from interviews with senior U.S. military officers A and B, Washington, D.C., and Brussels, 2007.

17 Donald Rumsfeld, "Weekly Meeting on Afghanistan" (memo), March 28, 2002, http://www.rumsfeld .com, accessed February 25, 2012.

18 See Gordon and Trainor 2006; Ricks 2006; and Woodward 2002, 2004. Franks's memoir (2005) suggests he was much more focused on Iraq than Afghanistan in late 2002 and early 2003.

19 Donald Rumsfeld, "Memo on Afghanistan," May 2, 2003, http://www.rumsfeld.com, accessed February 25, 2012; David Rohde and David Sanger, "How a 'Good War' in Afghanistan Went Bad," *New York Times*, August 12, 2007. See also Martin Strmecki, "Winning, Truly, in Afghanistan," *National Review*, May 20, 2002.

20 The White House, "Joint Statement between the United States of America and Afghanistan," February 27, 2003, http://georgewbush-whitehouse.archives.gov/news/releases/2003/02/print/20030227-22.html, accessed September 12, 2011.

2003, Rumsfeld was calling for doubling the pace of ANA training as well doubling the number of provinces within which ANA units were operating.[21] Again, these were the orders of a principal focused on achieving outcomes. Lieutenant General Dan McNeill, the commander of Combined Joint Task Force 180 during 2003, was given a relatively free hand as long as he achieved Rumsfeld's priority goals.[22]

## Abizaid and Barno

As NATO took control of the International Security Assistance Force (ISAF) around Kabul in August 2003, there were significant changes in the U.S. chain of command. Franks retired in July 2003, to be replaced by General John Abizaid at CENTCOM. Abizaid was among the first senior officers personally selected by Secretary Rumsfeld, who had expressed concern over some of the senior general officer selections made by the army and CENTCOM, particularly as it related to Lieutenant General Ricardo Sanchez's appointment to Iraq in 2003. As a result, Rumsfeld became more heavily involved in the selection process for general officers, later noting in his memoir, "The problem of the McKiernan to Sanchez transition caused me to change the nature of my involvement in assigning officers to senior positions. Previously, the chairman and the vice chairman of the Joint Chiefs, the deputy, and I had been principally involved in promotions at the four-star level. Now we decided to increase our involvement in decisions regarding key service appointments" (Rumsfeld 2011: 502).

Abizaid took over command at CENTCOM in July 2003. He was a known quantity to the civilian leadership, having served as Deputy CENTCOM commander under Franks as well as Director of the Joint Staff before that. Abizaid also had many of the qualities needed for the job, according to Rumsfeld, which included a facility with Arabic language and a master's degree in Middle East studies (Rumsfeld 2011: 502). In November 2003, Lieutenant General David Barno became the new overall U.S. commander in Afghanistan.

The guidance given to Barno upon assuming command was outcome-oriented. He was ordered to continue the missions given to McNeill: counterterrorism operations and training the ANA, all in the name of getting out of Afghanistan as soon as possible.[23] Activities associated with nation building were not part of that mission, which was consistent with the administration's long-standing opposition to activities that would tie down the United States for extended time periods

---

21 Donald Rumsfeld, "Memo on Afghanistan," May 2, 2003, http://www.rumsfeld.com, accessed February 25, 2012.
22 Interviews with senior U.S. military officers, Washington, D.C., and Brussels, 2007.
23 Interviews with senior U.S. military officer A, Washington, D.C., 2007. Neither Abizaid nor Barno shared Franks's penchant for fluid chains of command. Indeed, Barno's guidance from Abizaid was to stand up a new three-star command with a span of control over the whole of the country.

(Barno 2007: 33–34).[24] For instance, a mid-2003 Office of the Under Secretary of Defense for Policy (OUSDP) memo argued that "the coalition will maintain security forces in Afghanistan for as long as is necessary to accomplish our goals, and no longer." The memo continued, "We do not want to create over-dependence on the U.S. or others."[25] General Abizaid understood his mission, and committed to "maintain focus on the kill/capture OEF mission."[26]

Secretary Rumsfeld became increasingly impatient with the slow pace of ANA training during the latter months of 2003 (Rumsfeld 2011: 685). Administration sources have since blamed that pressure on the need for more combat troops and enablers for the Iraq War (Jones 2009: 127–29). In successive memos at the time to Under Secretary of Defense Doug Feith, Chairman of the Joint Chiefs Richard Myers, and General Abizaid, Rumsfeld repeatedly demanded recommendations for accelerating the formation of the ANA.[27] Lieutenant General Barno did not believe he was subject to significant direct oversight during the initial months of his tenure in late 2003 and into 2004. He would initiate informal calls to Abizaid two to three times per week to inform CENTCOM of developments in Afghanistan, but this was not a formal requirement and seemed to be based on a personal affinity between the two men.[28]

All this would change in 2004. Upon taking command in late 2003, Barno and his staff engaged in a comprehensive review of U.S. policy in Afghanistan. They decided that existing policy was not working and devised a fundamentally new strategy that departed in significant ways from established guidance. The new "Five Pillars" strategy contained many components of classic counterinsurgency doctrine and required significant nation-building activities over an extended time frame. The strategy focused on helping the Afghan people rather than simply capturing or killing terrorists, and divided the country into regional commands whose commanders had responsibility (and authority) for all operations in their region.[29] In Barno's words, "The late 2003 shift in strategy from an enemy-centric

---

24 See, for example, Francis Fukuyama, "Nation-Building 101," *Atlantic*, January 2004, http://www.the atlantic.com/magazine/archive/2004/01/nation-building-101/302862/, accessed April 23, 2013; and Mark Burgess, "Afghanistan: From War to Complex Emergency," Center for Defense Information, March 8, 2002, http://www.cdi.org/terrorism/nation-building.cfm, accessed March 16, 2008.

25 Office of the Under Secretary of Defense for Policy, "Principles for Afghanistan—Policy Guidance," July 7, 2003, http://www.rumsfeld.com, accessed February 25, 2012.

26 General John Abizaid, "Memorandum for the Secretary of Defense," November 10, 2003, http://www .rumsfeld.com, accessed February 25, 2012.

27 See Donald Rumsfeld, "Snowflake to Doug Feith," October 22, 2003, http://www.rumsfeld.com, accessed February 25, 2012; Donald Rumsfeld, "Snowflake to Gen. Dick Myers," October 21, 2003, http://www .rumsfeld.com, accessed February 25, 2012; and Donald Rumsfeld, "Memorandum to Gen. John Abizaid on Afghan Security Forces," December 19, 2003, http://www.rumsfeld.com, accessed February 25, 2012. Rumsfeld would continue to ask Feith and Myers for progress reports on ANA and ANP training in the first half of 2004. See "Afghan Security Forces" (memo) February 2004, http://www.rumsfeld.com, accessed February 25, 2012.

28 Abizaid and Barno were long-standing friends.

29 See Barno 2007: 34, 37–39 for the details of the "Five Pillars" strategy; see also Jones 2009: 141–42.

counterterrorist strategy to a more comprehensive, population-centered COIN [counterinsurgency] approach marked a turning point in the U.S. mission" (Barno 2007: 42). In short, Barno had changed the mission from one with an outcome-oriented approach to one focused on the behavior of OEF forces.

Despite the fact that Barno's strategy was not consistent with Rumsfeld's vision, Barno did not ask permission from the Pentagon to change U.S. policy.[30] Instead, some in the Pentagon learned of the strategy via the media. In a late December 2003 interview, Barno said, "We are looking at a significant alteration of our strategy in the south and east."[31] OEF forces began to fully implement Barno's strategy in March 2004.

The oversight situation changed dramatically two months later. In June 2004, Secretary Rumsfeld initiated "intense personal management" of Barno under a very active oversight scheme.[32] From June to September, Barno was required to participate in weekly video teleconferences (VTCs) with Rumsfeld, and CENTCOM focused on the degree to which Barno was meeting administration ANA training goals and how he planned on increasing the pace of training. Rumsfeld's tone in the VTCs was highly contemptuous of Barno and his strategy according to two regular, senior VTC participants. Rumsfeld's focus was on shifting resources to Iraq: how fast could troops be drawn down from Afghanistan, how quickly could the ANA replace U.S. troops, how quickly could ISAF take over U.S. missions.[33] In Rumsfeld's words, "our goal is to not have our military in Afghanistan forever. We need to have a detailed plan and timetable."[34]

In the words of one regular VTC participant, Rumsfeld "did not trust either CENTCOM *or* Barno at this point." Lieutenant General Barno's VTC briefing slides had to be approved in advance by Under Secretary of Defense for Policy Doug Feith, and any requests for forces or money had to go to the Office of the Secretary of Defense (OSD).[35] If approved, those requests were forwarded to CENTCOM by OSD staff. In addition, the OSD required that U.S. forces in Afghanistan report directly to *both* Barno and to the OUSDP rather than to Barno alone, as had been

---

30 Interview with senior U.S. military officer A, Washington, D.C., 2007.

31 Stephen Graham, "New U.S. Commander Plans Tactical Change in Afghanistan," December 20, 2003, http://news.google.com/newspapers?nid=1980&dat=20031216&id=-YkiAAAAIBAJ&sjid=r60FAAAA IBAJ&pg=1141,2915671, accessed August 9, 2011.

32 Interview with senior foreign officer, Washington, D.C., 2007. Jones (2009: 167–68) does not mention the confrontational tone when discussing these VTCs.

33 Interviews with senior U.S. Officers A and B, Washington, D.C., and Brussels, 2007. See also Jones 2009: 244–45. This position was consistent with the priorities expressed by President Bush. In early 2007 he would reflect back on the Afghan campaign thus: "I made Baghdad the top security priority. And I sent reinforcements to our troops so they can accomplish that mission." See The White House, "President Bush Discusses Progress in Afghanistan, Global War on Terror," February 15, 2007, http://georgewbush -whitehouse.archives.gov/news/releases/2007/02/20070215-1.html, accessed August 30, 2011.

34 Donald Rumsfeld, "Afghanistan" (memo), July 2, 2004, http://www.rumsfeld.com, accessed February 25, 2012.

35 For an example of Rumsfeld's requests for information associated with these VTCs, see "Afghanistan Update Brief" (memo), August 27, 2004, http://www.rumsfeld.com, accessed February 25, 2012.

the case earlier. Barno's VTCs with Secretary Rumsfeld continued, but at a slightly reduced rate of roughly once every two weeks through May 2005.[36] CENTCOM officials were largely silent during VTCs, deferring to Rumsfeld. In short, oversight was conducted by the secretary himself, and the OUSDP in his absence.[37]

Secretary Rumsfeld remained focused on achieving the outcomes of training the ANA and getting U.S. soldiers out of Afghanistan. By early September 2004, he was asking interagency partners and Pentagon subordinates to come up with a new strategic plan for Afghanistan.[38] Part of this could have been the result of his dissatisfaction with Barno's "Five Pillars" strategy. Another factor could have been that ISAF took operational control of northern Afghanistan on October 1, 2004. The expectation was that ISAF would expand its coverage to much of Afghanistan over the next eighteen to twenty-four months. As a result, the U.S. government began serious discussions as to how to coordinate OEF and ISAF efforts. In mid-October, the OUSDP drafted a concept paper that argued that the OEF-ISAF merger would accelerate ANA training and could "facilitate a reduction in U.S. force levels and an increase of force contributions by other nations." At the same time, the OSD advocated naming a U.S. general to be in charge of both operations, as this would facilitate the adoption of more robust rules of engagement and better coordination across provincial reconstruction teams (PRTs) run by ISAF nations.[39] Throughout this period, Rumsfeld remained firm in his desire to accelerate the training of indigenous forces in both Afghanistan and Iraq, and made that known across the U.S. government in a series of memos through the winter and into the spring of 2005.[40]

## Abizaid and Eikenberry

On May 4, 2005, Lieutenant General Karl Eikenberry replaced Barno as OEF commander. Eikenberry's selection was consistent with Rumsfeld's desire to personally select senior military officers for promotion and positions, and was one of

36 Interview with senior foreign officer, Washington, D.C., 2007.

37 Ibid.

38 Donald Rumsfeld, "Strategic Plan on Afghanistan," September 2, 2004, http://www.rumsfeld.com, accessed February 25, 2012; Donald Rumsfeld, "Afghanistan Funding," September 15, 2004, http://www.rumsfeld.com, accessed February 25, 2012.

39 Mira Ricardel, *Concept Paper on Merging ISAF and OEF into a Single Command*, October 13, 2004, http://www.rumsfeld.com, accessed February 25, 2012; Donald Rumsfeld, "Stability Operations" (memo), January 28, 2005, http://www.rumsfeld.com, accessed February 25, 2012; Richard Myers, "Stability Operations" (memo), February 25, 2005, http://www.rumsfeld.com, accessed February 25, 2012.

40 Donald Rumsfeld, "Numbers in the Petraeus Report" (memo), February 5, 2005, http://www.rumsfeld.com, accessed February 25, 2012; Donald Rumsfeld, "Afghan National Police" (memo), March 4, 2005, http://www.rumsfeld.com, accessed February 25, 2012; Donald Rumsfeld, "Training and Equipping Security Forces" (memo), March 18, 2005, http://www.rumsfeld.com, accessed February 25, 2012; Donald Rumsfeld, "Recommendations on Iraq and Afghanistan" (memo), March 25, 2005, http://www.rumsfeld.com, accessed February 25, 2012; Donald Rumsfeld, "Petraeus" (memo), April 20, 2005, http://www.rumsfeld.com, accessed February 25, 2012.

a series of changes in the senior military leadership that Rumsfeld was considering during 2005 and into 2006.[41] Eikenberry represented a realignment of principal and agent preferences. He was a known quantity, both to his civilian superiors and in the Afghan theater of operations. Most important, he had been in charge of building and training the Afghan National Army as a major general in 2002. The thinking was that he could bring the same skills to the Afghan mission.

The missions he was given by CENTCOM and Secretary Rumsfeld were similar to those originally given to Barno: counterterrorism policy, training and equipping the ANA, and coordinating special operations (usually on counterterrorism missions).[42] In congressional testimony, for example, Assistant Secretary of Defense Peter Rodman noted that the priority components of U.S. strategy for Afghanistan included training the ANA and ANP and counterterrorism operations.[43] There was no mention of continuing counterinsurgency (COIN) activities or Barno's "Five Pillars" strategy, despite the recently released Department of Defense directive that established stability operations as a core military mission.[44] Eikenberry's assignment was consistent with the administration's desire to decrease U.S. troop commitments and their initial aversion to nation building in Afghanistan.[45]

According to several U.S. military officers, Eikenberry embraced those military missions, replacing much of the COIN strategy devised and implemented by Barno in favor of a counterterrorism orientation for units under his command.[46] This led to two changes in the U.S. principal-agent contract. First, direct oversight relaxed dramatically with Eikenberry's assumption of command. He was required to participate in relatively few VTCs with Rumsfeld in comparison to Barno. Some have argued that Iraq took all of the OSD's and CENTCOM's attention, leaving no time for Afghanistan.[47] Another complementary explanation was that Eikenberry needed less oversight because he was a known quantity who sought to

41 Donald Rumsfeld, "Rotations" (memo), May 31, 2005, http://www.rumsfeld.com, accessed February 25, 2012; Donald Rumsfeld, "Stan McChrystal" (memo), September 29, 2005, http://www.rumsfeld.com, accessed February 25, 2012; Donald Rumsfeld, "Memo on the Most Important Jobs in Afghanistan and Iraq," January 4, 2006, http://www.rumsfeld.com, accessed February 25, 2012.

42 Interviews with senior U.S. military officer B, Brussels, 2007. See also American Forces Information Service, "Eikenberry Takes Command of Coalition Forces in Afghanistan," May 4, 2005, http://osd.dtic.mil/, accessed August 31, 2011.

43 "Situation in Afghanistan," *CQ Congressional Testimony*, June 22, 2005. Rodman also noted that NATO PRTs were playing a greater role in Afghanistan's future.

44 See Department of Defense Directive 3000.05 on Stability Operations, November 28, 2005.

45 Barno 2007: 43; Donald Rumsfeld, "Troop Commitments" (memo), May 13, 2005, http://www.rumsfeld.com, accessed February 25, 2012; Donald Rumsfeld, "Iraq and Afghanistan" (memo), June 20, 2005, http://www.rumsfeld.com, accessed February 25, 2012.

46 Eikenberry advocated that civilian agencies increase their support of nation-building projects rather than having the military take on these responsibilities. Interviews with senior U.S. military officers and senior foreign officer, Washington, D.C., and Brussels, 2007. See also Barno 2007: 43.

47 Interviews with senior U.S. military officer B, Brussels, 2007. The little attention spent on Afghanistan in Rumsfeld's memoir supports this position.

advance his principal's goals by using acceptable means. That said, he was not left completely to his own devices. For instance, Rumsfeld advocated sending General David Petraeus to Afghanistan to advise Eikenberry on ANA training and then report back his findings to the OSD.[48] Rumsfeld eventually expressed a desire to know more about what Eikenberry was doing.[49] But again, Eikenberry did not face nearly the same amount of oversight through the end of his tour in February 2007 because his actions were more consistent with the intent of the U.S. proximate principal, Secretary Rumsfeld.

Second, Eikenberry was given more latitude by civilians in the Pentagon than had been Barno.[50] That translated into Eikenberry's ability to accelerate the equipping of ANA units, to the tune of an eightfold increase in funds for that purpose with no questions from Washington.[51] He was able to keep the Tenth Mountain Division in Afghanistan longer than the OSD wanted them to remain. He was even able to slow the pace of developing the Afghan army by arguing that it was more efficient to field fully trained and equipped ANA units than to pump out a large number of poorly trained and equipped forces.[52]

Three major facts were changing on the ground during Eikenberry's tenure. The first was the worsening Afghan security situation, particularly in the south and east. Enemy-initiated attacks were more frequent in 2005 than the year before. The second was the handover of two regional commands, RC-West and RC-South, to the ISAF chain of command. The third was that U.S. troop numbers in Afghanistan actually decreased between 2005 and 2006.[53] These three facts were related. The farther expansion of ISAF operations into the south was announced at the December 2005 NATO foreign ministerial meeting. This so-called stage 3 was to take place in the first half of 2006. Eikenberry's tasking from the OSD and CENTCOM was to make the transition work in a way that did not curtail U.S. actions on the ground while not committing the United States to doing everything as it was shifting its forces to the Iraq theater.[54]

Unfortunately, the security challenges in the south were much worse than what ISAF had expected. National caveats and their effect on ISAF operations

---

48 Donald Rumsfeld, "Idea of Petreaus Visiting Afghanistan" (memo), June 3, 2005, http://www.rumsfeld .com, accessed February 25, 2012. The idea of sending a "rival" agent for an independent opinion is similar to the rationale for creating multiple intelligence agencies (CIA, DIA, etc.), each of which can provide a check on the others.

49 Donald Rumsfeld, "Meetings with Eikenberry" (memo), June 23, 2006, http://www.rumsfeld.com, accessed February 25, 2012.

50 He was not given complete free rein, as witnessed in Donald Rumsfeld, "Eikenberry and Future Ops" (memo), June 21, 2005, http://www.rumsfeld.com, accessed February 25, 2012.

51 Interviews with senior U.S. military officer B, Brussels, 2007.

52 Secretary Rumsfeld agreed to this slower pace, but held the line at a 70,000 troops ANA rather than the 50,000 recommended by Eikenberry. See Rumsfeld 2011: 689.

53 Jones 2009: 204.

54 Interviews with senior U.S. military officer B, Brussels, 2007.

there were at the forefront of U.S. thinking, largely because of incidents like the one in Meymana, mentioned at the beginning of chapter 1. From the U.S. perspective at the time, ISAF forces would not be ready to take on duties in RC-South, to say nothing of the East, without significant U.S. support.[55] In the view of senior U.S. officers, too many ISAF nations saw their role in Afghanistan as one of peacekeeping rather than war. Rumsfeld's reaction was, "Without deploying tens of thousands of U.S. military forces, we could use a parallel structure of civil, nonmilitary support teams to help Afghans" (Rumsfeld 2011: 689).[56]

Through the end of his tenure as secretary of defense, Rumsfeld remained convinced that the United States could "increase the NATO alliance's involvement in Afghanistan to lessen the burden on our troops as well" (Rumsfeld 2011: 689). He remained focused on achieving his desired outcomes in Afghanistan while the OEF-ISAF transition was occurring, particularly with regard to the metrics associated with building the ANA, as well as other measurable outcomes.[57] He again sent an "outside" agent, this time General Martin Dempsey, to Afghanistan to check up on the ANA training program.[58]

Finally, Rumsfeld accelerated his search for the next set of general officers to be sent to Afghanistan. In his words, "I want to sit down and go over who we want heading up the military functions in Afghanistan and what their tenure is going to be. I want to interview them and make sure they are the right people. I don't want it done automatically."[59] This was particularly important from the U.S. perspective, as control over the majority of U.S. forces in Afghanistan would pass from OEF to ISAF command with the October 2006 implementation of stage 4 in the ISAF rollout. (The political quid pro quo was that ISAF would have responsibility for the whole country but would be led by an American flag officer.) One of Rumsfeld's last appointments as secretary of defense was for General Dan McNeill to take over as COMISAF.[60] McNeill's choice fit well with the secretary's priorities; he had previously commanded American

---

55 Ibid.

56 Donald Rumsfeld, "Afghanistan Memo," July 21, 2006, http://www.rumsfeld.com, accessed February 25, 2012; Martin Strmecki, *Afghanistan at a Crossroads: Challenges, Opportunities, and a War Ahead*, August 17, 2006, http://www.rumsfeld.com, accessed February 25, 2012.

57 Donald Rumsfeld, "NATO Forces in Afghanistan" (memo), March 21, 2006, http://www.rumsfeld.com, accessed February 25, 2012; Donald Rumsfeld, "Energy Behind NATO Train and Equip in Afghanistan" (memo) May 11, 2006, http://www.rumsfeld.com, accessed February 25, 2012. In a July 11, 2006, press conference, for instance, Rumsfeld commented, "If you look at the number of terrorists and Taliban and al Qaeda that are being killed every month, it would be hard for them to say that the Coalition forces and Afghan security forces were losing." Rumsfeld, quoted in Woodward 2006: 482.

58 Donald Rumsfeld, "General Dempsey Look at Train and Equip in Afghanistan" (memo), May 11, 2006, http://www.rumsfeld.com, accessed February 25, 2012.

59 Donald Rumsfeld, "Meeting on Military Functions in Afghanistan" (memo), June 13, 2006, http://www.rumsfeld.com, accessed February 25, 2012.

60 McNeill was nominated to be COMISAF on September 21, 2006, and would take command in February 2007.

forces in Afghanistan in 2002–3 when the focus was on counterterrorism and starting to build the ANA.[61]

To sum up the first five years of U.S. intervention in Afghanistan, Secretary Rumsfeld acted as the president's proximate principal with regard to deployed U.S. forces. We would expect principals in single-principal countries to tailor their principal-agent contract depending on whether they valued military outcomes in the target country or the behavior of their deployed troops. Rumsfeld clearly valued outcomes more than behavior. He acted accordingly. Whenever possible, he selected officers that shared his vision and focused oversight on metrics associated with those preferred outcomes. Oversight varied in intensity depending on the performance of the agent, with agents that diverged from desired outcomes being subject to stringent oversight. All this is consistent with the model introduced in chapter 3.

## THE GATES YEARS: BEHAVIOR, AGENT SELECTION, AND INCENTIVES

Robert Gates became secretary of defense on December 18, 2006, and would continue in that office through the end of the period covered in this study. Gates's tenure spanned the last two years of the Bush administration and the first two years of the administration of President Barack Obama. Two things were notable immediately upon Gates becoming secretary. First, the Bush administration's goals in Afghanistan began to evolve. The administration conducted a significant review of Afghan policy in the late fall of 2006 and into the early winter of 2007. The review resulted in five goals for Afghanistan, among which were tasks associated with classic COIN strategies, such as improving provincial governance and Afghanistan's rural economy, curtailing poppy cultivation, and helping the Karzai government fight corruption.[62] This represented a significant change from the Rumsfeld years.

Second, Gates had a different philosophy and used different means to exert control over military agents. He focused on oversight and incentives to ensure that deployed troops engaged in the appropriate behavior in Afghanistan and elsewhere. Rumsfeld had focused on agent selection and episodic oversight to ensure that his outcomes were achieved. Gates's first move in terms of agent selection was to fire Secretary of the Army Francis Harvey over the Walter Reed Army

---

61 Some in NATO were concerned that McNeill would be too aggressive militarily, given his background. See Carlotta Gall, "American Takes Over Command of NATO Forces as Its Mission Grows in Afghanistan," *New York Times*, February 5, 2007.

62 See The White House, "President Bush Discusses Progress in Afghanistan, Global War on Terror," February 15, 2007, http://georgewbush-whitehouse.archives.gov/news/releases/2007/02/20070215-1.html, accessed August 30, 2011.

Medical Center scandal. Gates remarked at the time, "Accountability is obviously very important to me. Leadership is more than just making decisions about budgets and administrative decisions; it's about setting a tone."[63] The top brass got the message.[64] By 2009, Gates had removed "a half-dozen senior officers and civilian secretaries for underwhelming performance or just plain arrogance."[65] That would include an ISAF commander in 2008. He would continue holding senior officers accountable through the end of his tenure as secretary of defense, removing a second ISAF commander in 2010.[66]

## McKiernan and Petraeus

The situation in Afghanistan deteriorated during 2007, Gates's first year in office and General McNeill's first year as COMISAF. Attacks on ISAF soldiers had increased during 2007. Casualties were up. The situation in Helmand Province was dire enough that the Bush administration was forced to deploy an additional 3,200 marines in early 2008 to shore up ISAF forces there. Gates recommended two personnel changes that would affect the conduct of the war in Afghanistan. With these personnel decisions, Gates accelerated the shift from the outcomes-based counterterrorism and ANA training mission of late 2006 toward a defense, diplomacy, and development COIN strategy whose metrics would be based on the behavior of troops on the ground.

First, Secretary Gates decided to replace McNeill as ISAF commander in January 2008, less than a year after McNeill had taken command. The situation in Afghanistan had clearly deteriorated during McNeill's tenure, with even higher levels of violence predicted for 2008.[67] Additionally, McNeill had been chosen by Secretary Rumsfeld, and had been given Rumsfeld's default command guidance: build the ANA and engage in counterterrorism activities. Gates did not have the same aversion to COIN efforts as had Rumsfeld (Hodge 2011). It was widely believed that Gates replaced McNeill because McNeill was taking a too-cautious, traditional approach to counterinsurgency and was moving too slowly to embrace the new command objectives.[68] As President Bush would note in a

---

63 Robert Gates, "Interview with Secretary Gates," *Pentagon Channel*, March 13, 2007, http://www.defense.gov/pdf/Gatesinterview031307.pdf, accessed August 17, 2011. See also "Secretary Gates: Embrace Accountability, Return to Standards of Excellence," *Air Force Print News Today*, http://www.schriever.af.mil/news/story.asp?id=123102254, accessed August 17, 2011.
64 Tom Ricks and Ann Tyson, "Defense Secretary Sends Stern Message about Accountability," *Washington Post*, March 3, 2007.
65 Gordon Lubold, "Afghanistan War Decision: How Robert Gates Thinks," *Christian Science Monitor*, November 2, 2009.
66 Mark Thompson, "The Military's New Surge in Accountability," *Time*, February 17, 2010.
67 Ann Tyson, "A Sober Assessment of Afghanistan," *Washington Post*, June 15, 2008; Josh White, "U.S. Deaths Rise in Afghanistan," *Washington Post*, July 2, 2008.
68 Lubold, "Afghanistan War Decision."

White House press event with McNeill after McNeill left command in June 2008, a COIN strategy was now seen as appropriate for Afghanistan. "Helping rebuild this society after years of tyranny is in all our interests. And it's also a moral duty we have."[69]

Army General David McKiernan was picked as McNeill's replacement and took command of ISAF in June 2008. This was a milestone of sorts, in that McKiernan was the first U.S. officer in charge of both ISAF and OEF forces. In the words of President Bush, "This newly created position and realignment of the command structure provides General McKiernan authority over nearly all U.S. forces in Afghanistan, ensuring greater coordination in operational planning and execution."[70]

McKiernan seemed to have embraced the behavioral focus advocated by Gates.[71] One of McKiernan's most notable command directives was an attempt to change the *behavior* of ISAF forces in Afghanistan. Specifically, he issued a directive in early September that aimed to limit civilian casualties. As quoted in the press, the directive read, "We will demonstrate proportionality, requisite restraint and the utmost discrimination in the use of firepower. We will only use such munitions against Afghan houses or compounds when there is an imminent threat and when the on-the-scene commander determines there is no other way to protect the force."[72] While the directive aimed to reduce one of the main points of friction with the Afghan people from allegedly indiscriminate air strikes, raids into private homes, and unobserved indirect fire, it was only marginally successful at changing behavior on the ground.[73] That said, these were the orders of a commander trying to change how the battle was being fought, not just whether his forces won the battle.

Second, President Bush nominated General David Petraeus as CENTCOM commander, which was important in that the CENTCOM commander was the combatant commander the newly double-hatted McKiernan would report to when wearing his OEF hat. General Petraeus was widely respected for his success

---

69 The White House, press release, June 17, 2008, http://georgewbush-whitehouse.archives.gov/news/releases/2008/06/20080617-3.html, accessed August 30, 2011.

70 The White House, press release, October 2, 2008, http://georgewbush-whitehouse.archives.gov/news/releases/2008/10/20081002-8.html, accessed August 30, 2011.

71 The official Defense Department position in 2008 was that "the U.S. continues to pursue a comprehensive counterinsurgency (COIN) campaign, which utilizes the military, government, and economic expertise of the U.S. and the international community." See U.S. Department of Defense, *Progress toward Security and Stability in Afghanistan: Report to Congress*, January 2009, http://www.defense.gov/pubs/OCTOBER_1230_FINAL.pdf, accessed April 23, 2013.

72 John Burns, "Afghanistan Airstrike Threatens to Deepen Anger in an Uneasy Populace," *New York Times*, October 17, 2008.

73 U.S. Department of Defense, *Progress Toward Security and Stability in Afghanistan*, 9; Burns, "Afghanistan Airstrike." According to one knowledgeable former Bush administration official interviewed in 2009, the order raised the perception among troops on the ground that they were fighting with one hand tied behind their backs, which may account for the directive's mixed success.

in Iraq using a behaviorally focused, population-centric COIN strategy, a strategy that combined a troop surge and kinetic operations with intense interactions with local officials and steps to protect the Iraqi population.[74] Petraeus would take command of CENTCOM in October 2008, and one of his first tasks would be to conduct a very large commander's assessment of the entire CENTCOM region.[75] That review would point to the need for a much more proactive COIN effort in Afghanistan, among other things. Petraeus would remark that the 2008–9 CENTCOM assessment pointed to a need for new ideas and operating concepts in Afghanistan, new organizational structures, different military leaders, and more resources devoted to Afghanistan.[76]

## Obama, Petraeus, and McChrystal

The Obama administration took office knowing that U.S. policy toward Afghanistan was in grave peril but getting different recommendations as to what to do about it. There were 32,000 U.S. military personnel in the country at the time. The intelligence community had recently completed a very grim national intelligence estimate that warned of a downward spiral in the security, governance, and poppy cultivation situation in Afghanistan.[77] The aforementioned Defense Department review released in January 2009 painted an equally grim picture. The CENTCOM assessment was ongoing, as was a review of Afghan policy by Admiral Mike Mullen, chairman of the Joint Chiefs of Staff (CJCS). Lieutenant General Douglas Lute, a member of the Bush National Security Council staff, had led a Bush administration review in late 2008.

The new administration conducted its own review of Afghan policy, led by Bruce Riedel of the Brookings Institution.[78] The review found that the coalition was losing the war in Afghanistan, but that the war was not yet lost; that changing Pakistani behavior with regard to Taliban sanctuaries was a key to success; and, most important, the United States needed to engage in major COIN operations in both countries.[79] A key point of contention within the administration that motivated the review and flowed from it was how many additional troops to commit to Afghanistan. Senior administration officials were divided. The vice president elect, Joe Biden,

---

74 For a summary of his Iraqi strategy, see David Petraeus, "Multinational Force-Iraq Commander's Counterinsurgency Guidance," *Military Review*, September–October 2008, 2–4.

75 Sean Naylor, "Petraeus Team to Review CENTCOM," *Army Times*, September 19, 2008; see also Woodward 2011: 76–79. David Auerswald participated in that assessment process.

76 John Banusiewicz, "Petraeus Explains Afghanistan Strategy," *Armed Forces Press Service*, September 3, 2010.

77 Mark Mazzetti and Eric Schmitt, "U.S. Study Is Said to Warn of Crisis in Afghanistan," *New York Times*, October 8, 2008.

78 Woodward 2011: 88–90; see also The White House, press briefing, January 28, 2009, http://www.white house.gov/the-press-office/press-briefing-12809, accessed August 30, 2011.

79 Interview with senior U.S. military officer C, Washington, D.C., 2009.

advocated for essentially giving up on Afghan nation building and instead opting for counterterrorism missions when necessary. Such a strategy would allow for a much-reduced troop presence. Others in the administration, particularly Generals Petraeus and McKiernan, advocated for a much larger troop presence. McKiernan had reportedly lobbied the incoming administration quite strongly that he needed 30,000 additional troops right away. "We're not losing," he is reported to have said to Biden during a trip to Afghanistan, "but to get off the fence to where we're actually winning we need these additional troops."[80] The White House pushed back, questioning the logic behind those numbers. Upon further review by Secretary Gates himself, it seemed that only 17,000 were needed in early 2009.[81] President-Elect Obama agreed to that amount, noting, "This increase is necessary to stabilize a deteriorating situation in Afghanistan."[82] Then, on March 27, 2009, President Obama unveiled a new U.S. strategy for the region based on the Riedel review, with a renewed focus on a whole-of-government counterinsurgency plan, an additional 4,000 deployed troops, and a significant emphasis placed on the role of Pakistan.[83]

McKiernan would remain in command for only eighteen months, until June 15, 2009, rather than the two-year tour that was originally envisioned. Rumblings about McKiernan's future had begun in early 2009. Some believed that McKiernan was simply too "regular army" for a COIN operation and moved too slowly to engage with local officials.[84] He was more comfortable with a kinetic counterterrorism approach, which would not work in the Afghan theater, argued retired army general Jack Keane to newly appointed secretary of state Hillary Rodham Clinton (Woodward 2011: 82–85). CJCS Mullen was not altogether comfortable with McKiernan's leadership either (Woodward 2011: 118). Secretary Gates knew that McKiernan had been behind the questionable 30,000 troop request in late 2008 that Gates had had to disavow to the new administration. And finally, the situation did not seem to have improved in Afghanistan during 2008.[85] With the secretary's penchant for accountability, such a track record would not bode well for McKiernan.

In principal-agent terms, the decision to replace McKiernan was consistent with a principal, in this case Gates, using *incentives* to ensure correct agent

80 Joe Biden, quoted in Woodward 2011: 70.
81 "We don't have the numbers right. The complaints you raise, I went back and looked into. And I've got to tell you, I now don't have confidence in those numbers. So please pull the package from the president, and I'll get you the right numbers." Robert Gates, quoted in Woodward 2011: 95.
82 The White House, press release, February 17, 2009, http://www.whitehouse.gov/the-press-office/statement -president-afghanistan, accessed August 30, 2011.
83 The White House, "Remarks by the President on a New Strategy for Afghanistan and Pakistan," March 27, 2009, http://www.whitehouse.gov/the_press_office/Remarks-by-the-President-on-a-New-Strategy -for-Afghanistan-and-Pakistan, accessed August 30, 2011.
84 Elisabeth Bumiller and Thom Shanker, "Commander's Ouster Is Tied to Shift in Afghan War," *New York Times*, May 12, 2009; and Ann Tyson, "Top U.S. Commander in Afghanistan Is Fired," *Washington Post*, May 12, 2009.
85 U.S. Department of Defense, *Progress toward Security and Stability in Afghanistan*, 7–10.

behavior. Secretary Gates and CJCS Mullen went to the president in April 2009 and advocated replacing McKiernan with General Stanley McChrystal, arguing that McKiernan was not providing the best leadership available in Afghanistan.[86] Gates announced the change on May 11, 2009: "Our mission [in Afghanistan] requires new thinking and new approaches from our military leaders. Today we have new policy set out by the president. We have a new strategy. I believe that new military leadership is also needed."[87] Gates was also using *agent selection* to ensure that military behavior was consistent with his expectations. McChrystal was in many ways an ideal choice as a military agent to run a COIN operation. He had significant exposure to COIN strategy, having commanded the Joint Special Operations Command (JSOC) from 2003 to 2008. He also was a relatively known quantity to Secretary Gates, both from McChrystal's time at JSOC and his more recent service as a senior Joint Staff official.

Gates's use of incentives and agent selection seemed to work. McChrystal quickly embraced the population-centric COIN mission from his first days as COMISAF. For example, he issued a tactical directive to all troops under his command on July 1, 2009, that put limits on when lethal force could be used and described steps to ensure that civilian casualties were minimized. McChrystal then conducted an extensive review of U.S. policy in Afghanistan and Pakistan, and released an unclassified version at the end of August 2009.[88] His review pointed to two problems: "a resilient and growing insurgency" and "a crisis of confidence among Afghans . . . that undermines our credibility and emboldens the insurgents."[89] His solution was to argue for "a significant change to our strategy and the way that we think and operate. This new strategy must be properly resourced and executed through an integrated civilian-military counterinsurgency campaign."[90] ISAF should focus on areas where the population was threatened. "Our objective," argued McChrystal, "must be the population."[91]

The president agreed to deploy an additional 30,000 troops to support McChrystal's strategy. Those 30,000 would be in addition to the 68,000 U.S. and 39,000 non-U.S. ISAF troops already in the country by the end of the year. When announcing the deployment in a December speech at West Point, President Obama said, "Afghanistan is not lost, but for several years it has moved

---

86 This was one of the first times a general had been removed from a combat command since Douglas MacArthur during the Korean War. McKiernan reportedly resisted Mullen's demand that he retire, saying that Mullen would have to fire him before he would step down. See Woodward 2011: 119.

87 Woodward 2011, 119; Bumiller and Shanker, "Commander's Ouster"; Tyson, "Top U.S. Commander in Afghanistan Is Fired." The related Pentagon press release on May 11, 2009, http://www.defense.gov /transcripts/transcript.aspx?transcriptid=4424, accessed August 30, 2011, would note, "Implementation of a new strategy in Afghanistan called for new military leadership."

88 Stanley McChrystal, "COMISAF's Initial Assessment," August 30, 2009, unclassified official assessment document provided to the authors.

89 Ibid., 1-1.

90 Ibid.

91 Ibid. See also Jones 2009: 335.

backwards . . . and the Taliban has gained momentum. The status quo is not sustainable."[92] This "Afghan surge," as it was referred to, was aimed at stopping the insurgents' momentum and protecting the Afghan population, both consistent with a population-centric COIN approach.[93] By all accounts, McChrystal made every effort to implement this approach to the best of his ability through January 2010, the end of our study's time frame.[94]

In conclusion, presidents serve as the ultimate principal in the U.S. civil-military system. We expect presidents to use a combination of agent selection, oversight, and incentives. Presidents Bush and Obama appear to have delegated that authority down one level to their respective secretaries of defense, allowing Rumsfeld and Gates to serve as the proximate principal for deployed U.S. commanders. Rumsfeld focused on achieving particular outcomes associated with training the ANA and ANP, counterterrorism actions, and minimizing the U.S. footprint in Afghanistan. He used agent selection and episodic oversight in an effort to achieve those outcomes. One could argue he also curtailed agent discretion, if indirectly, in that he refused to provide the resources many deemed necessary for the fight. Gates took a different track, focusing on ensuring that the U.S. military engaged in behavior appropriate to a COIN strategy. He famously insisted on accountability for his senior officers, and willingly supported more troops and improved capabilities, all of which constitute incentives of one form or another. Finally, he too occasionally used agent selection to achieve desired behavior. Overall, then, the U.S. story in Afghanistan supports the expectations for a presidential government identified in chapter 3.

## The French in Afghanistan: Chirac versus Sarkozy

French operations in Afghanistan spanned two presidential administrations: those of Jacques Chirac and Nicolas Sarkozy, both representing the conservative-leaning Union for a Popular Movement party.[95] But before exploring each president's policies in Afghanistan, we should review the rules governing civil-military relations in

92 The White House, "Remarks by the President in Address to the Nation on the Way Forward in Afghanistan and Pakistan," December 1, 2009, http:www.whitehouse.gov/the-press-office/remarks-president -address-nation-way-forward-afghanistan-and-pakistan, accessed August 30, 2011.

93 The White House, "Fact Sheet: The Way Forward in Afghanistan," December 1, 2009, http://www.white house.gov/the-press-office/way-forward-afghanistan, accessed August 30, 2011.

94 He, too, would be removed from office in June 2010 for inappropriate comments and behavior published in *Rolling Stone* magazine. At the time, President Obama would remark, "This is a change in personnel, but it is not a change in policy." See The White House, "Statement by the President in the Rose Garden," June 23, 2010, http://www.whitehouse.gov/the-press-office/statement-president-rose-garden, accessed August 29, 2011; David Jackson, "Obama Fires McChrystal, Picks Petraeus to Lead in Afghanistan," *USA Today*, June 23, 2010, accessed August 10, 2011; and Shaun Waterman, "McChrystal Resigns Afghan Command," *Washington Times*, June 23, 2010.

95 The scope of this study ends before Francois Hollande took office with a promise to get out of Afghanistan.

France. The French system empowers the president to make all significant deployment decisions. The French have a premier-presidential government system, with both a president and a prime minister (Elgie 1999, 2009; Roper 2002; Shugart 2005). The president serves a fixed term of office and holds virtually all of the foreign policy powers of the national government.[96] The premier is chosen by a parliamentary majority and has some influence over domestic legislation. This was by design. The Fifth Republic's constitution was written to correct the shortcomings of the previous regime, when governments would regularly fall over foreign policy issues, particularly related to Algeria (Keeler 1993). Presidents in the Fifth Republic were given broad discretion on security policy and were insulated from public backlash via a long fixed term of office. Thus, the starting point of the 2008 *French White Paper on Defense and National Security* is this statement by President Sarkozy in the foreword: "As Commander in Chief of the French armed forces, I have the duty to protect the vital and strategic interests of our nation. It is *my responsibility* to choose the strategy and assets France needs. . . ." (Republic of France 2008: 9; emphasis added).

The French military chain of command runs from the field to the Joint Staff (État-Major des Armées) to the president. Neither the prime minister nor the minister of defense has a mandatory role in military operations, although they may be consulted.[97] Indeed, one senior French officer suggested that the minister of defense was nearly out of the loop with regard to Afghan policy.[98] Within the Elysée, the president has a small military staff including a senior military officer, the chef d'état-major particulier (who frequently becomes the head of the French military), which coordinates with the Joint Staff. As a senior joint officer notes, "The French military is quite privileged. We are close to the president. The bulk of decisions are made at the Joint Staff, working hand in hand with military advisers in the Elysée."[99] Consequently, we should not be surprised that the significant shifts in French deployments and restrictions in Afghanistan coincided with the change from Jacques Chirac to Nicolas Sarkozy as president. The remainder of this section focuses on the caveats placed on French forces, as that was the primary means by which the president exerted control over his agents in the field.

## JACQUES CHIRAC: BEHAVIOR AND CAVEATS

Jacque Chirac held the presidency from the beginning of French involvement in Afghanistan until May 2007, and was very much focused on controlling the *behavior* of his deployed troops. Chirac authorized French participation in Afghan

---

96 Interview with Thomas Krau, European Council on Foreign Relations, Paris, June 9, 2009.
97 There is surprisingly little written on French civil-military structures and relations; see, however, Vennesson 2003.
98 Interview with Joint Staff officer, Paris, June 2009.
99 Interview with senior Joint Staff officer, Paris, June 2009.

operations, but did so in a way that maximized French freedom of action, regardless of the outcomes produced, and minimized the political risks at home.

The key factors shaping Chirac's outlook seem to have been his desire for a greater French role in European defense policy and his poor relationship with the Bush administration, particularly after the start of the Iraq War.[100] The initial French decisions in the aftermath of 9/11 were much more assertive and supportive than the ones that took place during and after the invasion of Iraq. Chirac kept France in Afghanistan after his split with Bush, but minimized the French commitment and its public exposure. The French had only 750 troops in Kabul in 2005, then 1,100 by the end of 2006, a relatively small contribution given France's military capabilities and much smaller than that of the other major European countries. He initially resisted the expansion of NATO from the Kabul area to covering the rest of the country.[101] His refusal to deploy a PRT was part of a larger view toward restricting the U.S.-led NATO military efforts, and protecting the European Union's role, over which France has more influence, as a civilian agency to support development, reconstruction, and governance.

The main French military contingent remained in Kabul when NATO spread across Afghanistan in 2004–6, where it shared command of RC-Capital with German and Turkish troops. French troops were restricted to this part of Afghanistan and were unavailable to reinforce NATO troops elsewhere.[102] The French refused to send their regular combat troops to the south or east, and were publicly opposed to the U.S. counterterrorism mission.[103] Being limited to Kabul essentially prevented the French battalion from engaging in combat since there was relatively little violence in Kabul from 2005 through 2009. While other countries set up PRTs to combine security, governance, and development efforts around the country, France refrained. According to a senior French officer, they refused to form a PRT because of the long-term commitment entailed by a PRT.[104] Oversight was relatively tight. French commanders had to report back through the French Joint Staff, up through the chief of defense to the president, and had to do so "on any action that could possibly appear in the press."[105] Combined, these actions suggest a country that cared more about directing the behavior of their troops rather than achieving outcomes on the ground.

---

100 Leo Michel, "Quelle place pour la France dans l'OTAN ?" Le Monde, June 6, 2007.
101 "Chirac Assures Karzai of Continuing French Presence in Afghanistan," Pak Tribune, October 4, 2005, http://paktribune.com/news/Chirac-assures-Karzai-of-continuing-French-presence-in-Afghanistan-121277.html, accessed April 23, 2013.
102 Interview with senior French officer, Tampa, Florida, February 2009.
103 Ron Synovitz, "Afghanistan: France Wants to Keep Separate Commands for ISAF and Combat Forces," Radio Free Europe/Radio Liberty, October 4, 2005, http://www.rferl.org/content/article/1061875.html, accessed March 10, 2012.
104 Interview with senior French officer, Tampa, Florida, February 2009. The public rationale was that it was too difficult to coordinate PRTs run by different national contingents.
105 Interview with senior French officer, Tampa, Florida, February 2009.

French forces were also restricted from other types of behavior; for instance, they could not engage in counternarcotics operations. Counternarcotics are an interesting indicator of a leader's focus on behavior or outcomes, and are generally geared toward an outcome-oriented strategy. Poppy production is easily measurable, but often forces the military to engage in dangerous, open-ended, and sometimes morally questionable behavior. French officers argued that their refusal of counternarcotics operations was not relevant given the absence of the drug trade in eastern Afghanistan.[106] This seems like a hollow argument, as a French officer who served as the senior military representative invoked the red card when asked to engage in just such operations.[107] More likely, the French leadership did not want to be involved in this type of behavior. A similar restriction was placed on France's participation in crowd control in Kabul. Crowd control would have meant backing up the Afghan National Police, and the Afghan style of crowd control was not something with which the French wanted to be associated.[108] French forces engaged in combat also faced a series of restrictions on their behavior, to include using proportional force when attacked, avoiding civilian infrastructure, and requiring visual recognition before calling in air strikes.[109]

The anomaly was that a small two-hundred-person contingent of French special forces was attached to Operation Enduring Freedom from 2003 to 2007. French special forces engaged in significant combat in and near Spin Boldak, a town on the border with Pakistan. But even here the special forces units had limits put on their behavior.[110] While they were allowed to engage in short-term counterterrorism and counterinsurgency raids, they were not allowed to engage in long-term counterterrorism missions, such as tracking insurgent movements over time, and were not allowed to accompany Afghan units as advisers during military operations.[111] The other interesting thing to note about this deployment was that Chirac kept special operations force (SOF) deployments highly secretive. That is, SOF could operate but not tell anyone about it, a form of restricted behavior. Public exposure would raise an implied commitment and increase political costs at home. Interview subjects agreed that, under Chirac, combat missions were cloaked in secrecy. The most visible units—the forces in Kabul—were doing very little, and the least visible units were doing a great deal. The French government put out very little information, and the French media did not provide much coverage.

106 Interviews with senior French officers, Paris, June 2009.
107 Interview with senior French officer, Paris, June 2009.
108 Interviews with French officers, Paris, June 2009.
109 Interview with senior French officer, Tampa, Florida, February 2009.
110 There is some dispute, even within the French military, as to why the SOF deployment ended in 2007. Some believe that the SOF agreement was for a specific time frame not to exceed four years. Others believe the deployment ended because of a 2007 Franco-American dispute over the role of French SOF in RC-East. Interviews with senior French officers, Tampa, Florida, and Paris, February and June 2009.
111 Interview with senior French officer, Tampa, Florida, February 2009.

In sum, the French under Chirac kept their main troop deployment deliberately out of harm's way. At the same time, they had small, almost invisible but highly kinetic units sent for an apparently fixed term. Both actions seem to be those of a leader concerned more about behavior than about outcomes.

## NICOLAS SARKOZY: OUTCOMES AND FEW CONSTRAINTS

Nicolas Sarkozy took office on May 16, 2007. As part of a larger rhetoric of change (Szarka 2009), Sarkozy broke with Chirac's policies and pledged to increase France's involvement in Afghanistan shortly after he was elected. Rather than opposing or limiting the transatlantic alliance, Sarkozy wanted France to be more involved in NATO, and specifically to become reintegrated into the NATO command structure (Cogan 2010; Ghez and Larrabee 2009). As the 2008 French *White Paper* notes, "There is no competition between NATO and the EU—the two are complementary. This reality leads us to advocate the full participation of France in the structures of NATO" (Republic of France 2008: 8). Analysts will debate how much of a shift this is, given that France was already participating in key NATO efforts in the Balkans and then Afghanistan, but there is no doubt it was a major political move at home (and was opposed by two former prime ministers), in Europe, and in the United States.[112] While part of this might have been driven by a desire on the part of Sarkozy to contradict anything Chirac did (Cogan 2010), there is more to it than that.

Where Chirac was motivated to limit most French behavior in Afghanistan, Sarkozy seems to have been motivated to achieve particular *outcomes* on the ground and with regard to the NATO alliance. In particular, Sarkozy wanted more influence in NATO decisions as his ultimate goal. According to our interviews, Sarkozy realized that French influence within NATO depended on making a greater commitment to the ISAF effort in Afghanistan and actually achieving positive outcomes. He also seemed to have formed a bond with U.S. president George W. Bush.[113] The immediate result was that France doubled its participation in ISAF, to 2,200 troops by early 2008, and raised that again to 2,700 by September and to 3,300 by February 2009.[114]

---

112 Michael Moran, *French Military Strategy and NATO Reintegration*, March 12 2009, http://www.cfr.org /france/french-military-strategy-nato-reintegration/p16619#p2, accessed March 11, 2012.

113 See Philip Gordon, "France Learns How to Say Yes," *Newsweek*, September 25, 2007; and Moran, *French Military Strategy and NATO Reintegration*. For an example of the chemistry between the two leaders, see The White House, "President Bush Participates in Joint Press Availability with President Sarkozy," June 14, 2008, http://georgewbush-whitehouse.archives.gov/news/releases/2008/06/20080614-2.html, accessed April 23, 2013.

114 Interview with senior French officer, Tampa, Florida, February 2009.

Rather than merely being present in a low-risk environment, France moved a battalion in 2008 to a more dangerous area under the United States in RC-East: Kapisa, an area close to Kabul but with significantly greater risks and, ultimately, more frequent combat. France later moved the rest of its Kabul combat forces to eastern Afghanistan.[115] This allowed the redeployment of some American units from RC-East to RC-South, which made it easier for the Canadians to renew their mission's mandate.[116] The French also were willing to assist in southern Afghanistan when needed. They deployed observer, mentor, liaison teams (OMLTs) outside of Kabul, including one to Uruzgan in southern Afghanistan to support the Dutch units there. This OMLT was almost twice as large as normal, a French requirement given how far the OMLT was from France's other commitments, making logistical support more difficult.[117] Despite the greater logistical challenges, France's OMLTs, unlike their German counterparts, were allowed to move with their kandaks out of the French areas of operation (Kapisa, Kabul, and Uruzgan), although a phone call was required to gain permission from Paris.

To be clear, a phone call requesting permission was not a trivial issue and had implications for mission success. In the aftermath of the Kandahar prison break in the summer of 2008, one of the Afghan kandaks the French were mentoring was redeployed to help clear the Taliban from the Arghandab area north of the city. According to several Canadian officers involved at the time, the French OMLT had to wait until it received permission from Paris to redeploy, with the call going all the way to Sarkozy. As a result, the kandak went into battle with a hastily summoned group of American Marines, and the kandak broke after the first shots were fired. The French OMLT arrived the next day after permission had been granted from Paris, and the effort went much more smoothly thereafter. A one day's delay thus had a mixed impact. The delay risked the mission's initial success. On the other hand, France did redeploy one of its OMLTs to a different regional command despite the team being put directly in harm's way.

Finally, French fighter planes were moved to Kandahar Airfield in 2008. French planes had been flying over Afghanistan since 2002 from a base in the central Asian republic of Tajikistan. Redeployment to within Afghanistan shortened their flight times to Kapisa, which made them much more effective and responsive, even if they could only operate during daylight hours.[118]

These actions are consistent with a coalition partner making every effort to contribute to the ISAF cause. In short, Sarkozy was making a significant effort to

---

115 Interview with senior French officers, Tampa, Florida, and Paris, February and June 2009.
116 See chapter 6 for the Canadian mandate renewal of 2008.
117 Interview with senior French Joint Staff officer, Paris, June 2009.
118 French Embassy in London, "Michèle Alliot-Marie on Reorganization of French Forces in Afghanistan," http://www.ambafrance-uk.org/Michele-Alliot-Marie-on.html, accessed April 23, 2013.

ensure that NATO succeeded. As a result, he lifted French geographic caveats,[119] and France, never shy about using force in its other deployments, operated very much like its more active allies. In sum, France moved from being among the most restricted to among the least restricted national contingents, corresponding to a change in presidential priorities.

# The Poles: Out in Front

Poland has a premier-presidential system of government.[120] The president is directly elected every five years and is not dependent on legislative confidence for his tenure in office. The president selects the prime minister, with that selection having to be ratified by the Sejm, the lower chamber of the parliament. The prime minister has frequently represented a governing coalition in the Sejm, rather than just a single party. The president has the majority of foreign policy powers and must approve all international deployments of Polish troops. Such decisions are taken by the president and the Council of Ministers. The parliament has no role in deployment decisions, which was fortunate for Polish participation in that public support for the ISAF mission has been very low in Poland, providing individual Members of Parliament with an electoral incentive to oppose Polish participation in the ISAF mission.

## THE KWASNIEWSKI PRESIDENCY

Poland was led by President Aleksander Kwasniewski from 1995 until October 2005. President Kwasniewski represented the Sojusz Lewicy Demokratycznej (SLD), or Democratic Left Alliance, a center-left party. He had three different prime ministers between the start of the Afghan intervention and the end of his term of office, all SLD members. His defense minister, Jerzy Szmajdzinski, was also an SLD member. The president's foreign policy priorities at the time were to join the EU, which would occur in 2004, and to solidify the Poles' ties to the United States, their chief patron within NATO.

Presidential systems have a number of techniques to control their deployed military forces. As discussed earlier, nations can place limits on what their troops can do when deployed through caveats or through limitations on the capabilities given to those troops. Both seem to have been in play during Poland's initial

---

119 Natalie Nougayrède, "En Afghanistan, la France réaménage son dispositif pour affronter les talibans," *Le Monde*, June 22, 2009.
120 This section draws heavily on interviews between 2007 and 2012 with senior Polish officials in Brussels, Krakow, Warsaw, and Washington, D.C., including a minister of defense and a military chief of defense; senior members of the Polish delegation to NATO; and the U.S. and Polish representatives to CENTCOM. None of these officials wanted to be quoted or identified. Additional background information was provided by U.S. desk officers in the Departments of Defense and State.

deployment to Afghanistan. The Poles deployed just over one hundred people to Afghanistan in March 2002. These troops were limited to demining activities, operations at Kabul International Airport, and various engineering tasks. They were not given authority to engage in offensive operations nor given the equipment or support elements to do so. President Kwasniewski would focus most of Poland's efforts in Iraq, as that seemed to be the higher priority for the United States.[121]

The Poles also used two other techniques to control their deployed troops: oversight and agent selection. In terms of oversight, they created a new operational command in 2003 with responsibility for oversight and control of operations abroad. They also created a new special operations command in 2004, comprised of SOF elements from the land, air, and sea services of the Polish military. Both were created to foster joint operations. They also served as useful oversight tools. Deployed commanders were required to report back to the operational command, and to the special operations command if a SOF unit, on a daily basis. The Poles also used extensive agent selection. Initially, military units were put on a rotational schedule for six-month tours in Afghanistan. Their commanders would not necessarily go with them, however. Specific officers were selected for overseas command by name, and inserted into whichever unit was scheduled next for deployment abroad. Poland soon learned that this did not work well in that it set up a situation in which a commander would be leading troops into harm's way with little knowledge of that unit. They soon changed agent selection procedures so that commanders were chosen by name and deployed with their existing units.

## THE KACZYNSKI PRESIDENCY

Lech Kaczynski won the 2005 presidential election representing the strongly conservative Law and Justice party. Like his predecessor, Kaczynski initially chose ministers from his own party.[122] Poland went through a short period of cohabitation from November 2007 through April 2010, when Donald Tusk of the more centrist Civic Platform party became the prime minister and Bogdan Klich became defense minister.[123] These would remain the key officials in office through our period of study.[124]

The Kaczynski government was more pro-American and less trusting of their European neighbors than was the Kwasniewski regime. For example, Kaczynski

---

121 Poland would contribute 2,500 troops to Operation Iraqi Freedom in 2003–4, decreasing to 1,500 in 2005, and 900 in 2006–7, before withdrawing all troops in 2008.

122 Between 2005 and late 2007, Kazimierz Marcinkiewicz and Jaroslaw Kaczynski (brother of the president) each served as prime minister, and Radislov Sikorski and Aleksander Szczyglo served as defense minister. All were Law and Justice members.

123 The 2007 parliamentary elections resulted in the Civic Platform party winning a large plurality in the Sejm, with 209 of the 231 seats needed for a majority. Law and Justice won 166 seats.

124 President Kaczynski and many other senior Polish officials would tragically die in a plane crash in 2010.

was a strong advocate of U.S. missile defenses in Poland, and was behind attempts to bring Ukraine and Georgia into NATO.[125] Prime Minister Tusk shared the view that Poland should take on a greater role in Europe (O'Donnell 2012: 4). Both men were strongly pro–United States and believed that the U.S. government was their main protector against the Russians. President Kaczynski was more skeptical of Poland's western European neighbors, going so far as to delay ratification of the 2007 Lisbon Treaty on the EU because it was allegedly a threat to Polish values.[126] He had relatively poor relations with Germany, particularly as Poland saw increasing economic ties between Germany and Russia (O'Donnell 2012: 2).

The Kaczynski regime would institute two large changes in Poland's mission in Afghanistan. First was a dramatic increase in the size of the Polish contingent and where they would operate. In September 2006 it had roughly 100 soldiers stationed in Bagram. By the end of the year, 1,000 Polish troops would deploy to Ghazni in the American-led RC-East, bordering on Pakistan in some of the most hotly contested territory in Afghanistan. More than 1,200 Polish troops would serve in Ghazni in 2007; 1,600 in 2008; 2,000 in 2009; and 2,500 in 2010. They deployed 11 helicopters in 2008, and more than 110 armored personnel carriers by 2011. Polish troops were involved in five OMLTs and eight Afghan police OMLT training missions, SOF activities, and active patrols.

In interviews, we were told different but complementary rationales for this dramatic increase. The Poles wanted to stay engaged in NATO military operations, and particularly in U.S.-led military operations. They also firmly believed in UN-approved NATO Article V missions. Iraq met the former criteria but not the latter, and Prime Minister Tusk advocated withdrawal from that theater of operations. Afghanistan met both criteria, and was a deployment upon which both President Kaczynski and Prime Minister Tusk could agree. Poland, therefore, shifted emphasis from the Iraqi to the Afghan theater of operations. As the Poles drew down their forces in Iraq in 2007–8, they dramatically increased their deployments in Afghanistan.

The second development was that there were minimal caveats on Polish troops in Afghanistan. The relaxing of Polish caveats is consistent with our explanation in chapter 3 as to both the role of ideology and the outcome versus behavioral focus of the president on the use of force. The conservative, outcome-oriented Kaczynski placed fewer restrictions on Polish troops than did the more liberal Kwasniewski. The result was that Poles had no caveats on their behavior when operating within RC-East or when operating with the United States outside of RC-East. Operating outside RC-East without working with U.S. forces required approval from Polish operational command. The exception was helicopters,

125 Judy Dempsey and Diane Cardwell, "Kaczynski Often a Source of Tension within E.U." *New York Times*, April 10, 2010.
126 Stephen Castle and Judy Dempsey, "Poland Won't Sign European Treaty," *New York Times*, July 2, 2008.

which could support ISAF forces outside of RC-East in emergencies without approval from Warsaw. Polish SOF had no caveats beyond a prohibition against operating outside Afghanistan.

At the same time, however, there was no decrease in oversight of Polish troops. Deployed commanders were still required to report back to the operational command on a daily basis. Whether that oversight was effective is subject to debate. The reason was that Polish troops were held accountable to civilian courts for their actions in the field. In late 2007, Polish troops developed a perception of negative repercussions for civilian casualties, even if that was not the intent of the government, stemming from a November 2007 Polish mortar attack that killed unarmed civilians in the town of Nangar Khel. Polish prosecutors charged the unit responsible with war crimes, despite vigorous protestations from Defense Minister Klich. The soldiers involved were eventually acquitted in 2011, but not before damage had been done in the field. In the words of a U.S. military officer working with the Poles, "Polish soldiers are now less inclined to report the use of lethal force." Some U.S. officials charged that Polish troops "were being micromanaged by Warsaw" to the detriment of troop morale and initiative.[127] That said, the principal in the Polish principal-agent relationship actively worked to rectify the situation, and by 2011 had changed a number of personnel policies to better support and protect Polish troops.[128]

Poland, like France and the United States, had large swings in what it was willing to do in Afghanistan when the individuals making decisions changed. Kwasniewski and his government were much more cautious and limited the Polish deployment. Poland contributed, but did so in a minimal fashion. Kaczynski shifted the primary Polish mission from Iraq to Afghanistan and deployed more soldiers into some of the hardest parts of Afghanistan with a focus on achieving battlefield outcomes in conjunction with American troops.

## Conclusions

We began this chapter with the expectation that single principals will focus on agent selection and incentives to direct their agents. Both tools are well-suited to single-principal government systems. Presidential systems empower individual decision makers. Changes in individuals can produce significant changes in how a country operates in a multilateral mission, and change can happen quickly and quite significantly, as table 4.1 illustrates.

---

127 See Aleksandra Kulczuga, "Poland's 'Vietnam Syndrome' in Afghanistan," *Foreign Policy*, July 7, 2011.
128 Apparently the Poles started the conflict with outdated policies for veterans, which discouraged Polish soldiers from taking risks in the field for fear of being wounded but not cared for after they left the army.

**Table 4.1.** Presidents and Means of Control

| Country | Key Principal | Focus | Means of Control |
|---|---|---|---|
| United States | | | |
| | Rumsfeld, 2001–6 | Outcomes | Agent Selection, Oversight |
| | Gates, 2007–10 | Behavior | Agent Selection, Incentives |
| France | | | |
| | Chirac, 1995–2007 | Behavior | Restrictive Delegation |
| | Sarkozy, 2007–11 | Outcomes | Fewer Restrictions |
| Poland | | | |
| | Kwasniewski, 1995–2005 | Behavior | Limited Capability, Restricted Delegation, Oversight |
| | Kaczynski, 2005–10 | Outcomes | Increased Capability, Fewer Restrictions, Oversight |

We found this to be the case with the U.S. experience in Afghanistan. Secretary of Defense Donald Rumsfeld focused on selecting agents, negative incentives in the form of restricted budgets, and episodic oversight to ensure that the U.S. military achieved his desired outcomes. Secretary Robert Gates focused on incentives to foster COIN-related behavior. Gates matched the negative incentives of firing poorly performing agents with positive incentives associated with budgets and troop levels. French leaders used different tools available to single principals. President Jacques Chirac used restricted delegation contracts (i.e., caveats) to ensure that his troops avoided specific behaviors. President Nicolas Sarkozy relaxed those restrictions in order to increase the chances of achieving positive outcomes on the ground that could translate into greater French influence in NATO. Polish President Aleksander Kwasniewski kept the initial Polish contribution small and constrained through restricted delegation and limitations on material capabilities. President Lech Kaczynski would dramatically expand the mission and relax Polish caveats while maintaining oversight to monitor agent actions. Our results demonstrate that individuals matter a great deal in presidential systems, as changes in key actors produced relative sudden and dramatic changes in behavior.

# 5 Single-Party Parliamentary Governments

## The British and Canadians

We argued in chapter 3 that prime ministers in countries led by single-party governments should behave much like their presidential counterparts when establishing principal-agent contracts during military operations abroad. The prime minister or his designee (usually the defense minister or the chief of defense) is the principal in the principal-agent relationship, as there is no other entity within the government that has direct authority over the military. In the parlance of chapter 2, these systems most closely resemble the single-principal model.

As we argued in chapter 3 and demonstrated for presidential systems in chapter 4, we expect single principals to focus on agent selection and incentives to direct their agents. Both tools are well-suited to single principals, and parliamentary governments led by a single party should be no exception. Whether prime ministers restrict discretion or rely on oversight should depend on the degree to which they prioritize the behavior of their military contingents or the battlefield outcomes reached by those troops. Behavior-oriented premiers are likely to restrict discretion and utilize more active oversight, while outcome-oriented premiers are likely to utilize passive oversight.

This chapter reviews in detail British and Canadian actions in and debates over their military involvement in Afghanistan. These countries are attractive foci of analysis for a number of reasons. Both countries traditionally have been led by single-party parliamentary governments. Both played crucial roles in Regional Command–South (RC-South), with the Canadians in Kandahar and the British in neighboring Helmand Province, resulting in high-intensity military operations. And both countries have very close military, economic, political, and cultural relationships with the United States. We find that the leaders of each country organized their principal-agent contracts with the military in ways that are consistent with our expectations from chapter 3. We end the chapter with shorter reviews for Spain and Turkey, two other single-party parliamentary governments that had operations in Afghanistan.

# The British in Helmand Province

The British were among the first to deploy to Afghanistan's Bagram airfield in November 2001.[1] The British contribution increased to roughly 1,700 troops through the middle of 2002, operating in the capital and toward the Pakistan border. The British next led a provincial reconstruction team (PRT) in the northern city of Mazar-e-Sharif in mid-2003 and then a second PRT in Meymana. They would continue to operate in the north until the International Security Assistance Force (ISAF) extended operations to Helmand Province in RC–South in 2006. This section focuses on the Helmand operation, as it represented a dramatic escalation of the British presence in Afghanistan and took place in an extremely dangerous province. The British have traditionally been led by a parliamentary cabinet run by a single political party, a product of their majoritarian electoral system. This was the case between 2002 and early 2010, the period of our study. Prime Minister Tony Blair of the Labour Party led the government until late June 2007, when he was succeeded by Gordon Brown, also of the Labour Party, until May 2010. Blair governed under a large parliamentary majority in the House of Commons from the 2001 elections through the 2005 elections, with a smaller majority from 2005 to 2010. In the 2010 elections, the Conservative Party won a plurality of seats and formed a coalition government with the Liberal Democrats, as we discuss in chapter 8.

We would expect left-leaning governments to be concerned more about the behavior of their troops rather than achieving specific outcomes on the ground. For left-leaning, single-party governments, we would expect them to focus on less kinetic operations, a moderate amount of caveats, active oversight, and incentives geared toward behavior (see tables 3.3–3.6). As discussed in this chapter, British deployments were confronted with fairly active oversight and were constrained by indirect caveats, consistent with our expectations. As the Labour Party moved from the moderate, "third-way" ideology of Tony Blair to the more traditionally left-wing ideology of Gordon Brown, the British government focused more attention on less kinetic, more population-centric counterinsurgency (COIN) strategies, with a renewed focus on appropriate behavior for soldiers in the field. All this is consistent with our expectations.

## OVERSIGHT

Throughout the period of our study, authority over British troops involved in ISAF operations worked as follows. Brigade commanders reported up through two chains of command, a national chain and the ISAF chain, just like all ISAF

---

1 This section is largely based on a series of interviews with most senior British military officers who commanded in Afghanistan as well as a handful of key politicians.

units. The national chain flowed from the brigade to a veritable alphabet soup of decision-making bodies. Purely military issues were considered by the Permanent Joint Headquarters (PJHQ), to include requests for military forces or capabilities. Unresolved questions were forwarded from PJHQ to the Afghanistan Senior Officials Group when necessary, which consisted of one-star officers and civilian equivalents from various foreign policy agencies. Important decisions or unresolved issues would next be considered at the Afghanistan Strategy Group, a body with two-star representatives from the military, the foreign office, and the British Department for International Development (DFID). From there decisions moved to the cabinet subcommittee on National Security, International Relations and Development chaired by the prime minister or the foreign minister, and finally to the full cabinet when necessary.

All this is to say that the British Ministry of Defence (MOD) and the cabinet did not normally get involved in day-to-day tactical decisions involving operations in Afghanistan. Policy decisions were normally handled by the PJHQ, with daily oversight of deployed forces occurring at the PJHQ level. Indeed, each of the brigade commanders deployed between 2006 and 2010 reported back to the PJHQ on a nearly daily basis. Daily reports were often in the form of informal calls or e-mails, with more formal reports happening on a regular, if less frequent, basis. For example, Brigadier General Ed Butler, in command of the first British deployment to RC-South in 2006, talked to PJHQ officials on a daily basis. Brigadier General Mark Carlton-Smith, in charge of the fifth rotation of British forces in mid-2008, talked to the PJHQ at least five times per week. In short, oversight of deployed forces was relatively intensive, though as we will see, the more effective shaping mechanism for British military behavior was the contingent delegation contract implicit in the government's choice of capabilities to deploy to the fight.

## DISCRETION

The British relied less on formal caveats and more on informal restrictions and specific capabilities to shape the discretion of their commanders. They had only two clearly delineated caveats on what the troops could and could not do, making them one of the forces with the fewest caveats in ISAF, at least when it came to formal caveats.[2] They could not hold prisoners longer than a specified number of hours. They could not operate outside of RC-South without permission from home, and not outside of Afghanistan at all. There were other, less clearly defined caveats implied to commanders. The Defense Ministry frequently, if episodically, informed the PJHQ—and through them the deployed brigade commanders—of

---

2 The British government would repeatedly rail against caveats on other country's forces. See, for example, Hutton 2009.

political concerns with regard to Afghan operations. In the words of one senior MOD official with responsibility for Afghanistan policy, those concerns translated into "soft caveats" on deployed forces—things that the politicos at home would rather the military not do and that astute commanders would understand should not be done. These shifted as dictated by circumstances, and were almost never translated into formal orders. Poppy eradication, for instance, was an issue that commanders were warned away from by officials in London.[3]

Capabilities decisions were a third form of restriction on deployed troops, if an indirect one, and arguably had more impact on British behavior than hard and soft caveats combined. Requests for capabilities from the field could come through either the national channel (i.e., from deployed commanders) or via the ISAF force generation process (described in chapter 2). Requests from both chains were bundled by the PJHQ into a semiannual theater capabilities review (TCR) for consideration by higher authorities.[4] The TCR gave priority to different requesting chains, depending on to whom one talked. Senior civilian officials told us that capabilities requests from the brigade commanders were given priority in the TCR. Senior military officials at the MOD told us that ISAF requests were given priority over those from the UK commander in the field, largely because ISAF requests were more useful in internal UK bureaucratic fights over money and priorities with non-MOD decision makers, such as DFID, the treasury, and Parliament. Regardless of which was true, the result was a continual set of controversies over force levels and limited capabilities provided to British soldiers. If the former was true, then one can only conclude that limiting capabilities was a deliberate attempt by the PJHQ, the MOD, or the cabinet to limit agent discretion. If the latter was true, then inadequate capabilities would seem to be a byproduct of an interagency fight within the British government as to which agency's priorities would drive the mission (i.e. the MOD, DFID, or the foreign office), the result of which was to place limits on the military agent's discretion by non-MOD agencies represented in the cabinet.

Either way, capabilities seemed to be used as an indirect restriction on deployed British troops, an outcome that could not have occurred without the acquiescence of the prime minister. Both the Blair and Brown governments were repeatedly accused of shorting the troops of needed equipment and weapons, particularly improvised explosive device–resistant vehicles, helicopters, infantry fighting vehicles, and artillery. British Army General David Richards, the first

---

3 Interviews with British military and civilian officers, London, 2009.
4 For a detailed review of this process, see UK Ministry of Defence, "Memorandum Submitted by the Ministry of Defence, the Foreign and Commonwealth Office and the Department of International Development," http://www.publications.parliament.uk/pa/cm200809/, accessed October 14, 2009.

overall ISAF commander with responsibility for all of Afghanistan, would argue that logistical constraints were a key limitation on British forces in Afghanistan.[5]

## TONY BLAIR

The British government under Tony Blair was rhetorically very forward-leaning when it came to Afghanistan. There was a consistent pattern of aggressive statements coming from various senior ministers during Blair's tenure. In April 2004, for example, Jack Straw, the foreign secretary, notified international partners that the British were willing "to lead the expansion process in the north of Afghanistan."[6] In late 2005, Defense Secretary John Reid argued in favor of the alliance taking offensive combat operations across Afghanistan.[7] The British backed this rhetoric with actions, if largely symbolic ones. In a November 2006 trip to Afghanistan soon thereafter, Blair signaled that the United Kingdom was committed to the fight "for as long as it takes" for Afghanistan to be stable.[8] He asked alliance partners for more NATO troops to deploy to Afghanistan, noting, "We have to make sure that not just the United Kingdom, but all our NATO partners are doing their utmost to stabilize the situation in Afghanistan." He added, "The credibility of NATO rests on us doing everything we can to help the people of Afghanistan in the search away from the Taliban and in favor of democracy."[9]

British military officers in the field, however, were given decidedly mixed signals from their government when it came to operations in Helmand Province during Blair's tenure. Numerous interviews with British civilian and military officials repeated the idea that the Blair government was focused almost exclusively on stabilizing the situation in Basra, Iraq, temporary home to the British contingent to Operation Iraqi Freedom. Afghanistan was much less central to Blair's thinking. Certainly, bad news continued to emanate from Basra even while the British were deploying into Afghanistan's RC-South.[10]

The result of this attention on Iraq was that British troops in Afghanistan were to some extent left to fend for themselves, according to several British senior

---

5 Interview with General Sir David Richards in Washington, D.C., October 12, 2007.

6 "International Community Will Defeat 'Forces of Darkness' in Afghanistan, Says British Foreign Secretary," http://www.gov-news.org/gov/uk/news/international_community_defeat_39forces_darkness39/78576.html, March 31, 2004, accessed March 12, 2012.

7 "British Defense Official Downplays NATO's Differences in Afghanistan," *Voice of America*, October 2, 2005.

8 Benjamin Sand, "British Prime Minister Blair Vows to Aid Afghanistan 'For as Long as It Takes,'" *Voice of America*, November 20, 2006.

9 Tom Rivers, "British Prime Minister Urges Renewed NATO Commitment to Afghanistan, Sudan," *Voice of America*, November 22, 2006.

10 The Basra deployment was controversial in Britain within the Labour Party, and with the United States, producing a phased withdrawal in 2006–7. See Kim Murphy, "The Conflict in Iraq: British Troop Drawdown," *Los Angeles Times*, February 22, 2007; and "Timeline: UK troops in Basra," *BBC News*, March 23, 2009, http://news.bbc.co.uk/2/hi/uk_news/6977914.stm, accessed May 5, 2012.

military officials. On the one hand, they were given relatively wide discretion to operate in Afghanistan without explicit direction from London. On the other hand, British commanders believed they were denied the capabilities needed to make real progress in Helmand Province. Those capabilities were locked in Iraq, with the result that British commanders in Afghanistan faced a series of indirect limitations on their actions.

Consider the situation faced by Brigadier General Ed Butler, commander of the Sixteenth Air Assault Brigade from April to October 2006 and the first British brigade operating in RC-South. Butler felt that he had tremendous latitude to tailor operations as he saw fit. From his perspective, he received almost no strategic direction or operational guidance from either the MOD or the PJHQ before deploying to Afghanistan. He was told to operate consistent with the Joint Helmand Plan of 2005, but received no direction from the PJHQ on what military actions were appropriate for that plan given his circumstances.[11]

On the other hand, Butler's brigade faced a series of indirect or soft caveats that limited what they could do, largely because they were sent to Afghanistan with an inappropriate mix of forces for the situation and, more important for our purposes, were denied the supplementary forces needed to adapt to that situation. The Sixteenth Brigade thought it was going into Helmand to establish the British bases (particularly Camp Bastion) that would be needed for an extended deployment—essentially an engineering task. They initially deployed with only 3,150 people, and were not supposed to engage in offensive operations until July 2006 when they would be at their full strength of 4,500. Instead, they faced significant combat requirements almost immediately without the appropriate kinds or number of forces for that situation.

The Sixteenth Brigade theoretically could have operated without geographic restrictions, in that it had no written prohibition on that front, but it lacked the transportation and logistical capabilities, particularly helicopters, to move. It could have gotten involved in counternarcotics efforts, but was told not to get involved in search and destroy counternarcotics missions, which Butler interpreted as guidance to avoid counternarcotics altogether because they could easily escalate and turn into a politically risky mission. In short, this was an example of a principal engaging in contingent delegation by controlling the material capabilities given to that agent rather than via explicit caveats on behavior.

The resulting contradiction was embodied in Butler's actions in the town of Musa Qala. The townspeople and nearby British units were under siege by Taliban forces for weeks at a time. There was no way to evacuate large numbers of wounded, or even effectively supply British troops, to say nothing of taking the

---

11 The Joint Helmand Plan set out very broad guidance that lacked operational specifics and assumed that "everything would go right," in the words of one British brigade commander. Interview, London, September 2009.

battle to the enemy, given the limited capabilities Butler's force possessed. Butler reached an agreement with Taliban and local leaders for a cease-fire and withdrawal of all forces from Musa Qala, which made sense to him for tactical and logistical reasons and was within his discretion to order. Yet that decision left him the subject of criticism in London when the Taliban reneged on the deal once British troops were out of the town.

Brigadier General Jerry Thomas faced roughly the same situation as had Butler when the Third Commando Brigade deployed to Afghanistan from October 2006 until April 2007. Thomas, too, was given little guidance. Where the previous brigade had largely been on the defensive, Thomas decided that his force would take the offensive. He created mobile strike teams whose purpose was to hunt down and engage the Taliban in force-on-force encounters.

Yet Thomas confronted many of the same capabilities constraints as had Butler before him. Though Thomas had a larger force at his disposal, with a 5,500-person deployment, he only had about 650 combat soldiers in his mobile battle groups. That meant that the limited capabilities restricted what he could do. He could not engage in poppy eradication because that could lead to significant combat. He could not operate effectively outside of Helmand due to transportation and logistical shortfalls. There were times when he could not even operate in all parts of Helmand Province due to capabilities shortfalls, such as when the Dutch commander of RC-South wanted British forces to engage in a significant operation in Sangin. Thomas refused, given his limited combat troops, until he could garner sufficient U.S., Estonian, and Danish forces to fill out a 1,000-person battle group.

The final British commander under Prime Minister Blair was Brigadier General John Lorimer, who commanded the Twelfth Mechanized Brigade from April to October of 2007. Lorimer had two advantages over his predecessors in term of his delegated power. First, he was one of the architects of the Joint Helmand Plan (Farrell and Gordon 2009: 674). In principal-agent terms, Lorimer was a known agent who shared the preferences of his principal, at least when it came to the Joint Helmand Plan. Second, the British increased Lorimer's combat power to approximately 6,500 soldiers under his command. From a principal-agent perspective, a greater delegation of power to a known agent is not surprising. Of course, it did not hurt that the press got wind of Lorimer's November 2006 request—six months before his deployment—for additional troops and equipment for his brigade. The press jumped on the story as it closely followed a Blair promise that "If the commanders on the ground want more equipment, armored vehicles for example, more helicopters, that will be provided. Whatever package they want, we will do."[12]

---

12 Christopher Leake, "Army Fury as Chief in Afghanistan Is Told He Won't Get Vital Armor," *Mail on Sunday*, November 18, 2006.

With his larger force, Lorimer was the first commander to act consistent with the Joint Helmand Plan's ink-spot design. He attempted to secure strategic towns along the Helmand River, hold those population centers, and then spread to fill the intervening space (Farrell and Gordon 2009: 674). The problem was that he did not have enough troops to hold for any length of time the territory he had seized. And that meant that he had to repeatedly fight large-scale battles for control of the same territory, one example being Operation Pickaxe Handle against Taliban forces in Sangin and the Gereshk Valley in mid-September 2007.[13]

If forced to sum up the Tony Blair years in Afghanistan, one would have to say that they combined significant discretion to field commanders tempered by limitations on capabilities that effectively limited the actions of those commanders. Factored together, military agents under Blair's leadership were given only moderate overall discretion in Afghanistan. The result was that, to quote a House of Commons Foreign Affairs Committee report, "the initial UK strategy failed primarily because of a lack of manpower, and a poor understanding of the local situation and the level of resistance that would emerge" (Foreign Affairs Committee of the House of Commons 2009: 86).

## GORDON BROWN

There have been a great many analyses of British doctrinal innovation and lessons learned during the Afghanistan campaign.[14] Among the best is the work of Theo Farrell (2010), who argues that there were two periods of British military innovation in Afghanistan, both implemented during Prime Minister Gordon Brown's tenure. The first took place when Brigadier General Andrew Mackay was in command of the British contingent in late 2007. The second was under Brigadier General Gordon Messenger in late 2008. Farrell argues that these senior officers innovated in the absence of top-level guidance. We take a slightly different, though not contradictory, view. From our perspective, only marginal innovation was possible during Blair's tenure given the constraints on deployed forces from inadequate equipment and training. More substantial innovation was possible only when the terms of the principal-agent contract were revised at the beginning of Brown's government and force levels and capabilities improved. The lesson here is that in single-party parliamentary governments, just as in their presidential counterparts, a change in leaders can substantially change that country's performance on the ground.

---

13 "British-Led Forces Launch Anti-Taliban Offensive in Southern Afghanistan," *Voice of America*, September 19, 2007.

14 See, for example, Farrell and Gordon 2009; Tatham 2009; and Thruelsen 2008.

Gordon Brown became prime minister on June 27, 2007, and immediately made apparent that his foreign policy priorities differed from those of Tony Blair. Blair had supported the Iraq intervention as the central front against terrorism. Brown wanted out of Iraq as soon as possible and more resources devoted to Afghanistan.[15] Where Blair had supported the rhetoric from the administration of U.S. president George W. Bush on the War on Terror, Brown was said to believe terrorism was a law-enforcement problem. While Blair was vocally supportive of the United States, Brown leaned toward the European Union.[16] In terms of Afghanistan, Brown was a much more vocal supporter of a population-centric COIN strategy than had been Blair. Brown's priorities for Helmand included supporting and strengthening Afghan authorities so they could take responsibility for their own security and better provide basic services for their people, and supporting political reconciliation, economic growth, and local governance.[17]

The British military's approach to its efforts in Helmand changed in the late fall of 2007. The Brown government demonstrated more active direction of commanders in the field and more active oversight of those commanders by the PJHQ.[18] From our perspective, this was not a surprise given both Brown's ideology and his policy proclivities, which emphasized a certain form of behavior on the part of troops in the field. The Brown government also got lucky with the assumption of command of Brigadier General Andrew Mackay, who was a near perfect agent to achieve the new Brown government's priorities. Mackay had been put in command of the Fifty-Second Brigade in October 2006 to prepare for a deployment to Afghanistan in October 2007.

Mackay focused on population-centric counterinsurgency strategy and away from the highly kinetic operations of his predecessors. He wanted "to place the population at the forefront of the operational design. It was determined that 52 Brigade would *Clear, Hold,* and *Build* where it could and concurrently *Disrupt, Interdict,* and *Defeat* where it could not. Underpinning this would be a commitment to ensure a singular focus on influencing the population of Helmand" (Mackay and Tatham 2009: 13; emphasis in the original). He devolved authority to decentralized platoon and company commanders, and focused on influence operations and understanding the local population (Mackay and Tatham 2009: 16, 24). Mackay and the Fifty-Second Brigade did not avoid danger, as the retaking of the town of Musa Qala in early December demonstrates.[19] But they made every effort to avoid conflict whenever possible, as their preparation

---

15 Interview with senior British military officer, London, September 16, 2009.
16 Maura Reynolds and Kim Murphy, "Brown Keeps It Formal with Bush," *Los Angeles Times,* July 31, 2007.
17 The details of Brown's overall guidance are reprinted in Foreign Affairs Committee of the House of Commons 2009: 80–81.
18 Interview with senior British military officer, London, September 16, 2009.
19 "British PM Visits Troops in Afghanistan," *Voice of America,* December 10, 2007.

for the battle and their overall relatively low casualty figures compared to other British brigades make clear.[20] This incorporated many of the classic tenets of population-centric COIN.

It should not be surprising then that Mackay did not perceive the same amount of restrictions as did his predecessors. He would be quoted as saying he was not given a strategy by his superiors when he deployed (Tatham 2009: 2), but his strategy was consistent with the aforementioned cabinet intent, embodied in the early policy statements coming from the Brown government. That translated into Mackay having more troops to work with than any of his predecessors; roughly 7,750 all told. It also meant that he was allowed to develop and implement the specifics of his strategy even with the increased scrutiny coming from the PJHQ and the MOD. That strategy would eventually become known as the Helmand Road Map.[21]

Contrast Mackay's circumstances with those of his successors. Consider Brigadier General Mark Carlton-Smith, who took over the British contingent in April 2008 and stayed through October. In his view, implementing the Helmand Road Map required more than the 8,000-person contingent he commanded, even though that was more than Mackay had. He could maintain the status quo with what he had but could not generate positive momentum in Helmand without more troops. For example, he believed he had enough troops for two ground-holding battle groups, which could secure accessible populations centers. His numbers, however, were not enough to secure the province as a whole, particularly its smaller towns and remote areas.[22] He wanted more rapid reaction troops, helicopters, linguists, counter–improvised explosive device capabilities, and armored vehicles, but in his words, "PJHQ did not want me to mortgage our military liability any further from that which we were already doing. The direction I received was to continue to build on the progress of the 52 Brigade, to consolidate those areas currently under Government control, and to be careful about being pulled out of shape."[23]

His cause was not necessarily helped by the ISAF-inspired operation to replace the turbines in the Kajaki Dam. This was the sort of large-scale, infrastructure-oriented, highly kinetic operation that the population-centric COIN strategy of the Helmand Road Map had de-emphasized. Indeed, the British Foreign Office was against the operation from the beginning.[24] It is perhaps no coincidence that

---

20 See the figures in Mackay and Tatham 2009: 34.

21 The Helmand Road Map would be formally approved April 1, 2008. See Farrell and Gordon 2009: 672–74 for details.

22 Interview with Brigadier General Mark Carlton-Smith, London, September 15, 2009.

23 Excerpted from an internal MOD document provided to the authors, titled "Lessons Capture Process," November 24, 2008, 6. The document included a transcribed interview with Brigadier Mark Calton-Smith.

24 Interview with Brigadier Mark Carlton-Smith, London, September 15, 2009.

Carlton-Smith's September 2008 recommendation that an additional brigade of approximately 4,000 troops be deployed to Helmand (Foreign Affairs Committee of the House of Commons 2009: 90) was rejected. The official reason given was that the Treasury had put a cap of 8,300 on the deployment for budgetary reasons.[25]

The British operation in Helmand would involve three more brigade rotations through April of 2010. Throughout that eighteen-month period, Prime Minister Brown's government would continue to focus on reconciliation and nonkinetic operations, consistent with a behaviorally oriented principal. Said Lord George Malloch-Brown, the Foreign and Commonwealth Office minister at the time (Foreign Affairs Committee of the House of Commons 2009: 90), "We cannot solve this through that classic counter-insurgency ratio of troops to population. That is another reason why we need a political-military strategy . . . to create conditions for successful reconciliation with the [Afghan] government."

The key limiting factor on British contingents would remain the number of troops deployed and the capabilities deployed with those troops. Claims that the government was still refusing to supply needed equipment continued during 2008, leading to the resignation of a number of mid- to senior level British military officers.[26] Through 2009, the Brown government was dogged by accusations that it was shorting equipment needed by the troops. Press reports and our interviews confirmed that the military had asked yet again for more soldiers in early 2009, this time for 2,000 additional troops, but that request was rejected by the British civilian leadership.[27] The government, in rejecting the troop requests, argued that more troops could not solve the problems of Helmand Province or Afghanistan as a whole, which essentially had to do with the legitimacy of the government and a political accommodation between the government and the Taliban.

The debate reached a peak in mid-2009, by which time the United Kingdom had over 9,000 troops in Afghanistan. A parliamentary report released in July noted that British troops were operating "with very limited resources and support" (Foreign Affairs Committee of the House of Commons 2009: 90). A second report (Public Accounts Committee of the House of Commons 2009) went into detail as to what was and was not being supplied to the troops in the field. In the words of David Cameron, the Conservative Party opposition leader and future prime minister, "It is a scandal in particular that they (military forces) still lack enough helicopters to move around in southern Afghanistan. The government must deal with

---

25 Ibid.

26 See, for example, "British Special Forces Chief in Afghanistan Resigns in Protest," *Voice of America*, November 1, 2008.

27 Interview, British senior military officer, Tampa, Florida, February 2009; and John Burns, "Britain Mired in Its Own Debate over Troop Levels in Afghanistan," *New York Times*, October 7, 2009, http://www.nytimes.com/2009/10/07/world/europe/07britain.html, accessed March 11, 2012.

that issue as a matter of extreme emergency."[28] Yet the deaths caused by Operation Panther's Claw, initiated by Brigadier General Tim Radford, the British contingent commander at the time, led to yet more public doubts over the wisdom of the Afghan operation, while at the same time leading to questions as to whether the troops had adequate and appropriate equipment.[29] This was followed a week later by a House of Commons Select Committee report that argued that British forces were being asked to do too much with inadequate equipment.[30] The divisiveness of the debate even allegedly caused the prime minister to deny a promotion in August to General Richard Dannatt, then the army chief of staff, to the position of chief of defense staff, because of Dannatt's push to deploy more troops.[31]

By mid-September, Prime Minister Brown's popularity had sunk to new lows, with 48 percent of voters saying that "literally anyone" from the Labour Party could do a better job, and projecting that the Conservatives would win a majority in the House.[32] In late September and early October, the Brown government was confronted with the protest resignation of Major General Andrew Mackay and a tell-all interview by the recently retired General Dannatt, both making the case that the Brown government was refusing military advice to deploy more and better-equipped troops to Afghanistan.[33] Even the mid-August surge of 17,000 additional U.S. soldiers and marines into RC-South did not help staunch the flow of criticism directed at the Brown government.

Under this sustained pressure, Brown promised that that he would deploy up to 2,000 additional troops to Afghanistan in mid-2010, but only after British parliamentary elections were completed, if the appropriate equipment was ready for those troops, and only if other NATO members also increased their deployments.[34] He quickly amended that number down to 500 additional troops, however, with the same conditions attached to a final decision.[35] Brown's promise, and his seeming change of heart, caused a further schism two weeks later, when the Labour Party chair of the House Committee on Intelligence and Security, Member of Parliament Kim Howells, broke with the government and called for a complete withdrawal from Afghanistan. According to press sources, "Howell's comments have inflicted damage on the deeply unpopular government of Prime Minister

---

28 "British Government Defends Its Strategy and Support in Afghanistan," *Voice of America*, July 13, 2009.

29 "Rising British Casualties in Afghanistan Sparks Growing Debate," *Voice of America*, July 17, 2009. These questions even began to divide the Labour Party. See Rob Gifford, "British PM under Fire for Deaths in Afghanistan," *Morning Edition*, National Public Radio, July 23, 2009.

30 "British Lawmakers Critical of UK's Role in Afghanistan," *Voice of America*, August 2, 2009.

31 Burns, "Britain Mired in Its Own Debate."

32 Peter Riddell and Philip Webster, "Give Us Any Leader but Brown, Say Voters," *Times (London)*, September 15, 2009.

33 See "Harry's Commander Quits over Afghan Concern," *Sky News*, September 25, 2009, http://news.sky .com/home/uk-news/article/15389267, accessed March 12, 2012; "Dannet Blasts at 'Pathetic' Ministers," *Sun*, October 6, 2009; and Burns, "Britain Mired in Its Own Debate."

34 Burns, "Britain Mired in Its Own Debate."

35 John Burns and Peter Baker, "British Plan Would Deploy Bigger Afghanistan Force," *New York Times*, October 15, 2009.

Gordon Brown."[36] By this point, the Brown government, and the Labour Party as a whole, was focused more on their political survival than they were on their agent's behavior.[37] As would happen with the Dutch, the deployment in Afghanistan would contribute to the routing of the Labour Party in the June 2010 election.

In Helmand, the British faced extraordinary demands with insufficient resources. While they could, in theory, be quite flexible in response to NATO requests, the British commanders found themselves restricted by significant limits on their capabilities. In this way, while Canada is a pretty close parallel to the United Kingdom in many respects, the key dynamic in the British case is similar to that of France—intraparty changes in leaders led to some significant changes in priorities and thus behavior on the ground.

# The Canadians in Kandahar

Canada is a second case of a single-party, parliamentary government operating in Afghanistan.[38] Though both the Canadians and the British operated in RC-South, two things differentiate their behavior. First, while the British were ruled by a majority parliamentary government, the Canadians were led by a series of minority governments during the intervention in Afghanistan. Second, Canada's behavior in Afghanistan varied quite widely, from being heavily laden with caveats and ineffective to barely restricted and aggressive, making British behavior appear relatively consistent in comparison. That this occurred largely at a time of Canadian minority government, a rare phenomenon in Canadian politics, made the increased delegation to the ground quite a puzzle. Because of both institutional legacies and the weakness of the Canadian opposition, however, the Canadian forces (CF) ultimately had significant control over operations in the field. Variations in delegation, oversight, and incentives were largely driven by the individuals at the top of the Canadian military.

## BEHIND THE WIRE AND OUT IN FRONT

Canadian forces in Afghanistan had very limited discretion for the first three years of the conflict. This was certainly the case when they served as part of American-led Operation Enduring Freedom (OEF) in 2002. Canadian ground commanders at the time faced the same rules as bomber pilots and special forces units: any

---

36 Ben Quinn, "British MP Calls for Afghanistan Withdrawal as Five UK Soldiers Are Killed," *Christian Science Monitor*, November 4, 2009. See also "British PM Brown Vows to Fight On in Afghanistan," *Voice of America*, November 6, 2009.

37 "British MP Defends Military Mission in Afghanistan," *Voice of America*, November 10, 2009.

38 This section is largely based on a series of interviews with most senior Canadian military officers who commanded in Afghanistan as well as a handful of key politicians. Because of the scope of the book, this section does not address the training mission, heavy with caveats, that began in mid-2011.

mission that might risk collateral damage needed to be approved ahead of time. This meant a phone call home anytime the Canadians were to leave the base, since collateral damage is always a possibility when hundreds of soldiers move out. Lieutenant Colonel Pat Stogran, CF commander in Afghanistan in the first half of 2002, feared that these conditions would dangerously restrict his ability to act when necessary and that micromanagement from home might create a disaster akin to events in Bosnia and Rwanda, where officers had to stand by and watch war crimes take place in front of them.[39]

After one six-month tour in Kandahar, the CF were withdrawn from Afghanistan, only to return in 2003 to Kabul where they helped to institutionalize ISAF. Lieutenant General Andrew Leslie became deputy commander of ISAF and the Canadian contingent commander in 2003.[40] Leslie had to ask Ottawa for permission for operations where there was a significant chance of collateral damage, or the potential for lethal force, significant casualties, or strategic failure.[41] He also called home whenever Canadian special operations forces engaged in any significant activities, even when operating outside of ISAF as part of OEF. Leslie found that approval was almost always granted, often immediately. Major General Peter Devlin, commander of NATO's effort in Kabul under Leslie, believed that the home office said yes to about half of the requests to use the special operations units.[42] Devlin considered the Canadians to be in the middle tier in terms of flexibility and restrictions.

In the next Canadian troop rotation, Devlin's replacement, Brigadier General Jocelyn Lacroix, received his official national guidance via a "Letter of Intent." That letter stated that "*NDHQ* [National Defence Headquarters] *authority is required*, prior to committing CF personnel to *any operations*, wherein there is a reasonable belief that CF units or personnel may be *exposed to a higher degree of risk*."[43] Officials in Canada were very slow to respond to field requests, sometimes taking up to twenty-four hours or more.[44] On a few occasions, Lacroix had to face

---

39 Interview with Colonel Pat Stogran (Ret.), when he was vice president of the Pearson Peacekeeping Centre, Ottawa, April 25, 2007.

40 This was a rare moment, as Canada has tended not to give their officers two hats: usually one person serves as the alliance commander and another serves as the commander of the contingent. Interview with Lieutenant General Andrew Leslie, Ottawa, March 8, 2007.

41 *Strategic failure* refers to the possibility of a tactical effort potentially undermining the NATO mission and/or the Afghan government. Interview with Lieutenant General Andrew Leslie, Ottawa, March 8, 2007.

42 Interview with Major General Peter Devlin, Ottawa, May 15, 2009. Yet permission sometimes took longer if the deputy chief of the defense staff (DCDS) had to consult with the chief of the defense staff (CDS) and perhaps the defense minister. The minister of national defense at the time, Bill Graham, did not recall having to give permission for any operations during Leslie's time. Interview with Graham, Ottawa, April 19, 2007.

43 DCDS Intent Task Force Kabul, 19 December 2003, A0241084, 6, acquired via Access to Information request; emphasis added.

44 Interview with Brigadier General Jocelyn Lacroix, Kingston, Ontario, February 6, 2007.

the galling situation of needing to find an alternative to the Canadian contingent while waiting for deliberations in Ottawa to conclude.

When Canadian Lieutenant General Rick Hillier became overall ISAF commander, overlapping with Lacroix's Kabul rotation, he faced a similarly frustrating situation. The leaders of the CF gave Hillier the authority to act as a NATO commander but little influence over Canadian forces in Afghanistan. Instead, a Canadian colonel was the commander of the nation's contingent, so Hillier was forced to call Ottawa should he want to override decisions made by this colonel. This was problematic, since the colonel was operating under relatively strict caveats. Hillier later referred to the Canadian contingents in Bosnia and Afghanistan as "CAN'T BATs" (instead of the traditional NATO term *CANBAT* for a Canadian battalion) because he frequently had to rely on other national contingents that were far more flexible.[45]

All this changed when Colonel Steve Noonan became the senior Canadian on the ground in 2005–6; he found himself having far more latitude than previous commanders—"wide arcs of fire," as he called it. The orders at the time authorized "full spectrum operations."[46] Instead of having to ask permission to engage in a variety of operations, Noonan found himself facing a new command philosophy, enunciated by the new chief of defense staff (CDS), none other than the freshly promoted General Rick Hillier (Maloney 2009). Noonan was allowed to act first and explain his actions later if necessary.[47] His successor, Brigadier General David Fraser, found a similar situation: "Everything I did over there was notification, not approval. . . . If I had to go outside the boundaries of the CDS intent, then I would have to get approval. I never got to a boundary."[48] In the official "Letter of Intent" given to Fraser by the CDS, Fraser was told "Within the bounds of the Strategic Targeting Directive, you have *full freedom to authorize and conduct operations as you see fit*. In the interest of national situational awareness, *whenever possible* you are to inform me in advance of the concept of operations for any planned operations, particularly those likely to involve significant contact with the enemy."[49] Fraser's freedom of action was particularly useful when he led Canadian forces during their most intense combat since the Korean War—Operation Medusa in the summer of 2006 (Horn 2010).

---

45 General Rick Hillier, "Canada's National Security Interests in a Changing World," speech to the Conference of Defense Associations Institute, February 22, 2008, attended by Stephen M. Saideman. See also Hillier (2010).

46 CDS Operational Order 800 (010/2005) Task Force Afghanistan, 11, acquired via Access to Information request.

47 Interview with Colonel Steve Noonan, Ottawa, April 20, 2007.

48 Interview with Brigadier General David Fraser, Edmonton, Alberta, January 29, 2007.

49 Commander's Directive to Commander, Task Force Afghanistan, Rotation 2, (3350-165/A37) A0232107, p. 14, acquired via Access to Information Request, emphasis added.

This pattern of increased discretion and delegation continued until the CF pulled out of Kandahar in mid-2011. Brigadier General Tim Grant replaced Fraser, and found that he "was empowered to make 99% of the ops-related decisions in theatre."[50] That other 1 percent never came up. This contrasted sharply with Grant's previous experiences in Bosnia, where Canadians could not move out of their sector and there were limits placed on whether and how allies could use Canadian assets in theater.[51] In Afghanistan, Grant could and did send Canadian troops out of Kandahar Province to the other parts of RC-South to assist the British in Helmand. At no point did Grant have to reject a NATO request, although he did engage in some discussions with his NATO commanders to "achieve the desired effect."[52]

Brigadier General Guy Laroche followed Grant and found few restrictions. He sent troops to Helmand despite having much to do in Kandahar, which he told the chain of command back in Ottawa.[53] His calls home about moving outside the province were for notification, not permission. Indeed, Laroche recalled that at no time during his entire tour did he have to call home for permission for any operation. Instead, when receiving requests from the NATO chain of command, the question was whether he had enough troops or time, as his "plate was always full."[54] Brigadier General Denis Thompson replaced Laroche and reported similar experiences.[55]

The next general to lead the Canadian forces, Brigadier General Jon Vance wound up serving two tours in Afghanistan, from February to November 2009 and again from June to September 2010; the second tour was due to the firing of Brigadier General Daniel Menard for improper relations with a subordinate. The two tours allowed Vance to see the evolution of the mission as RC-South headquarters became far more directive as McChrystal's efforts to regionalize the mission took hold. The empowering of the regional command was not a problem for Vance as he had plenty of discretion from back home.[56] He faced only one time where he was tempted to play the red card when he needed intelligence, surveillance, and reconnaissance support that RC-South was not giving him. Vance only had one significant restriction—he could not share the biometric data the Canadians collected on prisoners with NATO.

50 Interview with Major General Tim Grant, Ottawa, February 7, 2008.
51 Ibid.
52 Ibid. Grant did point out that allies not only had caveats but their own agendas, of which one had to be conscious.
53 Interview with Brigadier General Guy Laroche, Montreal, September 21, 2010.
54 Ibid.
55 We knew Brigadier General Thompson years prior to his deployment, when he was director of the CF Peacekeeping Office, so we kept in touch before and after his deployment. We did not formally interview him, but did ask a series of questions as reality checks.
56 Interview with Major General Jon Vance, Ottawa, June 22, 2011.

Instead, most of Vance's tensions resulted from conflict with civilians back home. Vance's efforts to redeploy his troops as the Americans surged into the sector meant more friction with Canadian civilians than with anyone else. There was pressure in the aftermath of the so-called Manley Panel to coordinate with other Canadian agencies (Foreign Affairs, the Canadian International Development Agency, etc.), but the civilians in Ottawa had developed maps, plans, and benchmarks in parts of the province for which Canadian forces no longer had responsibility. Vance's initiative to focus on key districts received support from NATO and from his military chain of command but created friction with civilians in other parts of the Canadian government.[57]

In sum, the pattern is quite clear—Canadian officers in Afghanistan initially had very little discretion, but midway through the effort they gained a great deal of room to make decisions. The key was, as we shall see below, the ascendance of a new command group who had worked under tight restrictions while serving in Bosnia and Afghanistan.

## INSTITUTIONAL CHANGE, INDIVIDUALS, AND VARYING OVERSIGHT

Rick Hillier not only changed how much discretion the commanders in the field had but also how they were overseen. Until 2005, the deputy chief of defense staff (DCDS), based in the Department of National Defence (DND) building in downtown Ottawa, oversaw all Canadian operations in North America and beyond. Hillier deliberately created the Canadian Expeditionary Forces Command (CEFCOM) and located it on the outskirts of Ottawa to move it away from the civilians at the DND and to give the operational commander much more latitude about how to oversee operations abroad.[58] This represented quite a break from the past, when the office of the DCDS had tightly controlled missions abroad (Maloney 2009: 67).

CEFCOM was designed to improve joint operations by giving one officer in Ottawa the responsibility for overseeing overseas operations, imitating the U.S. system of combatant commanders. From 2006 onward, the instructions given to CF commanders in Afghanistan were written and coordinated by CEFCOM, and the commander of CEFCOM became the key contact back home. As a result, the most significant changes in oversight were when one general replaced another in this key position.

---

57 Ibid.
58 Hillier's memoir (2010) is directly aimed at the civilians in the DND. See also Lagassé and Sokolsky 2009. In 2012, the command structure was reorganized again as Hillier's structures meant more personnel and money were committed to the various headquarters. Instead, a new joint operations headquarters was put into place, keeping with Hillier's idea that the operations job was too big for the DCDS.

Lieutenant General Mike Gauthier was the first person to occupy this office. He was viewed by commanders in the field as maintaining fairly tight oversight. He conducted over thirty visits to Afghanistan in the course of three years— essentially monthly visits.[59] While these visits could be viewed as showing the flag and building morale by demonstrating Canada's interests in its troops in the field, they were also clearly to assess progress on the ground and performance of the commanders in the field.[60] Gauthier held multiple secure video teleconferences per week with commanders on the ground, sometimes on a daily basis. When Lieutenant Marc Lessard replaced Gauthier, the pace of visits slowed and the frequency of VTCs dropped to once a week. Lessard, perhaps because of his prior experience as commander of RC-South, viewed visits as "creating havoc" and opportunities to "transfer anxiety," so he visited less often.[61]

Why did Lessard behave differently from Gauthier? One officer speculated that it was the difference between an engineer (Gauthier) and an infantry officer (Lessard). Each officer had a long history with Lieutenant General Rick Hillier and General Walter Natynczyk, and the CEFCOM commander is appointed by the CDS. So, Gauthier might have gotten instructions to engage in tighter oversight than Lessard, but in interviews with both, the differences seemed more of inclination and experience. The key, again, was that this was an entirely intra-CF affair with the civilians having no say in which general oversaw operations nor even really in the innovation that was CEFCOM. Indeed, the view of the minister of national defense at the time of CEFCOM's creation was this: "I counted on the military to decide how best to organize itself, and Hillier came up with restructuring to handle interventions abroad."[62]

We have not addressed agent selection in any depth here since the choice of Canadian commanders in Kandahar was left up to the military, but before moving on to address the politics of the mission more directly, we consider one last aspect of the delegation contract: incentives.

## PATTERNS OF PROMOTION

The striking thing about the Canadian case is that, with only an exception or two, nearly every commander of the Afghan mission came back and was promoted. Even those who commanded during periods of high casualties moved up the chain of command.

---

59 Interview with Lieutenant General Michel Gauthier, Ottawa, September 11, 2007; interview with Lieutenant General Marc Lessard, Ottawa, January 8, 2010.
60 This was reported by more than one of the Canadian officers who commanded in Kandahar.
61 Interview with Lessard, Ottawa, January 8, 2010.
62 Interview with former minister of national defense Bill Graham, Ottawa, April 19, 2007.

- Hillier became the chief of the defense staff.
- Leslie, and later Devlin, became chief of the land staff (head of the army).
- Lacroix became deputy of Canada Command.
- Walt Semianiw became head of Canada Command.[63]
- Noonan eventually became a major general and deputy commander of Canadian Joint Operations Command (CEFCOM's successor).
- Fraser was promoted to major general.
- Grant became deputy commander of CEFCOM.
- Laroche became a major general and was responsible for Land Force Doctrine.
- Thompson became commander of Canada's Special Operations Command.
- Vance was promoted to lieutenant general and deputy commander of the Allied Joint Force Command, Naples.
- Milner was promoted to major general and went on exchange to Fort Hood to serve as its deputy commander, a post that former chiefs of defense staff Hillier and Natynczyk had each held.

Only Pat Stogran and Daniel Menard did not move up. Stogran was known for being outspoken and critical, which has since been proven again in other government positions.[64] Menard was discharged dishonorably as a result of his affair with a subordinate, and also made the news for a negligent discharge of his weapon while the CDS was visiting Kandahar. This pattern makes sense: the Canadian forces saw Afghanistan as a success, helping to redefine the military's identity as warriors and not just peacekeepers (Hillier 2010). While the Canadian public might disagree and regret the deployment to Afghanistan,[65] the military viewed itself as making a difference, so those commanding the effort did well in their careers after the mission.

The Canadian case has thus far been within the CF. We now need to consider the political context that gave the military officers much of the influence in how the mission was conducted.

## EXPLAINING THE EVOLUTION OF CANADIAN BEHAVIOR

At first glance, Canada presents a puzzle for our approach (and many others as well) given that it became one of the most forward-leaning efforts in the most dangerous areas of Afghanistan despite being led by a minority government from 2004 to 2011. Under a minority government, one would have expected coalition

---

63 Semianiw was the only Canadian officer who would not agree to meet with us.
64 Interview with Stogran, April 25, 2007.
65 This was reported in a series of surveys in 2012.

government–type behavior, with the party leading the government having to compromise with the other parties on the Afghanistan mission to stay in office and avoid or win confidence votes. However, Canadian minority governments were actually empowered by the inability of their parliamentary opponents to work together to restrict the CF in Afghanistan.

## Minority Government and Divided Opposition

In theory, the formal commander in chief of the Canadian forces is the governor general, who is technically an agent of the king or queen of Canada. In reality, the prime minister is empowered by Canadian governing institutions to make decisions in times of conflict and has generally delegated military decisions to the CDS. Usually, Canada's prime minister is quite powerful, having been delegated significant authority from the majority party in Parliament. The parliamentary rank and file have little influence over daily conflict decisions and exercise practically no oversight over military operations. Indeed, members of Parliament do not even have security clearances, greatly restricting their access to pertinent information.

That parliament was a relatively weak player when it came to military deployments may seem surprising given recent Canadian election results. The majority Liberal Party government elected in 2000 was followed by minority party rule under the Liberals in 2004 and the Conservatives in 2006 and 2008. One would think that minority government cabinets would be sensitive to opposition party concerns, if only to avoid no-confidence votes, giving Parliament significant influence over how the military was used (Lagassé 2010). That was not the case, however, in large part because the makeup of the four major political parties made it nearly impossible to form a stable opposition coalition. The two main parties, the Conservatives and Liberals, were on opposite sides of most issues. The Bloc Québécois party was not an appealing or viable partner due to its separatist agenda, and instead was a spoiler to the hopes of a left-leaning coalition of the Liberals and the New Democratic Party. The result was that Canadian prime ministers, even when leading minority governments, were in a strong position to make policy, or delegate that authority to a trusted surrogate—in this case the CDS.

That said, because Canada's was a minority government, Parliament had to periodically reauthorize the overall Canadian mission in Afghanistan, which, in theory, allowed it to exert some influence over the conduct of the Canadian mission in Afghanistan.[66] Prime Minister Stephen Harper had to ask Parliament to extend

---

66 This is not a constitutional requirement, as it is in Germany, but instead required by the politics of minority government. This process did create confusion in Canada about the role of parliament in authorizing deployments. See Lagassé 2010.

the mission in Afghanistan on a couple of occasions, with the last mandate expiring in 2011. The Liberals were sufficiently divided on Afghanistan that Harper was able to get enough votes for short extensions of the mission. Moreover, failing to authorize Canadian participation is a very blunt stick. Yet even somewhat less blunt alternatives, such as caveats, were not required by Parliament. There was some brief discussion during the 2008 mandate debate about restricting the CF from engaging in offensive operations, but this did not get very far. Instead, the day-to-day management of Afghan operations was left in the hands of the CDS and his subordinates.

Technically, the governor general selects the CDS, a four-leaf officer, upon the advice of the prime minister. In reality, the prime minister selects the CDS, who serves at the pleasure of the prime minister. The CDS then decides how Canadian forces operate. That said, the CDS must consider what the prime minister will tolerate or else be replaced. As such, the CDS consults the minister of defense and those under the minister. But when trying to understand Canadian behavior, then, we must look to the prime minister's trusted agent, the CDS.

Indeed, a striking feature of Canadian efforts in Afghanistan was that nearly all of the decisions and dynamics were intramilitary. When asked, Canadian civilians and officers largely concurred that the civilians delegated to the senior military leadership nearly all decisions except for those to deploy to particular places at particular times.[67] Recent Canadian deployments seem to meet the ideal type of Huntington's (1957) objective form of civil-military relations: the prime minister decides where the Canadian forces deploy and the CDS determines how they will operate once they get there. The CDS along with other top officers (the deputy chief of the defense staff prior to 2006 and the commander of the Canadian Expeditionary Forces Command since then) determined the flexibility of the forces on the ground, including caveats.

## Individuals in the Canadian Chain of Command

Explaining shifts in Canadian discretion on the ground requires considering the leadership personalities involved and their experiences. In our interviews with past and current military officers, former prime minister Paul Martin, and two former ministers of defense, it was quite clear that Canadian caveats depended on who was serving as the chief of the defense staff. Changes in caveats and other policies coincided with a change in the CDS from Ray Henault (2001–5) to Rick

---

67 Consequently, Harper has taken great care in how the missions were designed for the post-2011 training mission in Afghanistan, the Libyan air campaign, and the assistance the CF gave to France in Mali. In each case, the specifics of the deployment limited the risks greatly and limited how much discretion the CF had in conducting these missions.

Hillier (2005–8). Under CDS Henault and DCDS Maddison (2001–5), officers on the ground in Afghanistan were given little discretion, although their "left and right arcs of fire" became gradually broader as time went on. When Hillier replaced Henault in 2005, the officers on the ground quickly gained significantly more discretion, allowing them to beg forgiveness after controversial operations rather than having to ask permission beforehand. In short, Hillier imposed fewer and less restrictive caveats on theater commanders than did Henault.

The principal difference between these two officers was that their past professional experiences generated different attitudes toward risk and delegation. For Henault, the salient experience shaping his views seems to have been Somalia, according to his deputy, Vice Admiral Paul Maddison.[68] In that intervention, Canadian soldiers beat an arrested Somali to death, leading to a crisis within the military, the disbanding of the unit involved (the Canadian Airborne Regiment), and the resignations of consecutive chiefs of defense staff and the minister of national defense (Bercuson 1996). Maddison mentioned Somalia several times in the course of the interview, comparing it to the My Lai Massacre during the Vietnam War, and noted that the focus of the Henault-Maddison team was on avoiding similar incidents by managing the behavior of Canadian forces. Henault indicated that there were tight restrictions on the first deployment to Afghanistan because it was the first combat mission in a long time.[69] Conversations with senior civilians who served in the DND at the time support the view that Henault and Maddison were quite risk averse.

Hillier learned more from Canadian reactions to Somalia than from Somalia itself. That is, he and his entire command group had operational experience in Bosnia, Croatia, Kosovo, and Afghanistan. They all found the tight constraints of previous caveats, particularly in the Balkans, enormously frustrating. During the UN mission in Croatia, Canadians deliberately had to place themselves in harm's way before they could use their weapons. In Bosnia, the Canadians were in Srebenica before the Dutch, but redeployed because they saw what was coming and knew they could not respond given Canadian caveats and UN restrictions. In Afghanistan, as mentioned above, Hillier as commander of ISAF had to ask permission from a colonel to use the Canadian forces and was often refused.

Consequently, when Hillier replaced Henault, he established a "mission command-centric" philosophy in which the focus would be on managing risk rather than avoiding it. This philosophy focused on facilitating the success of the commander on the ground by giving him the authority to make the decisions and giving him the support needed (logistical, diplomatic, etc.) to have him achieve

---

68 Interview with Vice Admiral Gregg Maddison (Ret.), Montreal, June 19, 2007.
69 Interview with General Ray Henault (Ret.), Ottawa, November 4, 2010. Henault went from being CDS to Chairman of NATO's Military Committee.

success. This is very much an outcome-focused approach. The same language was repeated in nearly every interview of CF commanders who had served in Afghanistan and/or Ottawa since 2005. To Hillier, this approach was nothing more than common sense based on his earlier experiences.[70]

To be clear, Hillier mattered far more than the average CDS. His personal popularity made it hard for the minister of national defense to oppose him publically. Indeed, he outlasted one, Gordon O'Connor, a former general (Brewster 2011). Still, his entire generation of officers seemed to share the same outlook as the result of their experiences of commanding missions while under tight restrictions. Indeed, Hillier's replacement, General Walter Natynczyk, did not change how the CF operated in Kandahar.

The Canadian case demonstrates that minority governments can have as much flexibility as those with majority governments if the opposition cannot cooperate. The Kandahar mission ended precisely because this was something all four major parties could agree to, but because they could not agree on anything else, the conduct of operations during the six years was almost entirely shaped by CF leadership. In turn, we saw changes in how Canada operated due to a generational shift within the CF—from those officers that witnessed the mission failure in Somalia to those that experienced the restrictions produced by reactions to that scandal.

# Other Single-Party Parliamentary Governments

Two other NATO countries participating in ISAF had similar political structures as Canada and the United Kingdom: Spain and Turkey. These cases illustrate that politicians with significant authority and little need to bargain may still opt to restrict their forces. Parties and preferences come into play as prime ministers in Spain and Turkey were far less enthusiastic about the kinetic side of the Afghanistan effort.

## SPAIN

It is a challenge to address Spain's performance in Afghanistan precisely because it has been so very quiet compared to other countries. In 2004, the Spanish Socialist Worker's Party under José Luis Rodríguez Zapatero came into power just short of a parliamentary majority. Before assuming office, Zapatero and the party had been very critical of the previous government's participation in the Iraq War and immediately withdrew Spanish forces. Afghanistan was different because it was a UN-sanctioned effort and consistent with Spain's Article V commitments.[71]

---

70 Interview with General Rick Hillier, Ottawa, March 11, 2008. See also Hillier 2010.
71 Interview with Carlos Miranda, Spain's ambassador to NATO, Brussels, February 2, 2011.

Spain's behavior is consistent with a left-leaning minority government concerned about maintaining parliamentary confidence. The Zapatero government placed consistently strict limitations on what its forces could do in Afghanistan. When NATO expanded its coverage beyond Kabul, Spain chose to operate in relatively quiet Regional Command–West. The Spanish contingent was prohibited from leaving RC-West and was not allowed to engage in offensive operations.[72] Spanish troops were not allowed to participate in OEF missions, were prohibited from using lethal force if prisoners attempted to escape their custody, and could not even medevac Afghan civilians unless officers at Joint Operations Command in Madrid approved the flight with a phone call. Spanish forces were allowed to participate in observer, mentor, liaison teams (OMLTs) and would stick with the units they were mentoring during offensive operations, yet it was not clear whether Spanish OMLTs could follow their mentored units out of RC-West.

## TURKEY

Since 2002, Turkey has been governed by the Justice and Development Party (JDP), led by Prime Minister Recep Erdoğan.[73] Erdoğan has had significant discretion to manage participation in ISAF as he sees fit.[74] The JDP is a center-right Islamist party that maintained large majorities in the parliament during this mission. The mandate for the mission was renewed every year but was not controversial. The public continued to support the mission during our period of study, perhaps given the ethnic and historical ties between Turks and Afghans.

Turkey has had forces in Afghanistan, focused primarily on Kabul, since the beginning of the multilateral effort. Turkish forces were carefully chosen and given caveats. Their purpose in Afghanistan was not to fight insurgents but instead to help the Afghan people. Turkey's main contingent in Kabul remained there as NATO moved out to cover the rest of the country. Turkey was one of the very few countries to have staffed more than one PRT. The main Turkish force was restricted to Kabul, was not allowed to engage in offensive operations, and did not directly engage in counterinsurgency efforts.[75] Turkish troops were allowed to fire back if fired upon, could participate in OMLTs, and could even engage in

---

72 Interview with Miranda; interview with Rear Admiral Fernando Gea, Spain's CENTCOM representative, Tampa, Florida, March 2009.
73 This section is largely based on interviews with Turkish civilian and military representatives to NATO headquarters, Brussels, January 31 and February 2, 2011.
74 Thus far, the change in 2007 to a premier-presidential system has not changed the dynamics of who controls military deployments. The prime minister still seems to be the key actor.
75 Interview with Lieutenant General Veysi Ağar, Turkey's permanent military representative to NATO, Brussels, February 2, 2011.

**Table 5.1.** Single-Party Parliaments

| Country | Control of Parliament | Place on Spectrum | Focus | Means of Control |
|---|---|---|---|---|
| Canada, 2004–5 | Minority | Center | Behavior | Restricted Delegation, Oversight |
| Canada, 2005–10 | Minority | Right | Outcomes | Agent Selection, Incentives |
| Spain, 2004–10 | Minority | Left | Behavior | Restricted Delegation |
| Turkey, 2002–10 | Majority | Right | Behavior | Restricted Delegation, Agent Selection |
| United Kingdom, 2006–10 | Majority | Center, Then Left after 2007 | Behavior | Oversight, Restricted Capabilities |

offensive operations that their mentored Afghan units ran. No Turks were killed in Afghanistan due to hostile fire during the scope of this study.

Turkey combined these caveats with careful selection of commanders. Indeed, agent selection appeared to be a key means by which control over deployed troops was exerted. Rather than routine rotations, the vice chief of the defense staff nominated senior officers who deployed to Afghanistan.[76]

## Conclusions

The single-party parliamentary governments reviewed in this chapter were consistent with our expectations, as summarized in table 5.1. We expected them to focus on agent selection and incentives to direct their agents. The conservative Canadian government, via the CDS, utilized both from 2005 to 2010, and the Turks focused on agent selection throughout the period of our study. We further expected that left-leaning or behaviorally focused prime ministers would utilize restricted delegation contracts and oversight. The Spanish, the Turks, and the British restricted discretion one way or another, using caveats or capabilities, as did the Canadians from 2004 to 2005. To a large extent, this chapter demonstrated that single-party parliamentary governments, like their presidential counterparts, designed their principal-agent contracts bearing in mind the outcome or behavioral focus of their leaders, and to a lesser extent the ideological leanings of those leaders.

---

76 Interview with Miranda.

# 6  Coalition Governments in Combat

Coalition governments face far greater challenges when their countries are at war than do presidents or prime ministers supported by a single party in government. Keeping two or more political parties together in a coalition is no easy task under ordinary circumstances, but to do so while the country is facing casualties and an uncertain military mission is far more difficult. While one can make a variety of comparisons among NATO allies, the distinction between coalition government and other types of governments is far more important for conflict behavior than are distinctions between English speaking and non-English speaking countries or between continental Europeans versus non-European International Security Assistance Force (ISAF) partners.

In general, our expectation is that coalition governments behave differently from their presidential or single-party parliamentary peers. They should be especially likely to utilize restrictive delegation contracts and tough oversight when deploying troops internationally. Coalition governments have certainly received the most attention for such restrictions, with Germany serving as the focal point for debates over caveats. The need to keep less enthusiastic parties in support of the mission generates compromises that become embedded in the delegation contracts with their militaries, often in the form of the parliamentary mandates that permit initial deployments and their renewals. Efforts to oversee the troops should be more vigorous because a coalition government usually has every incentive to avoid behavior that could lead to the fracturing of the governing coalition, and oversight is a good method for catching problems early. That said, coalition governments may have trouble acting on that information, in that establishing proper incentive structures for the military—to include rewarding appropriate behavior or achieved outcomes, or sanctioning poor behavior or failed outcomes—relies on reaching agreement within the parliamentary coalition. These countries will also have difficulty selecting particular individuals to key military positions. More likely is that civilian leaders will default to established

141

bureaucratic processes (i.e., seniority; rotation among air, land, and sea services; etc.) for determining their military agents.

Yet we must not underestimate the variation that exists among coalition governments and how they influence operations in Afghanistan. In chapter 3 we argued that the nature of the coalition will be a significant determinant of behavior. Coalitions having ideologically aligned parties will require less bargaining and fewer internal compromises before engaging in military missions overseas than ideologically dispersed grand coalitions. Ideologically narrow coalition governments should give their troops a freer hand in the field, with relatively fewer caveats, somewhat less oversight, and a greater ability to use incentives than would an ideologically polarized coalition. Similarly, coalitions with fewer parties should be likely to delegate more robust power to their military agents and engage in less active oversight than might coalitions comprised of a large number of political parties. Finally, we hypothesize that left-wing parties are less likely to be enthusiastic about the mission.

We explore these expectations in three in-depth case studies in this chapter. While there are many coalition governments operating in Afghanistan, we closely consider Germany, the Netherlands, and Denmark. Germany has gotten the most attention for its restrictions on its troops precisely because it had a very large contingent and a reputation for a very capable military, though that reputation has been significantly degraded by Germany's ISAF experience. As one press report argued, "Germany has acquired the reputation of a discredited nation, a nation incapable of waging war, a cowardly nation."[1] The Dutch case demonstrates that coalition governments may collapse due to differences over the Afghanistan mission. The Dutch appeared conflicted as to their role in ISAF. Unlike most coalition governments, they were willing to send troops to southern Afghanistan, one of the most hotly contested regions in the country. At the same time, the Dutch were not very proactive when in the south. Of the countries operating there, the Netherlands had the reputation for the most stringent restrictions and oversight. Indeed, as we will see below, the leash from The Hague via phone calls was extremely tight. In our third case study, Denmark appears to have been an outlier for coalition governments. The Danish government deployed a relatively unconstrained military, acting freely in some of the most dangerous parts of Afghanistan. While most of the coalition governments we have studied placed significant restrictions upon their troops, Denmark did not. For that reason alone, it merits closer study.

We consider these three cases at length and then briefly examine other coalition governments that sent significant troops to ISAF: Belgium, Italy, and Norway.

---

1 Ulrike Demmer, Christoph Hickmann, Dirk Kurbjuweit, and Ralf Neukirch, "Fear of Rising Death Toll: Berlin Reluctant to Follow American Lead on Afghanistan," *Der Spiegel Online*, January 25, 2010, http://www.spiegel.de/international/world/0,1518,673790,00.html, accessed January 28, 2010.

Together, these cases demonstrate that coalition politics and multilateral warfare mix as well as oil and water.

# Explaining German Decisions: A Parliamentary Army

Coalition government and Germany's parliament play key roles in shaping how German troops operate in the field.[2] Germany has a federal system with the national parliament, the Bundestag, elected via proportional representation. The Bundestag contains four to six main political parties, depending on the year. The chancellor is chosen by a majority vote in the Bundestag, and serves a maximum of four years before new elections must occur. Chancellors can and sometimes do call for confidence votes before their terms expire, and if the vote fails, then the current parliament is dissolved and elections are called (Chancellor Gerhard Schröder did this in July 2005; see Johnston 2010). The only way opposition parties can dissolve the parliament is if a majority favors an alternative successor cabinet, which has only happened twice since 1949. All this is to say that it is very hard for parliamentary opposition to get its voice heard.

Yet it is clear that the parliament matters. The reason is that German electoral laws make it difficult for any one party to acquire an outright majority in the Bundestag. Coalition governments have been the rule. The Sozialdemokratische Partei Deutschlands (SPD), or Social Democrats, shared power with the Greens to reach a bare majority after the 2002 elections. The Christian Democratic Union (CDU) and the Christian Social Union (CSU) formed a grand coalition with the SPD following the 2005 elections. In 2009, elections produced a center-right coalition among the CDU, the CSU and the Free Democratic Party (FDP). Two things stand out with regard to these coalition governments. First, the governing coalition has shifted dramatically after each election, meaning that with the exception of the relatively stable CDU-CSU partnership, today's enemies could be tomorrow's allies. Such a system cannot help but bias the various parties toward compromise, power sharing, and collective decision making. In 2002, for example, Chancellor Schröder (SPD) had Joschka Fischer of the Greens as the foreign minister. In 2005, Chancellor Angela Merkel had Frank-Walter Steinmeier of the SPD as the foreign minister, and the allocation of cabinet posts was evenly split between the CDU/CSU and the SPD. Second, the cabinet coalition often has spanned a large swath of the ideological spectrum, particularly between 2005 and 2009 (corresponding to the heart of our study's time frame). As a result, all

---

2 For an examination of the evolution of Germany's politics and processes for foreign deployments, see Johnston 2010, which covers well not just the previous missions but also the earlier decisions over Afghanistan. For the sake of brevity, we focus more on the latter stages of the mission.

the trends in coalition governments that we expect should be exacerbated in the case of German deployments. In short, the German electoral system encourages collective decision making, and, by extension, restricted discretion for those in the field.

Little of this would matter, of course, unless the Bundestag had a voice in decisions related to military deployments. The Bundestag has such a voice (Ryjáček 2009). The 1949 German constitution was designed to constrain German armed forces from extraterritorial operations. A July 1994 constitutional court decision, in response to NATO actions in the Balkans, prohibited German troops from operating outside NATO territory without prior legislative approval. Absent such approval, it only takes one-third of the Bundestag members to appeal to the Federal Constitutional Court to halt the mission (Dieterich, Hummel, and Marschall 2010: 22–24). Indeed, many consider the armed forces to belong to the Bundestag and not the government.[3] This reinforces the desire to get widespread parliamentary support for each deployment-related vote.[4]

Thus, the Bundestag must approve each deployment, including adding units to existing missions, with an up or down vote. The Bundestag must also approve all funding requests for military operations abroad, either through the regular defense budget or via supplemental budget requests, though again, these requests cannot be amended (Dieterich et al. 2010: 23). The government, led by the Ministry of Defense, tries to anticipate what the Bundestag will accept and draft a mission statement that will get the broadest possible legislative support. The usual claim is that it wants broad support so that the troops know that the people and their representatives are behind them.[5] According to a news report from early 2010, "Officials at the Chancellery say that this is necessary because the Bundeswehr is represented by all parties in parliament, not just those in power."[6] Having all of the major parties support a mandate also limits the ability of anyone to criticize the policy and the other parties. In other words, all of the major parties become implicated. Consequently, "with the exception of the far-left Left Party, all of the parties in the German parliament . . . agreed to keep Afghanistan out of the campaigns for the September [2009] parliamentary elections."[7]

Officials in the MOD, the Ministry of Foreign Affairs, and other parts of the government consult with key members of the relevant legislative committees to ensure that the Bundestag will accept the proposed mandate, giving these

---

3 In presentations of this case study, we were told that the Bundeswehr is a parliamentary armed force.
4 Demmer et al., "Fear of Rising Death Toll."
5 This sentiment was repeated in several of our interviews.
6 Demmer et al., "Fear of Rising Death Toll."
7 Ulrike Demmer, "Do Poor Weapons Hinder Germany in Afghanistan?" *Der Spiegel Online*, June 29, 2009, http://www.spiegel.de/international/germany/0,1518,633274,00.html, accessed February 1, 2010.

parliamentary bodies a significant amount of power.[8] The necessity of maintaining parliamentary support seems to explain why casualty aversion was *the* top priority for German officers in Afghanistan, guiding decisions on almost every aspect of Afghanistan operations. Certainly, Defense Minister Franz Josef Jung (2005–9) tried to avoid using war-related terms for much of his time in office, often referring to casualties using the German words for killed by accident, rather than the word for a soldier fallen in battle (*gefallen*).[9] Defense Minister Karl-Theodor zu Guttenberg (2009–11) was more willing to call the conflict a war, and "his choice of words was perceived as an act of liberation."[10] Chancellor Merkel did not discuss Afghanistan in a major media or public event until after September 2009 in the aftermath of the German-ordered bombing that killed more than a hundred civilians in Kunduz.[11]

In our interviews, German officials noted that the minister of defense, on behalf of the cabinet, created specific instructions for the troops on the ground in anticipation of parliamentary reactions, because of the fragility of his own political position and due to instructions from the chancellor to keep Afghanistan off the front page. What seems clear is that German behavior was consistent with the governing coalition trying to anticipate the reactions of a collective decision-making body worried about the behavior of its troops overseas.

An example played out literally while we conducted our interviews in Berlin in June 2009: the deployment of NATO Airborne Warning and Control Systems planes (AWACS) to Afghanistan.[12] NATO had decided to send some of its jointly staffed planes to help manage the increasingly crowded airspace over Afghanistan, but it took about a year to get passage through the North Atlantic Council (NAC) due to French concerns about financing the effort. Once the NAC approved the AWACS, the Germans had to move quickly to get a mandate passed through the Bundestag before the summer preelection break. Parliamentary

---

8 Interviews with members of parliament and officials in the MOD and the Ministry of Foreign Affairs, June 2009.

9 This was repeated in nearly all of the interviews we conducted in Berlin. See also "Germans Blitz the Taleban. Just Don't Mention the Krieg." *Times Online*, July 24, 2009, http://www.timesonline.co.uk/tol/news/world/world_agenda/article6726192.ece, accessed August 6, 2009.

10 Gerhard Spörl, "Facing Reality in Afghanistan: It's Time for Germans to Talk about War," *Der Spiegel Online*, December 4, 2010, http://www.spiegel.de/international/germany/0,1518,688424,00.html, accessed August 13, 2010.

11 Charles Hawley, "Letter from Berlin: Germany Confronts the Meaning of War," *Der Spiegel Online*, April 2, 2010, http://www.spiegel.de/international/germany/0,1518,675890,00.html, accessed August 13, 2010; Siobhán Dowling, "The World from Berlin: 'German Soldiers Don't Believe In a Happy Outcome,'" *Der Spiegel Online*, April 23, 2010, http://www.spiegel.de/international/germany/0,1518,690826,00.html, accessed August 13, 2010. She only attended a ceremony for Germans killed in Afghanistan in 2010 after she had been criticized by the *Bild* newspaper. Judy Dempsey, "Merkel Tries to Beat Back Opposition to Afghanistan," *New York Times*, April 22, 2010, http://www.nytimes.com/2010/04/23/world/europe/23iht-germany.html, accessed August 13, 2010.

12 This was a coincidence that helped to illustrate the dynamics, but also impacted how long we could spend with the officers in the Ministry of Defense working on this issue.

discussions focused on whether these planes would be used for just NATO efforts or also for Operation Enduring Freedom (OEF).[13] Officials assured members of parliament that the planes would not coordinate OEF efforts—that "we don't do fire control"—but that was hardly realistic given the advanced technologies on these planes for close air support.[14] Despite these doubts, cabinet assurances were good enough to get an overwhelming majority to support the deployment. This example shows the acrobatics the government had to go through to get wide support for a trivial part of the larger war effort.[15]

Clearly this institutional design gives ultimate responsibility to the collective Bundestag. To maintain the mission and pass mandates with broad support, compromises must be made, and those compromises involve conditions placed on the behavior of the mission. The collective Bundestag, by design and historical precedent, is concerned about the behavior of the German contingent rather than on reaching some sort of goal or outcome. Clearly, the priority here for both members of the Bundestag and the MOD is do no harm, because there are significant political stakes if something goes wrong on a mission. Given that successful counterinsurgency requires acceptance of risks, it is not surprising that German politicians tried to avoid counterinsurgency and continued to define the Afghan mission as one of nation building despite the increasing violence facing them in Regional Command–North (RC-North).

## RESTRICTED DELEGATION

The German government placed significant restrictions on the authority delegated to their troops and coupled that with significant caveats on military behavior for most of their time in Afghanistan. Germany became notorious for its restrictions, perhaps more so than any other country operating in Afghanistan. The Germans did not help themselves by denying that they have caveats, calling them merely restrictions.[16] They made matters worse when they justified German caveats by saying that countries engaged in much more dangerous locales and efforts have caveats too.[17] To be clear, the Germans have done more in Afghanistan than drink

---

13 "A NATO Exit Would Be Devastating for Afghanistan," *Der Spiegel Online*, July 3, 2009, http://www
    .spiegel.de/international/world/0,1518,634135,00.html, accessed February 1, 2010.
14 Interview with Sascha Lange, research fellow, Stiftung Wissenschaft und Politik (German Institute for
    International and Security Affairs), Berlin, June 18, 2009.
15 A subsequent AWACS deployment met with far greater resistance with Germany declining to partici-
    pate. See "AWACS for Afghanistan: Germany May Refuse NATO Request for Help," *Der Spiegel Online*,
    December 14, 2010, http://www.spiegel.de/international/germany/0,1518,734279,00.html, accessed
    April 28, 2011.
16 This distinction was repeated in several interviews we conducted, including those with military officers
    and members of the Ministry of Foreign Affairs.
17 Reported by Canadian embassy officials in Berlin, June 2009.

beer,[18] and, contrary to popular mythology, the formal mandates passed by the Bundestag did not restrict the German troops as much as advertised. That said, the actual restrictions on German troops were still quite significant.

The most obvious caveat is that the German contingent was largely restricted from operating outside of RC-North, the sector it led and the one that was comparatively but not entirely peaceful through early 2010. The Bundestag's mandates gave the minister of defense the authority to permit troops to move outside the German sector if it was temporary and necessary for the success of ISAF. This allowed the Germans to deploy electronic warfare specialists to Kandahar Airfield in the summer of 2009. However, this was the exception that proved the rule: the Kandahar base was very large and well defended, so this unit faced minimal risks of being harmed or of harming others. A similarly exceptional (and relatively safe) circumstance was a temporary move of German troops just across the line into RC-West to support a Norwegian provincial reconstruction team (PRT) that was essentially in the seams between the two regions. More generally, however, unless the minister of defense permitted, the Bundestag's geographic restriction prevented the German contingent from doing two things: sending troops to reinforce allies who might need assistance,[19] or mentoring Afghan National Army units outside RC-North.

When the Afghan National Army (ANA) kandaks mentored by the Germans moved outside of the north to help in the south, east, or west, the German observer, mentor, liaison teams (OMLTs) did not go with them. "At the moment," notes a news article from that time, "the Bundeswehr is only permitted to come to the aid of its ISAF partners in the south in emergency situations. Former defense minister Jung *ruled out sending German trainers to the south*, because there was such a high likelihood that the *Bundeswehr would become involved in combat* there."[20] This was a serious impediment to the military performance of the ANA kandaks. It inhibited their development, which hindered the larger ISAF effort to transition to Afghan responsibility.

A similar geographic restriction impeded the effort to train the Afghan National Police. "I am totally ashamed of what we have not achieved regarding the police," commented one Bundestag member.[21] Germany was the lead nation in

---

18 Reports of German consumption of beer in Afghanistan appeared in newspapers around the world; see Craig Whitlock, "German Supply Lines Flow with Beer in Afghanistan." *Washington Post*, November 15, 2008, http://www.washingtonpost.com/wp-dyn/content/article/2008/11/14/AR2008111403512.html, accessed August 10, 2010.

19 German officials said that this was never tested—that NATO commanders never asked German troops to come to the aid of allies—and that the minister of defense could say yes in such a circumstance. Members of the aforementioned allies disagreed. Interviews, Berlin, June 2009.

20 Demmer et al., "Fear of Rising Death Toll"; emphasis added.

21 Interview with member of Bundestag committee on defense issues, Berlin, June 2009.

this effort for several years,[22] yet German police officers were not only restricted to RC-North but were also prohibited from leaving Germany's base in Kunduz.[23] This, again, was a serious problem since German mentors could not observe police units in their daily activities, which slowed the development of the rule of law in Afghanistan, another fundamental part of the ISAF state-building effort.[24]

The second notable restriction was that until the middle of 2009, German units were prohibited from engaging in offensive operations. It was widely known that German troops could not fire on adversaries once the enemy began to move, whether it was to retreat or to reposition. As a news report from July 2009 notes, "Up until last week it was, for example, forbidden to shoot a fleeing assailant, even though every civilian police in Germany has the right [to do so in a similar situation]."[25]

Germany added "special remarks" to the NATO documents broadening the alliance's rules of engagement (ROE) regarding offensive operations: "The use of lethal force is prohibited unless an attack is taking place or is imminent."[26] These special remarks indicated that Germany was opting out of a vital part of NATO's ROE. Instead, German forces were to be used only for self-defense. Of course, the relevance of this restriction depended on how one defined offensive operations, but the special remarks would seem to preclude efforts to go out and find Taliban leaders, bomb factories, and other key targets. In one case, German special forces refused to participate in an offensive operation because it was considered to be "tantamount to targeted killings."[27]

This caveat was modified in 2009. In April 2009, the U.S. troop surge in southern Afghanistan began to push insurgents north, into areas patrolled by the Germans, increasing dramatically the violence around Kunduz in the north and attacks on German forces. Minister of Defense Jung removed restrictions against some offensive operations and the strict limitation on heavy weapons at the behest of Major General Erhad Bühler, director of the Joint Commitments staff.[28] The list of ROE carried by each German soldier was shortened from seven pages to four.[29] (We will come back to this significant change below.)

22 See Jones 2009: chap. 14 for a discussion of the problems with the "lead nation" distribution of responsibilities.
23 Interview with senior official in Germany's Ministry of Interior, Berlin, June 2009.
24 The Dutch police mission that began in 2011 was designed to remedy this caveat. For more on the Netherlands police mission, see Saideman 2012.
25 "New Rules Let Germans in Afghanistan Stop Shouting and Start Shooting," *Times Online*, July 29, 2009, http://www.timesonline.co.uk/tol/news/world/europe/article6730996.ece, accessed August 6, 2009.
26 "Changing the Rules: German Troops Beef Up Fight Against Taliban." *Der Spiegel Online*, July 9, 2009, http://www.spiegel.de/international/germany/0,1518,635192,00.html, accessed July 23, 2009.
27 Matthias Gebauer, "U.S. to Send 2,500 Soldiers to German-Controlled Area," *Der Spiegel Online*, January 4, 2010, http://www.spiegel.de/international/world/0,1518,670085,00.html, accessed April 24, 2013.
28 Judy Dempsey, "German Party Calls for Plan for Removal of Troops From Afghanistan," *New York Times*, August 20, 2009, http://www.nytimes.com/2009/08/21/world/europe/21iht-germany.html, accessed August 26, 2009.
29 "New Rules Let Germans in Afghanistan Stop Shouting and Start Shooting," *Times Online*, July 29, http://www.timesonline.co.uk/tol/news/world/europe/article6730996.ece, accessed August 6, 2009.

Counternarcotics operations were a controversial issue for most NATO members and partners operating in Afghanistan. Germany was not alone in refraining from engaging in such efforts, and they had a "clarifying remark" restricting their troops from such activities. The decision to opt out of this when NATO decided to engage in counternarcotics operations was made at the very highest level.[30]

A different kind of restriction involved German military capability. Germany deployed only a handful of helicopters (reportedly six) to Afghanistan and only the armored version of the CH-53. This was quite a limitation on Germany's flexibility because some helicopters were not operational due to repairs and maintenance, they were required to fly in pairs, and one was always reserved for emergency medical evacuation. This meant that there were only one or two helicopter flights available at any given time, which significantly restricted the ability of German forces to move across very difficult terrain. The effect was that ISAF had little idea of what was happening in Badakhshan Province, since the German troops deployed in Feyzabad could only travel within twenty-five kilometers or so of their base.[31] When two more helicopters were sent as reinforcements to RC-North, no additional personnel accompanied them, producing little real improvement in capability and flexibility.[32]

It also seemed to be the case that German decision making on the ground was so cumbersome as to be ineffective. As the governor of Kunduz indicated, "When we call them to help with a conflict with the Taliban, they often need orders from the German headquarters in Mazar-e-Sharif first, and then they often come too late. Too much time passes, and help doesn't come."[33] This report was from one potentially biased Afghan politician, but it fits the larger pattern of restraint rather than flexibility.

Together, these and other restrictions impaired the effectiveness of German forces in Afghanistan. Given their large numbers, the large sector for which Germans were responsible, and their previous reputation as being among the best in NATO, this was a significant challenge for the commander of ISAF.

## AGENT SELECTION

We noted in chapter 1 that parliamentary coalitions are likely to defer to standard bureaucratic processes when selecting military agents, in large part due to the difficulties associated with reaching consensus on senior agents via internal political

---

30 Interview with Ministry of Foreign Affairs official, Berlin, June 2009.
31 Interview with senior officer at Joint Forces Command, Brunssum, Belgium, January 28, 2011.
32 Alexander Szandar, "Snafu in Afghanistan: German Troops Bemoan 'Critical' Deficits in Training and Equipment," *Der Spiegel Online*, August 31, 2009, http://www.spiegel.de/international/world/0,1518 ,646085,00.html, accessed February 1, 2010. Budgetary constraints have limited the flying hours of German pilots, further limiting capability as few pilots are qualified to operate in harsh conditions.
33 Governor Mohammed Omar, quoted in "Kunduz Governor Omar: 'It Would Honestly Be Better if They Left,'" *Der Spiegel Online*, November 23, 2009, http://www.spiegel.de/international/spiegel/0,1518 ,662824,00.html, accessed January 29, 2009.

bargaining. This seemed to hold true with regard to the selection of German military leaders. The commanders in the field were not selected for their stellar records or innovative tactics. Experts did not consider the set of colonels sent to command the PRTs, for instance, to be consistently among the best and brightest within the German military.[34] While other countries clearly selected officers to key positions by their potential to rise far in the ranks, this did not seem to be the case for the German process. Instead, senior German officers were known more for their political skills than for their talents in the field.

## BUTTRESSING RESTRICTIONS WITH OVERSIGHT BUT NOT INDUCEMENTS

German officials coupled their caveats with especially intense oversight, as we would expect with a coalition parliamentary government. Not only was there an annual mandate renewal process, but the Bundestag defense committee met weekly with the minister of defense in closed sessions to be briefed on the week's events.[35] This was not a trivial exercise, as the legislators took this task quite seriously.[36] Indeed, German members of parliament paid close attention to how many troops were in Afghanistan. They complained if the numbers exceed the force cap, making noise all the way to the Supreme Headquarters Allied Powers Europe in Mons, Belgium.[37]

There were few apparent rewards given to officers for achieving particular milestones and few penalties associated with failed outcomes. Instead, deployed troops were judged on their behavior, and then only for egregious individual violations of regulations. Soldiers in the field faced a very stringent form of accountability—German civilian courts. Soldiers suspected of violating German laws were tried in ordinary civilian courts with jurisdiction determined by where the soldier resided in Germany. Only late in the game was a special prosecutor in Potsdam (site of the German operational headquarters) given responsibility for investigating alleged crimes committed during a deployment.[38] This civilian court provided a significant check on the soldiers on the ground, and there were seemingly few inducements from the Bundestag for officers achieving political or military outcomes on the ground.

---

34 Conversations with Sascha Lange and Frank Kupferschmidt at the Stiftung Wissenschaft und Politik (German Institute for International and Security Affairs), June 2009, were especially instructive.
35 Interviews with members of the Bundestag defense committee, Berlin, June 2009.
36 Members of the Bundestag even registered some frustration that they could not monitor the U.S. special forces units operating in RC-North. "'Capture or Kill': Germany Gave Names to Secret Taliban Hit List," *Der Spiegel Online*, Feburary 8, 2010, http://www.spiegel.de/international/germany/0,1518,709625,00 .html, accessed August 12, 2010.
37 Interview with senior officer at SHAPE, February 2011.
38 This was reported in many of our interviews, including the interiew with Dr. Rainner Stinner, Liberal Democratic Party, member of Bundestag defense committee, Berlin, June 17, 2009.

## THE EXCEPTION THAT PROVES THE RULE: RELAXING GERMAN CAVEATS

As mentioned above, Germany changed the rules of engagement for its soldiers in the spring of 2009. Specifically, it dropped the language it had added, the "special remarks," to NATO's rules on the use of force. The ROE cards given to the troops were altered to read, "Attacks can be prevented, for example, by taking action against individuals who are planning, preparing or supporting attacks, or who exhibit other forms of hostile behavior."[39] These changes were not just symbolic. German troops started to engage in offensive operations.[40]

How was this possible, given the coalition politics at the time of a grand coalition? The answer is that politics changed in Germany as the situation in RC-North became more kinetic. With reports of soldiers stating that they were being put in harm's way with the limitations they faced, parliamentarians began to speak out, suggesting that the rules of engagement were endangering the troops. As violence increased in the German sector, the discourse changed (in part, but not entirely) from whether this was a war in which Germans might possibly kill people to an increased focus on the safety of the troops. So, "*at the behest of parliament*" the rules were changed.[41] At the time, SPD politician Rainer Arnold said, "It's good that the pocket card is now being amended to reflect the realities of the mission, thereby preventing uncertainty among the soldiers from arising in the first place."[42] To be clear, the story that these changes were made only came out a few months later. [43]

This decision shows that the politics of a dangerous mission can provide challenges for the politicians back home—how to avoid being responsible for the loss of their soldiers in the field while balancing the risk of collateral damage. As the conflict became more violent, the onus shifted toward the risks facing the troops. The quote above is striking since it comes from a left-wing politician. While our argument is that grand coalitions will be less likely to increase discretion, even a grand coalition will reduce caveats if the left wing sees the dangers involved in imposing restrictions.

In sum, the German case supports our intuitions regarding parliamentary coalition governments and international military operations. The German

---

39 "Germany Intensifies Mission in Afghanistan," *Der Spiegel Online*, December 22, 2009, http://www
    .spiegel.de/international/germany/0,1518,668404,00.html, accessed April 27, 2011.
40 Michael M. Phillips, "Germans Offensive Aims to Repair Reputation," *Wall Street Journal Asia*,
    August 12, 2010.
41 Ibid.; emphasis added.
42 Rainer Arnold, quoted in Phillips, "Germans Offensive Aims to Repair Reputation."
43 "New Rules of Engagement for German Troops in Afghanistan, July 26, 2009," *Deutsche Welle*, http://
    www.dw.de/new-rules-of-engagement-for-german-troops-in-afghanistan/a-4519627-1, accessed
    April 24, 2013.

government engaged in highly contingent delegation to its agents and imposed restrictive caveats on their behavior. To avoid risk, the government engaged in intrusive oversight, but had trouble acting on that information with incentives for appropriate behavior. It also defaulted toward the bureaucratic selection of agents, rather than selecting agents that were closely aligned with its collective preferences, in large part because parliamentary coalitions may not know their own preferences in the first place. Finally, when it relaxed its caveats it did so to protect its own domestic political interests.

# The Dutch in Uruzgan: Tied to the Telephone

The Netherlands was both more and less aggressive than one might have expected.[44] It agreed to deploy to southern Afghanistan despite significant risks, but was generally more restrained than the other countries in that region. Oversight was intense, but failed to prevent the government from collapsing over a proposed extension of the mission. As with the Germans, the Dutch utilized restricted delegation contracts, significant caveats, and active oversight. They did not utilize agent selection or robust positive or negative inducements, consistent with our expectations for parliamentary coalition governments.

## THE DOMESTIC DYNAMICS OF DUTCH DEPLOYMENTS

There is perhaps no better demonstration of the perils of military interventions for coalition governments than the Dutch government's 2010 collapse over a proposed extension of their mission in Uruzgan. This section will review the connection between constraints of a parliamentary coalition government and how the Dutch approached military missions abroad.

The Dutch have a bicameral parliament, the Staten Generaal, whose members are chosen by proportional representation. There are usually between four and six major parties represented in the lower house of the parliament, so coalition governments are the rule, with the last three governments comprised of three parties who together barely reached majority status. From 2003 to 2006, the ruling coalition contained the center-right Christen-Democratisch Appèl (CDA), or Christian Democrats; the moderate Volkspartij voor Vrijheid en Democratie (VVD), or People's Party; and the progressive Democrats-66 (D66), which was only included because its six seats gave this ideologically broad coalition a slim

---

44 We focus here on the mission to Uruzgan rather than the prior PRT effort in Baghlan because the Uruzgan mission not only illustrates the dynamics we want to explore but also because this effort is far more comparable to the other cases in this volume. For more on the Baghlan mission, see Rietjens 2008. For an excellent account of the Uruzgan mission, see Dimitriu and de Graff 2010.

majority. That arrangement proved too fragile to endure, and dissolved in mid-2006 when the D66 withdrew from the governing coalition. The country was led by a minority caretaker government of the CDA and VVD in the second half of 2006 until elections in late 2006 produced a new center-right coalition. From early 2007 until February 2010, the Netherlands was led by another coalition comprising the CDA, the moderate Partij van de Arbeid (PvdA), or Labor Party, and the socially conservative Christian Union (CU). As before, the 2007 coalition was only able to achieve a slim majority in parliament (80 of 150 seats). The CU was able to use its six seats to gain the defense minister post in exchange for its votes. Three years later, however, the government would fall when the Labor Party ministers resigned over extending the Afghanistan deployment.

The Dutch parliament has significant powers over military deployments and the use of force. Its principal means of influence is Article 100 of the Dutch constitution, as passed in 2000 in the aftermath of the Srebrenica debacle in 1995, and the Article 100 Review Protocol of 2001. This process specifies that the government must inform the parliament before deploying troops abroad via an "Article 100 Letter" that provides the rationale and estimated budget for the mission (Dieterich et al. 2010: 44–46). These letters range from between twenty-five and forty pages. The letter's contents usually include:

- the Dutch interests advanced by the deployment
- the assurance that the military deployment conforms with international law and is preferably based on a clear UN mandate
- the degree of solidarity, credibility, and sharing of responsibilities with allies or partner nations
- the assurance that the employment of military force will be done on a case-by-case basis, after consulting parliament and with sufficient societal support
- a statement that there is a concrete military mission and a clear command structure
- assurances that political and military goals are attainable and that tasks are feasible
- specification of available units
- assessments of the risks for the employed personnel
- a statement as to the needed financing and whether that financing has been budgeted
- the assurance that the military mission is done for a fixed term and that a new decision is needed to prolong the mission (Wessel 2008: 146)

The ministers of foreign affairs, defense, and development write the letter, anticipating what is acceptable and seeking broad support. For instance, in an interview with a Dutch representative, it became clear that there were issues left out of the Afghanistan letter because officials in the ministries of foreign affairs and defense knew that some issues, such as tanks, were "a bridge too far."[45] Once they submit this letter, parliament can hold hearings and debates, but a formal vote is not required. Instead, each party leader signals whether the party is for or against the mission. While the constitution does not prohibit the government from going ahead without some registration of support within the parliament, the political realities of coalition government and minority government require parliamentary support.

The parliament can hold closed hearings to debate the Article 100 letter, and parliamentary committees are empowered to read classified material. Yet the situation is not as intense as in Germany: Dutch mandates are for two-year terms, making the renewal process less of an ever-present reality in the field. Still, the parliament has significant power to oversee the mission, and the two-year time limits mean that parliament has to be taken seriously since extensions are always around the corner. There was definitely a sense that parliament watched the mission intently.[46]

Parliamentary power and influence was evident from the beginning of the mission to Uruzgan. Even at the start, there was significant uncertainty about whether there would be enough political support at home to deploy to Uruzgan. Deliberations began in May 2005, a ministerial decision was taken in September and October with an Article 100 letter, and finally the decision was sent to parliament in December.[47] The hesitation was not just about differences among the parties; significant ambivalence was also felt by the key actors: Prime Minister Jan Peter Balkenende (CDA), Defense Minister Henk Kamp (Liberals/VVD), and Foreign Minister Bernard Bot (CDA). This uncertainty deepened when it became clear that the Labor (PvDA), GreenLeft, and Social Parties were opposed to the mission, with the CDA and D66 wavering.

Foreign Minister Bot was nervous about the security situation, so he wanted more guarantees from the United States, although the latter had initially been reluctant to make such a commitment (Hazelbag 2009). This explains the language in the Article 100 letter about U.S. efforts continuing in Uruzgan. Divisions developed within the D66, the smallest but still crucial coalition partner.[48] Its leader, Boris Dittrich, announced his opposition to the mission. The cabinet met anyway, fudging the language to declare an intention to launch the mission rather than make a decision, with members of D66 in the cabinet taking a stance

---

45 Interview with Dutch representative at the Netherlands Embassy to Canada, Ottawa, November 2010.
46 This was reported in interviews with American and British diplomats based in The Hague who observed the process closely.
47 See Hazelbag 2009 for a thorough account of the 2005–6 decision-making process.
48 The D66 was described as a relatively amorphous party of somewhat left-wing intellectuals.

in opposition to its leader. This only led to more bickering among the parties, ultimately forcing the cabinet essentially to ask parliament to make a decision (Hazelbag 2009). This process made the news throughout the alliance, increasing the pressure felt by all.

Matters got clearer as the Labor Party leader, Wouter Bos, stated that "'the Cabinet is moving in the right direction with regard to a number of demands we (PvDA) have made,' pointing at the separation of ISAF and OEF" (Hazelbag 2009: 266). The parliamentary committee responsible for foreign affairs and defense got access to the NATO rules of engagement and the rules provided to Dutch commanders and soldiers in the field. After a week of briefings and information, the Liberal Party gave its support to the mission. The Socialist and the GreenLeft Parties remained opposed, while most of the smaller parties assented. In all, this process took about a year from the first discussions of taking on the mission to Uruzgan.

This process created a basis, albeit a fragile one, for a two-year mission to Uruzgan. There was still debate as to whether the deployment was a combat mission or a reconstruction effort, with the military essentially saying it was both, depending on the circumstances. The approval process left one party badly bruised, with the D66 leader leaving the party, and then that party eventually breaking with the rest of the coalition in June 2006.

The 2007 renewal was less politically heated than the 2005–6 process, but set a finite August 1, 2010, deadline for ending the mission. From 2007 until early 2010 there was speculation as to the need for another extension and the viability of any such request in parliament. When the time came to consider it, the government fell, as the Labor Party opposed any extension, even a police mission that was considered and ultimately approved in January 2011.[49] Still, it was clear that party differences about the mission were significant. The Labor Party had been wary of OEF and ensured there were restrictions against cooperating with the Americans even as Foreign Minister Bot of the Christian Democrats put in contradictory language focusing on the need for American help.

Before moving on, one party has largely escaped notice thus far: the Partij voor de Vrijheid (PVV), or Party for Freedom, a right-wing, populist party that has done well in various elections. It was a natural coalition partner for the Liberals and Christian Democrats except that its party program of anti-Muslim views, xenophobia, and Euroskepticism make it very unappealing. On foreign policy, one might expect it to be combative and support operations in Afghanistan, but

---

49 There were significant differences between the Labor Party and the other parties in the coalition, so Afghanistan was not the sole cause of its collapse. Indeed, the Labor Party may have used the Afghanistan issue strategically to bring the government down. This was the consensus at a workshop at the Hague Center for Strategic Studies, The Hague, January 26, 2011.

it was and is much more focused on "Fortress Holland" and isolation rather than foreign adventures. The various decisions along the way would have been far easier for the parties in government if they could have counted on the PVV for support on Afghanistan, but it was never a serious prospect. We raise the PVV now because it provides an important contrast to a similar party in the Danish case.

## DUTCH DELEGATION

Dutch officers were more open about their caveats than those in other countries, perhaps because they could and did feel good about comparisons with the Germans.[50] Those caveats were first contained in the Article 100 letter of 2005 associated with Uruzgan. As the letter noted, "The risks arising from this mission are considerable. It is sent to an area where the Dutch troops will contact the OMF [opposing military forces]. Taking into account attacks, both on patrol and in the logistics supply by air and road, and on the bases of the ISAF units . . . [it] cannot be excluded that in fighting, the Dutch side will have casualties" (Netherlands 2005: 12).[51]

The Article 100 letter specified the number of Apache helicopters (six) and F-16s (six) and the expected number of troops (1,200) to be deployed. The letter allowed ground forces to be moved to other parts of southern Afghanistan and acknowledged that offensive operations might be necessary. The document even specified, "A Dutch officer will be 'Red Card Holder' on behalf of the chief of defense (CDS) to ensure that they do not work in ways that conflict with ISAF instructions" (Netherlands 2005: 17; emphasis added).

The letter allowed the Netherlands to serve as the lead nation in Uruzgan, but prohibited Dutch soldiers from operating as part of OEF.[52] The challenge for the Dutch, given their OEF restrictions, was determining where the line existed between deconflicting and cooperation. For much of the Netherlands' time in Uruzgan, there were American units, particularly special forces, operating in their region under the OEF chain of a command with a focus on finding terrorists. Some of these units actually behaved in ways that were very similar to the Dutch and other ISAF units—based in a distinct area of operations and responsibility, meeting with the local elites, mentoring Afghan units and supporting the Afghan government. OEF and ISAF commanders in an area had no choice but to work together to prevent them from undermining each other. Indeed, Dutch officers on the ground met regularly with their U.S. OEF counterparts, exchanging

---

50 This was reported in several of our interviews.
51 We used Google's translation tool to get the gist of the Dutch document.
52 Avoiding the OEF is easier to talk about in The Hague and harder to do in Uruzgan. "The only people who think there is a division between OEF and ISAF are in parliament"; interview with Dutch officer, The Hague, January 2011.

information, attending meetings with local officials, and coordinating complementary missions.[53]

Emergency response was less controversial. Consider that Dutch F-16s were not supposed to participate on OEF missions yet could assist in emergencies (Netherlands 2005). The Dutch were allowed to help OEF units that were in trouble, but defining "in trouble" meant different things to the commanders in The Hague versus the officers in the field. For the former, "in trouble" did not just mean U.S. units in contact with the enemy—a firefight—but that the unit was at significant risk of being overrun.[54] For the Dutch officers on the ground, they would respond if the OEF units in question were in contact with the adversary.[55]

The second set of formal restrictions involved out-of-area operations. The air assets did not face significant geographic restrictions: Dutch Apache helicopters could go anywhere in RC-South, and the F-16s could go anywhere in Afghanistan.[56] On the other hand, the ground forces were almost entirely restricted to Uruzgan despite the Article 100 language. In 2006, the Dutch sent troops to Kandahar as part of Operation Medusa, but their role was to replace (i.e., backfill) Canadian troops pulled out of other missions for the fight rather than to be sent into battle.[57] Dutch OMLTs were restricted to the province, except for accompanying their kandaks on the occasional convoy to Kandahar Airfield. These trips required calls back home for permission.[58]

The 2007 letter for the extension of the mission until August 2010 was very similar (Netherlands 2007). The document again made clear that offensive operations were permitted. It was also quite specific about the number of air assets and OMLTs allowed. The letter tried to clarify when Dutch soldiers could be moved outside the province, but referred to different authorities in different parts of the letter—the minister of defense in one part and the chief of defense in another; we estimate this was not that significant in practice given how closely the two work with each other.[59]

## A SPECIFIC SET OF CAPABILITIES

The Dutch insisted on providing their own air support, largely to prevent another Srebrenica. The letter provided to parliament in 2007 was very specific: "We will continue to contribute five Apache combat helicopters and four F-16 fighter

---

53 This was reported by nearly every officer we interviewed.
54 Interview with senior Dutch officer in the Directorate of Operations, The Hague, January 2011.
55 Interviews with a series of Dutch officers who had served in Uruzgan, The Hague, January 2011.
56 We heard several stories that suggested that the Dutch helicopters operated under restrictive rules of engagement so that they would not fire in support of Australians in contact or pick up wounded on a few occasions where other countries' helicopters could. Interviews with diplomats based in The Hague, January 2011, and Dutch officers who served in Afghanistan, The Hague, January 2011.
57 Interview with Dutch officer who served in Uruzgan shortly after the operation, The Hague, January 2011.
58 Interview with two officers that served with OMLTs, The Hague, January 2011.
59 We are grateful to Rem Korteweg of the Hague Centre for Strategic Studies for clarifying the letter process.

planes to ISAF. In this way the security chain will remain in Dutch hands."[60] Indeed, in the newer police mission that started in 2011, the Dutch continued to deploy F-16s to Afghanistan. While these planes provided some useful reconnaissance capabilities to counter roadside bombs, the lessons of Srebrenica drove these decisions.

In 1995, Dutch units were part of the UN peacekeeping operation protecting the safe area of Srebrenica. When the Bosnian Serbs threatened to overrun the safe area, the Dutch asked for NATO planes to be used, but this was rejected by the French general running the UN effort at the time, as the planes were subject to a "double key" authorization process. As a result, the Dutch could not stop the offensive, which led to the worst atrocities in Europe since World War II. One of the lessons the Dutch learned was that in future operations they would bring their own air support with orders in place that would allow the Dutch commander to deploy these assets even if the multilateral chain of command was opposed.[61] The Dutch would never allow a "double key" situation again to stop the Dutch from protecting themselves.[62]

Thus, while other countries refrained from providing expensive and potentially risky air platforms, the Dutch embraced such units because of the specific lessons learned from the most dramatic Dutch failure of recent military history. Indeed, it is important to note that the governing coalition collapsed in 2002 when Prime Minister Wim Kok resigned in the aftermath of the official report on the events in Srebrenica seven years earlier. Bringing one's own air support was one lesson from this disaster, and the Article 100 procedure governing Dutch deployments was another.

## DUTCH AGENT SELECTION

As was the case with the Germans, agent selection was not something the Dutch emphasized as a means of controlling their deployed military's behavior. Commanders were not chosen for their affinity with one or another political party's international agenda. When the rank of task force commander went from colonel to brigadier general,[63] selecting new commanders for Afghanistan focused on whose

---

60 Consulate General of the Netherlands in Toronto, "An Informal Translation of Dutch Article 100 Letter, Re-authorizing Uruzgan Mission," http://www.mfa.nl/aspx/get.aspx?xdl=/views/post/xdl/page&SitIdt =65&VarIdt=50&ItmIdt=53388, accessed February 17, 2011. There was apparently a reduction in the number of F-16s required to protect the Dutch.
61 Reported in several interviews with Dutch officers, The Hague, January 2011.
62 Conversation with Dutch representatives at the Netherlands Embassy to Canada, Ottawa, November 2010.
63 The Canadians and Dutch both had colonels at first. As the mission progressed and intensified and as it became more necessary to have a general who could get attention and influence in NATO meetings, both countries upgraded the rank of the officer responsible for their respective task forces.

turn it was since there were a finite number of officers at that rank. The chief of the army would select a nominee, and then the chief of defense would approve it. The coalition cabinet and the minister of defense were out of this process of agent selection, but they did have a big hand in oversight.

## ROBUST OVERSIGHT: FIGHTING AT THE END OF A LEASH

As a coalition government, we would expect the Dutch to engage in active oversight. They did. The primary form of oversight between The Hague and Dutch commanders was via secure video teleconferences (VTCs).[64] In planning operations, if there was a reasonable possibility of contact with the enemy (level 1) or if there was probability of a confrontation (search and destroy missions, attempts to seize a cache, etc.—level 2), the Dutch task force commander had to contact the director of operations back home.[65] The chief of defense sat in on the level 2 conversations, so these conversations were not trivial exercises.[66] In addition, the minister of defense was notified of all level 1 and 2 operations. This tight process was seen as a benefit of being a small country—that there were "short lines" between the officers on the ground and their bosses back home, without a lot of layers of bureaucracy and command structures in between.[67]

Most operations would be planned days or weeks ahead of time, so getting permission was not problematic. However, sometimes operations would develop with only one or two days' lead time, requiring a fast response. While interview subjects reported that this need to get permission did not create pressure to reduce activities, there was also a repeated emphasis on having to get the story right before calling back home. The repeated focus on having a good story to get permission suggests that the Dutch officers in Uruzgan were willing to say no to the ISAF chain if they were not confident that they could convince their Dutch bosses. Such seeming reluctance led to the Dutch military gaining a reputation in ISAF for being less active.

The permission process was not always quick and efficient. In 2006, Dutch special operations units had a vehicle that got stuck.[68] They sought an air strike to destroy the vehicle so that adversaries would not be able to examine it and gain intelligence about its capabilities. This required approval from the Netherlands,

---

64 To be clear, in previous operations, the Dutch armed forces fell short of the ideal and rhetoric of mission command. See Vogelaar and Kramer 2004.
65 Level 0 refers to operations where contact is not likely or expected. Interview with Dutch officer who had commanded a company in Afghanistan, Royal Netherlands Defence Academy, Breda, Netherlands, January 2011. This process was confirmed in other interviews.
66 Interview with Major General T. A. Middendorp, Director of Operations, The Hague, January 27, 2011.
67 Ibid.
68 Interview with Dutch company commander, The Hague, January 2011.

where officers recommended sending a helicopter to lift the vehicle. They viewed it as expensive to waste a Hellfire missile to destroy an armored personnel carrier. While this haggling was going on, the special operations unit had to wait beside the vehicle, putting the unit at greater risk. Finally, the decision was made to destroy the vehicle. This example shows how slow the process was during the early stages of the Dutch involvement in Uruzgan.

The process got quicker and less intrusive as the military learned from experience. The first operational plans sent back with search and destroy missions generated some shock, but with repetition these became less surprising. Moreover, as the officers who had gained experience on the ground in Afghanistan came back and filled in the billets in the directorate of operations, trust and understanding developed. The director of operations that we interviewed, Major General Tom Middendorp, had previously served as the task force commander in Uruzgan, so he was quite familiar with the kinds of operations that were being planned.

The VTC procedures discussed above equated to intense reporting to The Hague and a commensurate limitation on the discretion of officers on the ground when it came to new operations. The commander on the ground knew that the chief of defense was not only informed of what was going on but was directly involved in overseeing every significant decision and had to brief the minister of defense every day about operations in Afghanistan. This equated to tight political supervision over the mission.

## DUTCH INDUCEMENTS

The Dutch oversight process was intense, but as with the Germans, there was little follow-through in terms of its effects on an officer's career. In our interviews we repeatedly heard from officers who exceeded their authority by going outside the wire or even outside the Dutch area of operations in order to do their jobs.[69] In these cases, the chain of command largely learned of these actions afterward, and, surprisingly, did not do much besides telling the officers to stop. In terms of positive incentives, most task force commanders have been promoted, including the current two-star general serving as director of operations. There were no ramifications for casualties during their tours, unlike their Australian partners (see chapter 7), perhaps because the mission approval process meant that each operation implicated the director of operations and the chief of defense.

---

69 Interviews with Dutch army officer and Dutch paramilitary officer (the *Marechaussee*, akin to the French *gendarmerie* and the Italian *carabinieri*), Royal Netherlands Defence Academy, Breda, Netherlands, January 24, 2011.

In sum, Dutch politicians faced tremendous pressure and controversy at the start the mission, with significant differences among the political parties about the feasibility of the mission, its value, and the challenges that lay ahead. These differences became embedded in the agreements governing the mission, especially the series of Article 100 letters. These then influenced the capabilities that were deployed and the rules under which the Dutch would operate. While the Dutch armed forces were sent to a dangerous area, the commanders on the ground worked very closely with the generals back home, with each significant operation vetted in The Hague.

The narrow discretion and the close oversight meant that bosses back home were as or more implicated by events on the ground than the field commanders. The tight leash allowed the Dutch armed forces to serve and make a difference in a difficult area, but only for as long as the coalition politics at home permitted. Still, despite the coalition politics and the tight leash, the Dutch effort in a tough Uruzgan assignment was far more forward-leaning than Germany's in a generally less dangerous area. Of the coalition governments operating in Afghanistan, one might consider the Netherlands to be among the most robust, second only to Denmark.

# The Danes as Modern-Day Vikings

The easiest way to demonstrate the contrast between Denmark and Germany is to note that when the two countries were deployed together in RC-North, the Danes found themselves not only doing most (if not all) of the patrolling, despite being dwarfed by the much larger German contingent,[70] but driving the German commander around Feyzabad.[71] From their initial deployment in RC-North, the Danes sent troops to help out the Lithuanians as they set up a PRT in Chaghcharan, in RC-West,[72] and a larger contingent to Helmand to deploy with the British as NATO expanded its coverage to southern Afghanistan. The latter became the focus of the Danish effort, providing the second largest contingent (until the U.S. surge) in the most dangerous province in Afghanistan.

The Danes made an early impression in RC-South by helping out the Canadians during Operation Medusa near Kandahar and the British at Musa Qala in the summer and fall of 2006. Since then, their focus has been mostly in the so-called

---

70 Interview with Danish diplomat, Ottawa, June 2010.
71 Roundtable with senior defense officials, Copenhagen, August 25, 2010. This section is based on interviews conducted largely in Copenhagen in August 2010.
72 Chaghcharan is in a fairly remote part of Afghanistan, and has the distinction of being twice refused by two larger NATO members for a PRT site. The Canadians, given the choice of here or Kandahar, chose the latter (see Hillier 2010; Stein and Lang 2007). The Spaniards originally were going to locate their PRT in Chaghcharan, but chose elsewhere, leaving it to the Lithuanians.

Green Zone in Helmand, where the poppies grow and the danger is extreme. Denmark paid a high price in casualties relative to the size of its deployment and the highest of all ISAF members relative to population size.[73]

The next section explains why Denmark appears to be an anomaly. After all, it was governed by coalitions for the entire mission, but enacted less restricted delegation contracts with its military than did either the Germans or the Dutch. The solution to the Danish behavioral conundrum lies in the nature of the country's parliamentary coalition dynamics—dynamics that differed significantly from other coalition governments explored in this chapter. Coalition politics allowed Denmark to play a risky role in some of the most dangerous parts of Afghanistan.

## A STABLE GOVERNMENT COALITION

Denmark superficially appears to be like Germany and somewhat like the Netherlands: parliament passes mandates for any mission, the Ministry of Defense drafts the language, the government seeks passage by appealing beyond the coalition and so forth. Yet important differences exist between these cases, ultimately producing far more discretion for Danish officers than we saw in either the German or Dutch cases.

The key to understanding Danish behavior is that the country had a stable coalition government that did not fluctuate significantly during the scope of our study.[74] We distinguish among three sets of parties in the Folketing, the Danish parliament: the two-party coalition, the supporting party, and the opposition. The coalition government consisted of the Liberals and Conservatives. The Danish People's Party (DPP) was the supporting party. The opposition included the Social Democrats and the Radical Liberals.

There was not that much ideological distance on foreign policy within the coalition. Despite their different names, the Liberals and Conservatives were on the same part of the political spectrum,[75] with similar outlooks on foreign policy, including the use of force in general and the mission in Afghanistan.[76] The prime minister for much of the relevant period, Andres Fogh Rasmussen, and Defense Minister Søren Gade, were both members of the Liberal Party and seen as assertive advocates of the ISAF mission. The foreign minister, a Conservative, was not mentioned in our interviews as a key actor in shaping Afghanistan policy.

---

73 See table 1.1.

74 We code Denmark as a coalition government because the cabinet includes two parties even though it is also a minority government.

75 A small piece of evidence of how right of center the Liberals are in the Danish context would be the posters and bumper stickers for the John McCain–Sarah Palin U.S. election ticket in the office of Michael Aastrup Jensen, the Liberal member of parliament we interviewed, Copenhagen, August 24, 2010.

76 Interview with Michael Aastrup Jensen.

Because the Liberals and the Conservatives fell short of a majority, they relied on an additional party, the DPP, for support. The DPP was seen as a xenophobic party, and only supported the coalition in return for strict policies on immigration. Before 2001, the DPP was relatively isolationist, voicing significant skepticism about the European Union. After 9/11 and the early 2006 Danish unrest over the cartoons depicting the Prophet Mohammed, the DPP became more interested in and supportive of the wars in the Mideast.[77] On that issue, then, circumstances narrowed the gaps between the governing coalition and the DPP. Thus, there was a stable majority in the parliament in favor of the Afghanistan mission, especially after 2006. Denmark went to war in Iraq with only a Liberal-CPP-DPP majority, breaking the Danish tradition of having a broader consensus before engaging in war.

For Afghanistan, the government was able to maintain a wider consensus in favor of the mission with the support of the other parties. The Social Democrats and Radical Liberals have been on board for the entire ISAF mission, and only in 2010 grew somewhat critical. The puzzle is why the opposition was not opposed to the Afghan mission.

To some degree, opposition parties, especially the Social Democrats, were trapped by their past. In the aftermath of the Cold War, the Social Democrats were in government, and directed the country toward an activist foreign policy.[78] The military was seen as an instrument by which Denmark could make a difference. The Social Democrats were in power in 2001 and committed to helping the United States in the aftermath of 9/11. The party broke with the government over Iraq, arguing that Afghanistan was the right war. Since then, the Social Democrats and their Radical Liberal partners have repeatedly committed to Afghanistan and the use of force as part of Danes making a difference in foreign policy. The governing parties would have every opportunity to accuse them of weakness and hypocrisy if the Social Democrats or Radical Liberals were to switch their stance.[79] Indeed, even the Socialists changed their stance to become more electable as a potential coalition partner to the other left-of-center parties.[80]

Consequently, there seemed to be a limit on what the less enthusiastic members of the parliamentary consensus could demand. The Social Democrats and Liberals asked for a 750-member cap on the troops sent to Afghanistan,[81] but that was not that much of a constraint given the small size of the Danish army. The two

77 Roundtable at Centre for Military Studies, University of Copenhagen, August 26, 2010.
78 This was the consensus in the interviews we had with politicians, government officials, and experts.
79 Interview with Peter Viggo Jakobsen, professor of political science, University of Copenhagen, August 26, 2010.
80 Interview with Holger Nielsen, foreign policy spokesperson for the Socialist People's Party, Copenhagen, August 24, 2010.
81 Ibid.

parties pushed the government to emphasize more training and to de-emphasize combat. The government accommodated these demands in the 2010 Helmand Strategy, but again, these did not impose restrictions on the troops and did not push the government very far from its own preferred positions. The Social Democrats and Radical Liberals only started to demand a timeline for an exit in 2010 in the aftermath of American and British leaders announcing potential exit dates, when it became more legitimate to raise such questions. Indeed, the government could not position itself as staying after the British departed, so again the left-wing parties were demanding of the government positions that the government had to take anyway.

These parliamentary dynamics translated into a predictable process when Denmark used force. Like Germany's, the Danish constitution requires parliamentary mandates to authorize foreign deployments. Parliament has to pass a resolution before force can be used (Dieterich et al. 2010). This gives the parliament the opportunity to impose conditions. A critical difference from the previous cases is that parliamentary authorization is not an annual requirement in Denmark; rather, the mandate is for the duration of the mission unless significant changes are recommended. The government did not have to be concerned about returning every year for parliamentary approval. The Afghan mandate limited the size of the force and where it operated, but the location was not specified as narrowly as in the German or Dutch processes: it limited troops to Afghanistan rather than just to Helmand Province.

Still, in terms of drafting the mandate, the Ministry of Defense and the government successfully sought consensus that went beyond just the coalition parties. Once the mandate was passed, the key decisions were made by the Ministry of Defense, Defense Command, and Army Operations Command. Our interviews with Danish officials made clear that operational decisions were not made at the level of the prime minister, even though the prime minister from 2001 to 2009, Anders Fogh Rasmussen, had a passion for foreign policy (and went on to become secretary general of NATO).[82] For major policy decisions, the minister of defense seemed to be the key actor. For much of this time, Søren Gade was defense minister (2004–10), and was seen by all as an assertive advocate for the ISAF mission. The chief of defense had "full national command," and delegated authority to the commander on the ground.[83] Defense Command, which is the Danish equivalent of the U.S. Joint Staff, made and implemented the authorization. Phone calls from the field went to Army Operations Command and occasionally up to Defense

---

82 At no point did our interview subjects focus on the prime minister for operational decisions, with a senior adviser in the prime minister's office clearly stating that decisions were made at the Ministry of Defense or below.
83 Roundtable with Ministry of Defense and Defense Command officials, Copenhagen, August 25, 2010.

Command. Unlike the Dutch case, this was said to be quite rare, as only extra-ordinary events required a commander to call home.[84]

## DANISH DELEGATION

The Danes, like the Dutch, are quite proud that they were more flexible than the Germans.[85] In the course of research, only a few significant restrictions became clear, and their nature says more about Danish flexibility than limited discretion. The first restriction was an initial reluctance to embed soldiers in an Afghan battalion—an OMLT. Other countries have been reluctant to participate in the OMLT program because the embedded troops face greater risks, engaging in combat within an Afghan unit rather than surrounded by their fellow national soldiers. For the Danes, however, several interviews explained Danish reluctance to mentor Afghan troops due to the risks of being present and perhaps even in command as Afghans commit atrocities.[86] This fits the larger pattern of deployments, in which the Danes have been willing to risk casualties.[87] They were more risk averse when it came to avoiding responsibility for the harm that others might cause.

Eventually, Danish decision makers agreed that training the Afghans was part of the exit strategy from Afghanistan. As of the fall of 2010, the Danes had an OMLT in Afghanistan, but strikingly, it was a garrison OMLT. That is, this unit was training Afghans on how to protect a headquarters or strong point rather than going out into battle with an Afghan battalion. The decision to change the position on OMLTs from having none to providing the garrison OMLT was clearly made by Defense Minister Gade.[88] It was explained that the decision was due to the shortage of kandaks in Helmand—that the Americans and Brits were taking all of the available units.[89] That seems somewhat hard to believe, as there was significant emphasis within ISAF to create more kandaks. Overall, then, the Danes were prohibited from mentoring Afghan troops in all but very controlled circumstances.

The second significant restriction was that the Danes were limited to having 750 troops involved in ISAF; this was a key part of the parliamentary mandate authorizing the effort. It was a relatively hard cap, limiting Denmark's ability to

---

84 Stated by Colonel Lars Møller, who would be on the end of the phone as Defense Command's assistant chief of staff for international operations, roundtable at Ministry of Defence, Copenhagen, August 25, 2010.

85 Interview with U.S. Navy captain Christopher McDonald, U.S. defense attaché, Copenhagen, August 23, 2010.

86 Interview with Peter Dahl Thruelsen, research fellow, Royal Danish Defence College, faculty in strategy and military operations, Institute for Strategy, Copenhagen, August 24, 2010.

87 Ibid. Thruelsen suggests that some of the OMLT reluctance was because Danish authorities were worried as to how to rescue Danes if they are deployed in a kandak that was distant from the main Danish force.

88 Stated by department head, roundtable at Ministry of Defense, Copenhagen, August 25, 2010.

89 Roundtable at Ministry of Defense, Copenhagen, August 25, 2010.

reinforce significantly its effort. This was not an unreasonable constraint given that Denmark has a small army, limiting how many troops can be deployed. Indeed, the garrison OMLT discussed above finessed the stress on the army by relying on Danish air force and navy personnel to fill out the ranks. The upshot was that the parliament, especially the less enthusiastic members of the group of parties supporting the mission, could feel that it imposed meaningful restraint while the reality was that the Danish army could not really do that much more.[90]

The Danes faced one more restriction. They were obligated to engage in self-defense. This may sound self-evident for a military force. The difference for the Danes was that Danish troops were required by royal decree to contradict NATO orders if necessary in order to defend themselves. This was an enduring lesson learned from World War II, when there was some confusion about how to respond to the German invasion.[91] Such an order might be problematic if it contradicted ISAF emphasis on protecting civilians even when that meant withholding fire in threatening situations where inaction might increase the risks facing Danish soldiers.

Denmark used the division of ISAF territories by areas of responsibility (i.e., regional commands and PRTs) as a key geographic caveat without having to formally specify it. By having control over their own sector, Danish forces controlled what they would do without having to say no to NATO commanders. They saw formal caveats as less necessary in such circumstances.[92] Indeed, as we shall see below, the Danes seemed to prefer not to provide their commanders with written instructions but instead relied on general guidance. Consequently, Danish commanders did not play the red card very frequently. They were instructed to cooperate with NATO commanders unless they were asked to do something that was illegal, inconsistent with the mission, or beyond their capabilities. In one notable incident, Canadian brigadier general David Fraser, commander of RC-South during Operation Medusa in 2006, ordered a Danish reconnaissance unit to enter the battle. The commander of that unit had to educate Fraser about the limits of their equipment and of this unit, essentially saying no. Fraser ultimately did not press the issue, so the Danish red card was not forcefully played.[93] Still, the Danish commander had the ability to say yes or no to the NATO commander without having to call home. For commanders of international missions, the Danes have this reputation: "For you, orders are orders."[94]

---

90 Interview with Jakobsen, August 26, 2010.
91 Colonel Lars Møller, assistant chief of staff for operations, Defense Command, roundtable with Ministry of Defense officials, Copenhagen, August 25, 2010.
92 Participants in roundtable at the Centre for Military Studies, University of Copenhagen, August 26, 2010, including Lars Bangert Struwe, Kristian Søby Kristensen, Henrik Breitenbauch, Esben Salling Larsen, and Mikkel Vedby Rasmussen.
93 Information on Fraser cited by Colonel Lars R. Møller, roundtable with Ministry of Defense officials, Copenhagen, August 25, 2010.
94 General Maurice Rose, the United Nations Protection Force, quoted by Colonel Lars Møller, roundtable with Ministry of Defense officials, Copenhagen, August 25, 2010.

In sum, the Danish military had significant amounts of discretion, with few caveats and rules of engagement that largely matched NATO's. Commanders were given significant leeway. Indeed, Danish commanders met with the senior decision makers (the minister of defense, the chief of defense, and so on) as they prepared to lead a mission to get unwritten instructions as they do not receive written ones, fitting the tradition of the Danish military.

## DANISH AGENT SELECTION

Agent selection was not emphasized by the Danes, and this is typical behavior for a coalition government. The selection of each military commander was an intra-military affair. The chief of the army chose officers seen as potential stars rather than how compliant they might be toward the governing coalition's policy preferences.[95] The Army Operations Command then chose which officers were sent to command units in the field. We found no evidence that civilian officials closely monitored or tried to influence the selection of commanders.

## DANISH OVERSIGHT

We would expect oversight to be a tool used by coalition governments. A clear distinction between the Danes and the other coalition governments, however, was that oversight by the Danish parliament or by the top of the military chain was simply not intense. In none of the interviews did we find much attention paid by the participants or the analysts toward how troops were monitored. The people responsible for operations within the military received the usual reports and briefed the people up the chain of command, but there was no sense that senior-level visits were very frequent. It was clear that there were no procedures for monitoring via regular phone calls.[96] Admittedly, it is hard to be certain about oversight since it was largely absent in our conversations. On this front, Denmark is quite different from either Germany or the Netherlands.

## DANISH INCENTIVES

How does the concern for career advancement influence Danish officers? The only tale of punishment for "bad behavior" in this case focused on an officer speaking out rather than behaving inappropriately in the field. Lars Møller, who had been a hero during the United Nations Protection Force effort in Bosnia for using force against the Serbs, was demoted temporarily when he criticized the government

---

95 Interview with Thruelsen, August 24, 2010.
96 Roundtable at the Centre for Military Studies, University of Copenhagen, August 26, 2010.

for not spending enough money on the military. His career eventually bounced back and he became the assistant chief for operations.[97] Otherwise, the officers who have served in Afghanistan and other deployments have advanced in seniority as one might expect in any other country.

In sum, the Danes maintained the most flexible contingent of all the coalition governments deploying troops to Afghanistan. Danish commanders faced few restrictions and relatively modest oversight when compared to their German and Dutch neighbors. Because of a relatively ideologically coherent coalition, Danish leaders faced fewer political restraints themselves. The opposition was implicated in the effort, demanding only that which the government did not mind doing. As a result, the desire to gain consensus from opposition parties did not mean that the government had to make significant compromises.[98] Instead, the focus clearly was on trying to make an impact on the ground and in the alliance rather than fearing what could go wrong.

## Comparisons

What distinguishes these three cases? First, we consider two factors drawn from chapter 3 that might differentiate coalition governments: the number of parties involved and the ideological spread of the coalition. These cases suggest that the number of parties did not seem to matter. The governments reviewed here had similar numbers of parties in decision-making processes. Each tended to have three parties in their coalition formally or informally (including supporting parties that did not have positions in the cabinet) during the relevant time frame, although Germany had only two parties in power (the Social Democrats and the Greens) until 2005.

Ideological spread seemed to make a significant difference. The contrast among the narrow Danish government, the broad German coalition, and the shifting Dutch cabinet is suggestive. The Danes have always had narrow cabinets, requiring only the right-wing populist, xenophobic Danish People's Party for support outside the cabinet. The Dutch government has required broader, less stable coalitions that have shifted over time. In the case of Germany, we not only find that the coalition of right (CDU/CSU) and left (SPD) imposed significant restrictions upon German forces but that German commanders more recently have greater discretion with a new coalition of right and center (FDP) parties. Broader and less stable coalitions require greater compromises, which are associated with more conditions placed on the deployment and more caveats for the troops. Broader and less stable coalitions also seem to use oversight as a tool more frequently. The constant VTCs home to The Hague are an example. None of the coalition

---

97 This was relayed to us in the interview with Jakobsen, August 26, 2010.
98 The need for consensus was not that compelling in Denmark, as the government went ahead with the Iraq deployment without the support of the opposition parties.

governments utilized agent selection or the tailored use of incentives, consistent with the expectations set forth in chapter 3.

In all three cases there was an avowed need for a broad consensus, both to demonstrate to the troops that they have support at home and to implicate all parliamentary parties, reducing the ability for any to play politics with the mission. The Dutch struggled to gain consensus, leading to repeated drawn-out processes and ultimately a collapsed government. To gain consensus, conditions were attached to the mission. The German government also sought broad consensus and gained it, in part, by putting broad conditions on the troops. The Danes stand out because consensus was not as problematic. The opposition had a greater need to demonstrate its international credentials and thus only demanded modest conditions.

A key difference between the Danes and Dutch should be addressed. In both cases, center-right coalitions could have used the support of a xenophobic party that was farther to the right. In the Danish case, the Danish People's Party supported the mission in Afghanistan as a part of fighting terrorism and confronting Islamist movements, despite an isolationist bent in its previous stances. In the Dutch case, the Party for Freedom opposed the mission and prioritized problems at home. That lack of support meant that the Dutch government was more fragile, depending on parties that were more distant ideologically. This comparison not only identifies a key difference between the stable and forward-leaning Danish positions and the fragile and more risk-averse Dutch stances but also that xenophobia is more complex than often averred (Saideman and Ayres 2008). In its European form, xenophobic nationalism can contain both isolationist and anti-Muslim strands with different implications for foreign policy.

# Considering the Other Coalition Governments in ISAF

The remainder of this chapter compares the three key cases with brief reviews of the remaining major ISAF participants also governed by coalitions: Belgium, Italy, and Norway. To preview, we generally see restricted forces serving in the less dangerous parts of Afghanistan—Regional Commands Kabul, North, and West; and we see coalition politics influencing delegation decisions across the board.

## BELGIUM

Belgium deployed to Afghanistan in early 2003 without public debate.[99] Its initial mission was to provide force protection at the Kabul International Airport. In the late summer of 2003, Belgium formed a PRT in Kunduz with the Germans,

---

99 This section draws heavily on interviews with three contingent commanders who asked not to be identified.

refusing to take on missions that risked casualties or put troops in harm's way. Belgian troops were subject to significant caveats: PRT staff were prohibited from leaving RC-North without express permission from the MOD, from working with American troops on OEF operations unless the mission was explicitly approved by the German RC-North commander as a joint ISAF-OEF operation, and from engaging in offensive operations. The Kabul Airport contingent was limited to a perimeter security mission at the airport facility, though they eventually were allowed to travel up to twelve kilometers if necessitated by a search-and-rescue operation for a downed aircraft.

The government coalition rejected repeated requests by the Belgian military's land component commanders in 2004–5 to deploy in larger numbers and with the authority to engage in offensive operations. At the same time, the air force wanted in on the NATO operation, both for the experience and to justify its share of an increasingly constrained Belgian defense budget. The government sided with the air force and sent four F-16s in 2005 to operate out of Kabul for six months, and then again for a year in 2007. From the government's perspective, the F-16 deployment demonstrated an increased commitment to ISAF while being relatively risk free compared to a larger ground contingent or offensive ground operations, to say nothing of operating with U.S. forces in the south or east. It also balanced Belgian service contributions to ISAF.

Belgian operations increased in size and risk in late 2008. They sent four F-16s to Kandahar in September 2008 as part of Operation Guardian Falcon, a deployment that lasted into late 2010. They also decided in September to create an OMLT in RC-North in addition to the ongoing PRT in Kunduz. The OMLT started operations in early 2009. Both deployments demonstrated an increased willingness to accept risk, but both deployments retained caveats. The F-16s could only support ISAF operations, not OEF operations. The OMLT faced identical constraints as did the Kunduz PRT, with a particular prohibition against participating in OEF operations. The problem with the OMLT restriction was that it had the potential to break the trust between the Belgian mentors and their Afghan kandak. As occurred more than once, the Belgian commanders were forced to choose between disobeying orders from home and keeping faith with their Afghan unit when that unit was engaged in joint Afghan-U.S. operations in the north. Belgian commanders participated when they felt able to *avoid oversight*. Other times they succeeded in getting the Germans to label the operation an ISAF mission, which circumvented the prohibition. Regardless, this was not an ideal procedure.

To explain this behavior, consider that Belgium has a parliamentary system that routinely returns coalition governments. Government decisions are made by the prime minster and the fourteen-person Ministerial Council. The key players on national security are the prime minister and the defense minister, with the foreign minister and the minister for cooperation and development having lesser roles. The chief of defense has no real decisional authority when it comes to military deployments other than as an adviser to the defense minister. The lower house of parliament, called the Chamber of Representatives, is relatively powerless on national security questions. Its sole authority stems from its ability to approve or reject the government's annual policy statement and to call for new elections in the absence of parliamentary confidence in the government. Neither situation held for the Belgian contribution to the ISAF mission.

From 1999 through late 2007, Prime Minister Guy Verhostadt from the Flemish Liberals and Democrats party led the Belgian government. Verhostadt led a left-leaning coalition of Socialist, Liberal, and Green Party members. His defense minister, Andre Flahaut, was a Socialist Party member. Consistent with our discussion in chapter 3, Belgian government policy at the time was to avoid military conflicts unless Belgian participation was authorized by the UN Security Council and posed few risks of combat or casualties. That led Belgium to join the French and Germans in vocally opposing the Iraq War in 2003. It also led the country to take a very cautious approach to Afghanistan. The airport security detail, the Kunduz PRT, and the Kabul F-16s were all relatively low-risk deployments, and all were heavily laden with caveats.

Belgium held elections in 2007 that would eventually move the government toward the right on the political spectrum after months of uncertainty and a short-term caretaker government. Pieter De Crem, a member of the Christen-Democratisch en Vlaams (CDV), or Christian Democrats and Flemish party, took over as defense minister on December 21, 2007, as part of that caretaker government. He would stay in that role under the new government of Prime Minister Yves Leterme, also of the CDV, when it took power on March 20, 2008. The CDV and the New Flemish Alliance, representing a more conservative government than Verhostadt's, led the new coalition. Defense Minister De Crem, in particular, was much more pro-NATO and pro–United States than was his predecessor, and believed that Belgium needed to demonstrate its commitment to NATO in a more visible manner. The F-16 deployment in Kandahar and the OMLT were both visible symbols of that commitment. At the same time, the Leterme government was a center-right coalition and could only be expected to move so far. Their policies would continue through January 2010, the end of our study period, despite significant political uncertainty during most of 2009 and into 2010.[100]

In sum, Belgium played a pretty consistent role in Afghanistan, with its forces largely based at the Kabul Airport until 2007. With a change of government and a

---

100 The Leterme government would fall in December 2008, replaced by a caretaker government led by Herman Van Rompuy until November 2009, when Leterme would again become prime minister. De Crem would remain defense minister throughout this uncertain period, providing policy consistency.

shift in the governing coalition's ideological stance to the right, the country subsequently deployed an OMLT to Kunduz and F-16s to Kandahar Airfield. Despite that, Belgium only engaged in ISAF operations and did not work with OEF forces. Overall, Belgian forces still faced significant caveats even after the 2007 election, as we would expect from a coalition government.

## ITALY

Italy has been among the largest providers of troops as the lead nation in RC-West and previously in a rotational command of RC-Kabul. Germany's caveats were more publicly infamous than were Italy's, but the Italians did not have appreciably more flexibility. Italy was responsible for the less accessible RC-West region, so there was much less international attention on its performance. At the same time, oversight appeared to be fairly robust. For instance, we were struck by the fact that the Italian defense attaché in Ottawa (a brigadier general) had to call back to Italy to gain permission to talk to us, which he did not get.

A parliamentary mandate limited Italy from sending troops to southern Afghanistan unless it was an emergency. Like Germany, Italy only deployed a handful of helicopters despite being the lead nation for an entire regional command. Moreover, the Italians apparently did not let Afghans fly on their helicopters, even if the Afghans in question were wounded army or police.[101] The Italian contingent was not allowed to conduct offensive operations on its own, but could apparently do so in support of Afghan units (Hale 2009).

Italian politics is a story of multiparty coalitions. The government has shifted from a center-right coalition with many parties from 2001 to 2006 to a center-left coalition with many parties between 2006 and 2008, and then a return to a center-right coalition in 2008. There was significant international concern in 2006 that the new, more left-wing government would lead to significant Italian foreign policy shifts (Davidson 2006). While the far left parties in the coalition opposed the ISAF mission, Prime Minister Romano Prodi was able to keep them on board by attaching support for the mission to a confidence vote. All this meant that the governing coalition wanted to stay in power more than it disliked the ISAF mission. The resulting environment was not conducive to reducing the restrictions placed upon the Italian forces by the previous government.

When Silvio Berlusconi came back into power in 2008, he did not have to worry as much about pacifist parties in his coalition. He asserted that Italian troops were more flexible. Italian leaders claimed to have changed the process by which a deployment outside RC-West could occur, reducing the turnaround

---

101 Reported by American officers who served in Afghanistan; interiews, Brussels, 2007, and Washington, D.C., January 2009.

time for permission from seventy-two to six hours.[102] The fact that Italy never sent significant troops to RC-South suggests the change in this caveat was symbolic. Moreover, leading a coalition of many parties meant the government remained constrained. When Italy agreed to deploy more than a thousand additional soldiers as part of the surge in early 2010, Minister of Defense Ignazio La Russa had to assert that the rules of engagement were not changing.[103]

## NORWAY

The Norwegian case reminds us that it is not only the ideological distance between coalition partners but also where they are on the left-right spectrum that is of importance.[104] The center-right minority government in Norway from 2001 to 2005 was less restrictive than the left-wing coalition that came after 2005. The 2005 government included in its coalition agreement language about both strengthening the country's participation in ISAF and not participating in OEF (Trønnes 2012). This should not be surprising since the new government included a party built on being anti-NATO and anti–United States: the Sosialistisk Venstreparti (SV), or Socialist Left Party. As the spokesman for this party commented in 2005, "If ISAF and OEF are combined or coordinated closer, or if the ISAF-forces change characteristics when they are expanding their area of responsibility southward, the Norwegian contribution will have to be reevaluated. The conclusion might be that SV will demand a full withdrawal."[105] Indeed, this party seemed to be at the heart of several Norwegian refusals to send troops to southern Afghanistan. Thus, there is a very clear connection between coalition politics and caveats in Norway.

Norway has been involved in many efforts in Afghanistan, including special operations units, quick reaction forces, a PRT, and mentoring, varying over time both in where they operated and how restricted they were. Initially, Norway's special operations units and F-16s could work with Operation Enduring Freedom with only modest differences in rules of engagement. This changed at approximately the same time that a new, more left-leaning government came into power in 2005.[106] As OEF transitioned to ISAF, the Norwegians prohibited their

---

102 "La Russa: 'Afghanistan combattiamo da un anno ma Prodi ha taciuto'" [La Russa: "Afghanistan Fighting For a Year but Prodi Has Remained Silent"] *Il Giornale*, http://www.ilgiornale.it/esteri/la_russa _afghanistan_combattiamo_anno_ma_prodi_ha_taciuto/01-07-2008/articolo-id=273064-page=0 -comments=1, accessed March 1, 2011.

103 "In Afghanistan altri mille soldati italiani Frattini: 'Ritiro truppe non oltre il 2013'" [Another Thousand Italian Soldiers in Afghanistan, Frattini: "Troop withdrawal no later than 2013"], *Corriere Della Sera*, December 3, 2009, http://www.corriere.it/politica/09_dicembre_03/afghanistan-invio-mille-soldati -larussa_a5592412-e037-11de-9712-00144f02aabc.shtml, accessed March 2, 2011.

104 This section relies heavily on the work of Otto Trønnes (2012), a Norwegian officer who had experience in Afghanistan and wrote a thesis about Norway's caveats in Afghanistan.

105 Reported in "Kan kreve norske styrker ut av ISAF" [May Require Norwegian Troops from ISAF], *Klassekampen*, September 26, 2005; translated by Otto Trønnes.

106 We must note that the changes in caveats became effective when the mandates for the previous missions had ended; the new government did not impose new restrictions during the middle of a rotation.

troops from supporting OEF with two key exceptions: in emergencies and the American-led ANA training effort.[107] Consequently, the F-16s sent in 2006 could only help out OEF units if they were at risk. Preplanned operations with OEF were no longer permitted (Strøm-Erichsen 2005). And even the F-16 exception was assisted by a traumatic event: American planes coming to the aid of the Norwegian PRT, helping prevent it from being overrun.

Geographic caveats became significant over time. At first, Norwegian special operations forces (SOF) could operate throughout Afghanistan, including in Helmand and Kandahar Provinces. This changed in 2006, when the new SOF mission to Kabul was clearly restricted to that area except in an emergency.[108] The team on the ground violated the letter of the caveats but perhaps not the spirit, as they were chasing down a network based near but not in Kabul. The officer in charge, Colonel Torgeir Gråtrud, asked for and received permission from the chief of defense and the operational headquarters.[109] Geographic restrictions prevented Norway from helping out its allies in the south, even to replace (i.e., backfill) Canadians at their bases so that they could be sent into battle during Operation Medusa.[110] After the Riga Summit, the Norwegian government promised to remove these restrictions, but they remained in place. To be clear, the Norwegians did on occasion operate in RC-West because their PRT was very close to a troublesome district in the neighboring area of operations. Eventually, this district was added to Faryab Province and into RC-North.[111] There is some confusion about the restrictions on the OMLTs. It appears to be the case that the Norwegians could accompany the units they mentored.

The PRT faced a significant restriction—the military was not to do any reconstruction or development. That was seen as a purely civilian task, but a problematic restriction given how little civilian capacity existed at this PRT until late in the mission. The commanding officer, Lieutenant Colonel Espen Arntzen, got into trouble in 2008 when he gave money for food distribution during a particularly nasty winter. The minister of defense, Anne-Grete Strøm-Erichsen, supported the minister of foreign affairs, who had criticized Arntzen. However, Arntzen was not

---

107 Like other countries, Norway did not consider the U.S.-led training mission out of bounds even though it was technically under OEF.

108 This was reinforced during the 2008 debate about sending the SOF back to Kabul, with the process clarifying that the chief of defense could allow the unit to respond to events, but would have to notify the MOD immediately (Trønnes 2012).

109 Berg Sveinung Bentzrød, "Go Back to Afghanistan," *Aftenposten*, November 8, 2007, http://www.aftenposten.no/nyheter/iriks/article2090464.ece, accessed February 25, 2011.

110 Otto Trønnes, personal experience, communicated via e-mail. Norway did send a medical team to serve at the Kandahar Airfield.

111 The Germans did not recognize this change (interview with senior officer at Joint Forces Command, Brunssum, January 28, 2011), and so the commander of RC-North strongly preferred that the Norwegians not go to Ghorwmach, even to help Americans and Afghans who were being ambushed, for fear that the Germans might have to leave RC-North to help the Norwegians rescuing the others (Trønnes 2012).

reprimanded, as the military thought it was permissible to overstep if lives were at risk (Trønnes 2012). One of the interesting things about the Norwegian rules is that the military was limited with regard to where to operate and they could not do civilian tasks, but they were able to engage in offensive operations.

## Summary

These cases support our expectations as expressed in chapter 3. Coalition governments differ from single-party parliamentary governments and presidential systems. The ideological dispersion within governing coalitions matters. Broad coalitions at home meant less discretion in the field for Belgian, German, and Dutch forces. The same has largely been true for center-left coalitions, reminding us that party preferences matter (Rathbun 2004). We see the greatest discretion when center-right coalitions govern, and when coalitions are relatively stable over time (as in Denmark). At the same time, most of these governments utilized relatively intense oversight, with frequent reporting, VTCs, and phone calls home. Coalition governments did not utilize agent selection or inducements to any appreciable degree. Both of these latter behaviors require a significant degree of consensus within the governing coalition, much higher than that needed for crafting the initial contingent delegation contract. Both also are labor intensive and require some measure of expertise among the civilian leaders.

Table 6.1 summarizes our findings on coalition governments. Overall, we find that coalition governments follow the patterns we predicted. In general, they

**Table 6.1.** Coalition Governments and Discretion

| Coalition Government | Coalition Type | Number of Parties | Pattern of Discretion |
|---|---|---|---|
| Belgium, 2001–7 | Center-Left | 5–6 | Tight |
| Belgium, 2008–10 | Center-Right | caretaker | Less Tight |
| Denmark | Center-Right | 3 | Loose |
| Germany, 2002–5 | Left | 2 | Tight |
| Germany, 2005–9 | Grand | 3 | Tight |
| Germany, 2009– | Center-Right | 3 | Tight |
| Italy, 2001–8 | Center-Right | 5 | Tight |
| Italy, 2006–8 | Center-Left | 5+ | Tight |
| Italy, 2008– | Center-Right | 3 | Tight |
| Netherlands | Grand | 3 | Medium |
| Norway, 2000-2005 | Center-Right | 3 | Loose |
| Norway, 2005- | Center-Left | 3 | Medium |

significantly restrict discretion on the ground. Restrictions tend to be tightest when countries are governed by grand coalitions, which are far more likely to have policy disagreements, and loosest when center-right coalitions govern. We see the most significant shifts when the composition of coalitions change, rather than when individual leaders change.

# 7  Does Membership Matter?

*Examining the Outsiders:*
*Australia and New Zealand*

Thus far we have only considered countries that are members of NATO. In this chapter we develop the implications of the alliance discussion in chapter 2 for nonmembers. We hope to discern whether and how NATO membership makes a difference. How do these outsiders manage their militaries when those militaries are in a command structure run by an organization to which they do not belong? Does alliance membership matter that much, or do the domestic dynamics of these partner states matter more than the international institution's imperatives? To preview our answer, we find that domestic institutions and individual inclinations matter more than international structures for nonmembers, just as they do for NATO members. Still, outsider status poses both constraints and opportunities, which we address below.

We consider the behavior and dynamics of Australia and New Zealand, two countries that are outside of NATO but have played significant roles in Afghanistan. Studying these two cases of parliamentary outsiders allows us to gain additional perspective via comparisons with the cases addressed in chapters 5 and 6.[1] We consider Australia and New Zealand in turn, focusing on each country's efforts in Afghanistan and how they were managed from Canberra and Wellington, respectively. We find that Australia managed to finesse a tough problem—how to maintain its reputation as a capable, flexible force and a good ally of the United States while minimizing casualties. New Zealand focused less on restricted discretion and more on using limited capabilities to control its deployed forces.

In chapter 2 we developed several different models of principal-agent (PA) relations to depict possible configurations of states during multilateral interventions. We argued that the hybrid PA model best describes the situation NATO members face during alliance interventions. Every NATO contingent faces two principals: a single principal in the form of its national command authority and a collective

---

1 We also examined Sweden, and found it quite similar to the coalition governments discussed in chapter 6. We omit discussion of this case for the sake of brevity.

principal in the form of the North Atlantic Council (NAC). Partners, such as the countries discussed here, do not have seats at the NAC or in the Military Committee (MC), although arrangements have been made to give them some voice but not a vote. So from a non–NATO member perspective, with no formal vote in alliance decisions, the NAC appears as a single decision maker. Consequently, military commanders from partner nations face a multiple principal, not a hybrid principal, situation. One principal is the national chain of command. The other is the NATO chain of command.

For nonmembers' deployed commanders, the national chain is far more powerful and influential than is the NATO chain. Who gets heard by nonmember military contingents is heavily influenced by that fact. In theory, having two masters can be quite complicated in the principal-agent literature, as agents can receive conflicting orders from each principal or try to play principals against each other. In the reality of NATO in Afghanistan, matters were far simpler for nonmember militaries because one principal, NATO, had much, much less power and authority than did the national chain of command.

We argued and found that in the hybrid situation, domestic dynamics of each member trumped the collective principal of NATO. This is even truer for partner states, since partners have few *direct* incentives to acquiesce to NATO decisions.[2] NATO members can worry about how today's actions affect tomorrow's standing within NATO structures, including the allocation of command billets (so-called flags to post) and other visible positions, such as secretary general and chair of the MC. For partners, these issues are entirely irrelevant; they can take or leave the orders they receive from the NATO chain of command. Thus, while we address some of the dynamics that apply differently to partners, the key processes driving outcomes are similar to those discussed in earlier chapters. In institutions and behavior, Australia and New Zealand are comparable to Canada and the United Kingdom.

## Understanding Australia's Deceptively Limited Effort

Australia is a bit of a puzzle.[3] It combined a history of and reputation for assertive war fighting with a mix of choices that significantly constrained efforts in Afghanistan. Australia has been amazing in its ability to project itself as engaged in a very assertive operation despite having placed significant restrictions

---

2 Partner states might listen to and be led by individual NATO members, particularly powerful members such as the United States, but that is more about bilateral relations and less about multilateral interventions per se.

3 This section is based largely on interviews with active and retired military officers, members of the Australian parliament, experts, and government officials in Canberra and Sydney in March 2010.

on its contingent. In the words of a senior Australian officer, "We are making a significant contribution. While Australia does not lead or control operations in Afghanistan, we are contributing capabilities that are important to the coalition."[4] A senior NATO military officer indicated at one time that caveats would not be so much of a problem in Afghanistan if NATO could just have more Australians, British, Canadians, and Americans and more helicopters to fly them around the country. This suggests that the Australians are just as flexible as their other English-speaking NATO counterparts. However, an Australian expert disparagingly referred to his country's effort as "the New French"[5] (which is, as we saw in chapter 4, a bit unfair since the French engaged in some of the tougher fighting once Nicolas Sarkozy became president). We subject Australia to the same analysis as the other countries in this study. We review who had authority to make decisions within Australia, their preferences, and then what the Australians did and did not do in Afghanistan. We focus attention on contingent delegation, patterns of oversight, and patterns of promotion that sent signals to commanders on the ground. We conclude our review of Australia by addressing how nonmembership in NATO has mattered to the country's behavior.

## CONCENTRATED AUTHORITY AND A BEHAVIORAL FOCUS

Australia, due to its British inheritance and approach to international relations, has developed institutions and capabilities akin to Canada's. The two countries' chains of command are nearly identical. Australian commanders on the ground reported to a one-star officer in Kabul and a two-star officer in the region, but were ultimately under the the commander of Joint Operations Command (CJOC), the Australian version of a combatant command. This was a relatively new position developed while troops were deployed in Afghanistan to centralize control of these and other overseas operations. The CJOC reported directly to the chief of the Defence Force (CDF), and was responsible for providing a joint effort via control of air, naval, and ground forces. Either the governor general or the queen is technically the head of state and commander in chief of the armed forces, but in practice the prime minister and the defense minister make the major decisions on the conduct of foreign and defense policy.

Prime Ministers John Howard and Kevin Rudd, and Minister of Defence John Faulkner and his predecessors, did not delegate authority to craft the civil-military

---

4 Lieutenant General Mark Evans, chief of Joint Operations Command, speaking at the International Conference on the Afghanistan Conflict and Australia's Role, Australia National University, October 22–23, 2009.

5 Clive Williams, "Showing Leadership in Afghanistan," *Australia Broadcasting Company*, March 10, 2010, http://www.abc.net.au/unleashed/stories/s2840440.htm, accessed March 30, 2010.

delegation contract to Chief of the Defence Force Angus Houston.[6] Interviews largely pointed to the level above Houston as the relevant locus of decision making for Australian defense policy. Though it is often hard to tell whether a senior military officer was anticipating what civilian leaders want, it was clear in this case that the behavior displayed by the Australian military in Afghanistan was dictated from on high.

Australia underwent a significant political shift during the Afghanistan conflict. It moved from a coalition of center-right parties (the Liberal and National Parties) to a majority center-left party (the Labour Party). Our theory would suggest that the earlier coalition government would have caveats due to the complexities of sharing control, while the newer Labour government would have felt less restrained. In reality, the Liberal-National coalition was not a product of post-election bargaining but a relatively permanent preelectoral coalition, acting more like a single-party than a coalition government. Moreover, as in Canada, the political shift to the left under the Labour Party did not signal a major change in the effort in Afghanistan, as the two major parties in Australia did not differ much on the mission. The pattern of restricted behavior owed more to the focus of both Prime Ministers Howard (Liberal) and Rudd (Labour) on the United States.[7] That is, both leaders viewed the mission as meeting a bilateral alliance commitment with the United States, so each was sensitive to U.S. interests while otherwise minimizing the domestic costs for the mission.

In every interview we conducted in Canberra and Sydney, fighting beside the United States was seen as crucially important. Australia has a vital security relationship with the United States, formalized by the ANZUS (Australia–New Zealand–United States) Treaty. Prime Minister John Howard invoked the ANZUS Treaty after 9/11, and Australia was one of the first countries to deploy troops into Afghanistan. But insiders consistently averred that Afghanistan itself was not worth expending too much blood or treasure on.[8] What mattered was the U.S.-Australian alliance, both for the history it represented and for the important role the United States could play in countering future threats to Australia from China, instability in Indonesia, and other potential challenges closer to home.

Besides alliance maintenance, the other clear concern to Australian politicians of both major policies was to limit risks. Casualty aversion was clearly a priority, exemplified by the lack of any Australians killed in action in Iraq. Despite affirmations of excellent training and equipment, this was clearly only partly about luck and skill and mostly about political instructions to the military. Although Chief of Defence Houston was reportedly cautious by nature, interviews consistently

---

6 This was reported widely, but most clearly by a senior advisor in the Department of the Prime Minister and Cabinet, March 2010.

7 Julia Gillard replaced Rudd as prime minister after the period covered in this study.

8 This was reported from both major parties in several interviews in Canberra.

reported that Howard and Rudd were more concerned with casualties than other dimensions of the deployment, and made that known to the military. In the parlance of chapter 2, interviews suggested that the Australian civilian leadership was strongly focused on behavior rather than on outcomes.

## Contingent Delegation

There was a distinct division of labor characterizing most of Australia's effort: the special operations forces (SOF) were responsible for nearly all of Australia's kinetic activity in Afghanistan, while the conventional forces were deployed in ways that minimized their exposure to risk. Once Australia partnered with the Netherlands in Uruzgan in 2006, it deployed a reinforced engineering unit, whose primary task was to build bridges, schools, and other infrastructure. As the limits of the Dutch became apparent (see chapter 6), Australia deployed an additional force—the Special Operations Task Group (SOTG)—to provide a force on the ground that could handle the violent side of the operation, such as patrolling, disrupting Taliban networks in the area, and so on. From that point on, there were two Australian forces deployed in Uruzgan: a SOF unit to do the fighting and another unit to do the noncombat mission of the day.

Australian SOF were among the first to enter Afghanistan after the Americans in the winter of 2001–2, and they provided the second largest SOF contingent after the Americans for much of the decade. The Special Air Service (SAS) and commandos had extensive training and excellent equipment, and were the product of a rigorous selection process. In addition, the SAS in particular had far more experience—from Iraq, East Timor, an earlier tour in Afghanistan, and elsewhere—than did Australia's conventional forces. Even when SOF were engaged in ordinary infantry work at times, they were seen as the better option for combat operations since they were far less likely to take casualties given their elite qualities, and developed a reputation for effectiveness. Indeed, one indicator of this respect is that the position of the International Security Assistance Force (ISAF) commander of SOF rotated between British and Australian general officers. The deployment of the SAS and commandos enhanced Australia's reputation for flexibility and forward-leaning operations.

The mission of the day for conventional forces was initially reconstruction. The conventional force was staffed and led by engineers, supplemented with some combat capability to provide security for the reconstruction effort, and called the Reconstruction Task Force.[9] In the middle of 2008, the emphasis shifted somewhat toward mentoring the Afghan National Army via observer, mentor, liaison

---

9 Interview with Colonel Stu Yearman, who commanded the Reconstruction Task Force in the first half of 2008, Canberra, March 11, 2010.

teams (OMLTs), so the conventional force was restructured and called the Mentoring and Reconstruction Task Force (MRTF). The SOTG and MRTF were commanded by different officers of equal rank (lieutenant colonel) who reported up the chain to a one-star officer in Kabul and a two-star officer for the Middle East. While the OMLTs working with the Afghan National Army (ANA) kandaks were engaged in combat and the MRTF included two combat teams that could engage in security operations, the bulk of the combat performed by Australians was still conducted by the SOTG. That is, the roughly three hundred special operations troops were doing much of the heavy lifting while the other twelve hundred Australians in Uruzgan were not as exposed to risk.[10]

To be clear, the move to mentoring increased the risks facing the conventional forces. As one Australian officer put it, this was the first serious combat conventional Australian forces faced since the Vietnam War.[11] Yet Australian decisions were focused on limiting the exposure of those conventional forces. The Australian OMLTs were significantly larger than those of other countries, as each OMLT carried more combat power via dedicated riflemen. This was to limit risk. Operations were kept to Uruzgan. In a series of interviews in Canberra, it became clear that commanders seeking to move outside of the province had to call home for permission. That call went through the chain of command from the field to Kabul to a Middle East command post to the CJOC to the CDF. This requirement applied to any forces seeking to operate outside of Uruzgan, be they engineers, special operators, or OMLTs.[12]

Consider the following example. During the fourth rotation of the Reconstruction Task Force from April to October 2008, ISAF needed bridges along Route 1 (the major road linking Kabul to Kandahar) to be repaired in and near Zabul.[13] Regional Command–South forces were asked to do the job since the bridges were at the intersection of RC-South and RC-East. The commander of RC-South asked the Dutch to do it, and in turn, the Dutch asked the Australians since the Australian armed engineering unit had the skills and combat power to do the job.

The Australians on the ground agreed to do the repairs, as it would give them a chance to make a difference, and they called home to ask for permission to perform the operation. The CJOC, Lieutenant General Mark Evans, went to the CDF, General Houston, who briefed Prime Minister Rudd. Rudd, Houston, and Evans

---

10 Interview with Raspar Khosa, research fellow at the Australian Strategic Policy Institute, Canberra, March 12, 2010.

11 Interview with senior officer, Canberra, March 10, 2010. This is a striking statement given the presence of conventional forces in Iraq in 2003 and again in 2004–5. The Iraqi deployment was notable for many reasons, including the fact that Australia lost no soldiers in combat.

12 Anthony Bubalo, "Obama's Surge: The United States, Australia, and the Second War for Afghanistan," Lowy Institute for International Policy Policy Brief, December 2009, 8.

13 This example was clearly delineated by Colonel Yearman.

agreed to permit the mission as long as the commander on the ground, Lieutenant Colonel Stu Yearman, was satisfied that there would be medical evacuation available in case of casualties. Yearman had to show to his superiors that helicopters would be ready in case something went wrong. This was a deal-breaker for Yearman's superiors. The engineering force was held in Kandahar for a day or two while awaiting final approval from Canberra. This episode illustrates that the unit could move outside of Uruzgan, but that it required clearance from the very highest levels.

More surprising, this geographic caveat also bound the Special Operations Task Group. In a conversation with a former commander of the SOTG, we learned that during his rotation, SOF were allowed to go out of Uruzgan about half the time they were asked to do so. Of course, with an Australian frequently serving as the commander of ISAF's special operations units, the SOTG was not often asked to do things it was not likely to receive permission to do. The Australian's restrictions unfortunately hampered ISAF effectiveness. There were several occasions when the SOTG commander wanted to go outside of Uruzgan but could not. Specifically, the Australians discovered that the Taliban leaders causing trouble in Uruzgan resided in Kandahar, but the Canadian and American special operators were otherwise engaged. Despite clear ties to the threat to security in Uruzgan, the Australian commander was denied by his superiors because of the increased risk of casualties inherent in the mission.[14]

More visibly and controversially, the Australian OMLTs were restricted to Uruzgan.[15] In our interviews it became clear that the idea of focusing on the ANA kandak in Uruzgan essentially restricted the Australian mentors to the province. During the first rotation of the Mentor Reconstruction Task Force (October 2008–June 2009), the OMLTs only left Uruzgan once, to go to Kandahar to resupply, and this effort required a couple weeks' notice to get authorization.[16] When asked if there was a procedure by which the Australian mentors could call home to ask for permission to accompany their kandak outside of Uruzgan, an Australian senior officer in the chain of command would not admit to the existence of such a procedure.[17]

This was a point of controversy, because each OMLT was a group of seventy or so Australians embedded in an Afghan kandak, and the ANA belongs to

---

14 The Australians deployed a small artillery unit to Helmand with the British and another to transport helicopters that moved around RC-South. These small units could cross provincial lines, but, not coincidentally, faced significantly lower risks of casualties.
15 Daniel Marston, who was a research fellow at the Strategic and Defence Studies Centre at Australia National University, said as much on ABC local radio on July 21, 2009. This was also reported in an interview with Senator Russell Trood, deputy chair of the Senate Standing Committee on Foreign Affairs, Defence and Trade, Canberra, March 10, 2010.
16 Interview with Colonel Shane Gabriel, commanding officer of MTRF 1, Canberra, March 9, 2010.
17 Interview with senior Australian officer, Canberra, March 2010.

Afghanistan. This seemingly obvious point means that if there was a need for the ANA to reinforce an operation outside of Uruzgan in nearby Helmand and Kandahar, it was quite possible that the kandak with whom the Australians were working might have been ordered to go. Restrictions on Australian forces could have resulted in either the brigade of Afghan soldiers in Uruzgan not being able to accommodate such a request or that they would have to go without their mentors. As we discussed in the case of the French in chapter 4, a kandak loses critical capabilities if its OMLT stays at home.[18]

Make no mistake, Australia was committed to Uruzgan, which is a far more dangerous place than many other provinces in Afghanistan. Any effort in RC-South was a significant commitment, and the Australian units operated throughout the province despite some significant dangers. Yet, the Australian forces on the ground were less willing to cross provincial boundaries than were the Canadians, British, or Danes.[19]

## Oversight

Australian commanders were subjected to a moderate amount of oversight. Lieutenant General Mark Evans, the CJOC, whose job it was to oversee Australian operations abroad, used a variety of means to oversee the mission in Uruzgan: occasional visits, a reporting system, various measures of performance, and phone calls.[20] Oversight did not seem particularly onerous, and none of the former commanders we interviewed felt that they had had somebody looking over their shoulder. The exception was in the case of casualties. Those officers selected for command were told informally that they were not to lose anyone.[21] When commanders took casualties, they were subjected to an onerous postincident investigation process. Investigators were even sent from Australia to Afghanistan in the event of soldiers' deaths (Palazzo 2008).

---

18 The week after our interviews in Canberra in March 2010, Minister of Defence John Faulkner made the following statement: "Most of the fighting our soldiers are involved in is in Oruzgan, where our primary base is located. Although concentrated on Oruzgan, elements of Australia's forces also participate in operations outside the province in response to operational requirements. In Operation MOSHTARAK, for example, Australian Defence Force personnel conducted operations in Kandahar Province to disrupt insurgent routes in Helmand, which will have a direct impact on security in Oruzgan." Nothing in this statement indicates that deployments no longer required a call home. Nor was it clear how often the answer coming back down the chain was a positive one. See Senator the Hon. John Faulkner Minister for Defense, "Ministerial Statement on Afghanistan," March 18, 2010, http://www.defence.gov.au/minister/93tpl.cfm?CurrentId=10055. Information also came from an e-mail conversation with a senior advisor in the Department of the Prime Minister and Cabinet, following up an interview held in mid-March 2010.

19 Australia, like most other countries operating in Afghanistan, did not restrict as significantly its air assets, especially transports that moved around the country.

20 Interview with Lieutenant General Mark Evans, chief of joint operations, Canberra, March 9, 2010.

21 This was reported in more than one of the interviews we conducted in Canberra in March 2010.

## Incentives

The Australians were more direct in their use of incentives, particularly in the signals sent by promotion boards. While operational experience was generally seen as a plus, it may have been outweighed in the Australian military by casualties borne during one's previous rotations.[22] That is, an officer with no operational experience may have had an advantage when it came time for promotion when compared to an officer who commanded an operation but lost soldiers during the mission. This sent a strong signal to commanders in the field that their career depended on avoiding casualties.

There was a consistent pattern shaping not just discretion but oversight and promotion: that avoiding casualties was of the highest priority, more so perhaps than success in Afghanistan. To be clear, the Australian effort has been significant, and its forces seemed to have tactical flexibility. They were not prevented from engaging in offensive operations or from working at night. So the concern with casualties was a restriction, but did not handcuff them so much that they could not be effective within Uruzgan. Instead, it increased the burden and operational tempo felt by Australia's special operations personnel.

## NATO MEMBERSHIP AS CONSTRAINT AND OPPORTUNITY

We chose to explore the Australian case because it was the largest non-NATO contingent operating in Afghanistan during our study period and could provide insight into whether NATO membership makes a difference for principal-agent contracts and resulting military behavior. The dynamics driving Australia's pattern of discretion and restrictions emanate from its chain of command and the interests of the prime minister and defense minister, and not from its non-NATO role. Instead, being outside NATO made for a mix of inconveniences and opportunities, but did not fundamentally affect Australia's principal-agent dynamics.

Working with NATO has posed challenges to Australia. Most notably, partner nations are "bastard children" in the NATO family.[23] To join the mission, the Australians had to be accredited by NATO; they had to pass NATO standards to be part of the mission, which was an embarrassing requirement. Australia had long practiced and developed high levels of interoperability with the United States, the United Kingdom, and Canada, and had developed a self-image as having one of the world's more effective fighting forces. To be placed in the

---

22 Interview with senior officer, Australia Defence Force, Canberra, March 2010.
23 Interview with senior Australian officer, Canberra, March 2010.

same category as Albania or Armenia was galling.[24] This was just the first taste of navigating the NATO bureaucracy. To manage the logistics in RC-South, the British had to act as a proxy for the Australians.[25] To get into a meeting of NATO defense ministers in Seville, Spain, in 2007, the Australian representative, Major General Vincent Williams, had to be smuggled in as part of the British delegation, as his Australian credentials were not sufficient for admission.[26] Even when admitted to alliance meetings, nonmembers were expected to be seen but not heard. French representatives have been known to ask why a nonmember was speaking at an alliance meeting. Perhaps the biggest problem was that Australia was a "strategy taker" rather than a "strategy maker."[27] As a nonmember, Australia did not have opportunities to shape ISAF plans. To be fair, most members beyond the Americans, British, French, and Canadians did not have much influence either.[28]

Lacking a voice in NATO affairs may have contributed to why Australia got involved in Uruzgan in the first place. As NATO spread from Kabul around the country, the Dutch agreed to be part of RC-South on the condition of having a good partner to share in Uruzgan. The Australians were working with the British on where they would be deployed, and Helmand Province appeared to be a likely candidate. Given the history of working with the British, exchange relationships, and consistent efforts to maintain interoperability, an Australian commitment to ISAF could reasonably be expected to be with the British. But with the Dutch deployment hinging on a reliable partner, Australia was slotted into Uruzgan.[29] Thus, intra-NATO dynamics to get the Dutch involved in the south resulted in the Australians working in a different sector than they had envisioned.

More positively, NATO eventually developed procedures to include nonmembers into decision-making procedures. Many "disconnections" reported early in the effort were worked out. Within RC-South, Australia developed significant influence as one of the major force contributors and was generally treated as an equal partner by the other nations operating in the command. Most important, nonmembership freed up Australian politicians to say no to alliance demands to do more. The clearest example of this revolved around the question of who would lead in Uruzgan after the Dutch withdrawal in 2010.

---

24 Interview with Major General Vincent Williams (Ret.), who served not only as Australia's defense adviser (attaché) to London, but also to NATO and to much of Europe at the time, Sydney, March 16, 2010.

25 Interview with senior Australian army officer, Canberra, March 2010.

26 Interview with Vincent Williams, March 16, 2010.

27 Interview with Raspar Khosa, March 12, 2010.

28 Interview with Ric Smith, Australia's special envoy to Afghanistan and Pakistan, Canberra, March 9, 2010. Steve Saideman witnessed this kind of process play out in 2002 when the five major contributors to the NATO missions in the Balkans met in Washington, D.C., to develop strategies and plans that would set the agenda for the rest of NATO.

29 Interview with Vincent Williams, March 16, 2010.

The Australians consistently refused to take the place of the Dutch. In a 2009 statement, Minister of Defence Faulkner said, "We have made it clear we cannot and will not lead in Oruzgan. At Bratislava, and in other international meetings before and since, I stressed that it is NATO's responsibility to resolve this issue as a priority."[30] Two arguments were used to justify this reluctance: that Australia lacked the capability to sustain such an effort and that NATO countries should lead NATO efforts. We briefly address both arguments here. In interviews with active military officers, we were told that Australia lacked sufficient "enablers" that would be required to run the NATO effort in Uruzgan—attack helicopters, intelligence assets, logistics, and the like. Perhaps the Australians could have led for one or two rotations, but they would not have been able to sustain the effort. In addition, Australia could not run a command headquarters in Afghanistan, as that would have exhausted its reserves dedicated to an emergency closer to home, either due to violence or calamity (a tsunami, for example).[31]

The first argument appeared like a rationalization to many. Retired Australian officers were confident in the abilities of the Australian Defence Force to lead in Uruzgan. Retired major general Jim Molan, who had commanded in Iraq, argued that the Australians should not only lead but more than double down by bringing six thousand troops to Uruzgan.[32] Other retired general officers agreed that Australia could have and probably should have taken the lead in Uruzgan and could have done so with a minor tweaking of the force mixture or a small reinforcement.[33] Given that the Dutch did not have to increase significantly their numbers when they took their turn in leading RC-South, and given that Australia had led missions closer to home with relatively small headquarters staff, these officers saw leading in Uruzgan as well within Australia's capabilities with one condition: the United States would have had to provide most, if not all, of the enablers that Australia lacked, but it was widely expected that the United States would do exactly that if Australia would take the lead.

The second argument for refusing to lead appeared to be at the heart of Australia's position. When asked if Australia could provide more, its representatives quickly noted that it was providing the largest non-NATO contingent to ISAF and that NATO leaders should ask members to step up before asking nonmembers. The argument was simply that Australia was not a NATO country, and it was

---

30 Ministerial Statement on Afghanistan, November 26, 2009, http://www.defence.gov.au/minister/92tpl .cfm?CurrentId=9761.
31 Interview with Lieutenant General Peter Leahy (Ret.), former chief of the Army, Canberra, March 8, 2010.
32 Molan repeated this recommendation in several places, including on the Lowy Institute's website. See Major General Jim Molan, "Afghanistan: The Case for 6000 Australian Troops," March 25, 2009, http:// www.lowyinterpreter.org/post/2009/03/25/Afghanistan-The-case-for-6000-Australian-troops.aspx, accessed April 24, 2013.
33 Interviews with retired officers in Canberra and Sydney, March 2010.

NATO's job to run the regional command since NATO had the lead in Afghanistan.[34] It is not entirely clear that there was a military logic to this argument, particularly as New Zealand and Sweden, non-NATO countries, ran provincial reconstruction teams (PRTs) and essentially served as lead nation for the provinces in which they were based. Instead, there was a political dynamic at work—that Australia should not be asked to fix NATO's problems. This was a consistent explanation for Australia's refusal to step in for the Dutch.[35] There could also have been a practical element: that non-NATO nations faced challenges operating in the alliance bureaucracy so that leading a province would have been too hard for them. A leading Australian defense expert, however, noted, "Neither of these problems is insurmountable."[36] In short, Australia did not want to lead because it was not a NATO member and did not *have* to lead.[37] The overall Australian pattern has been to help NATO where it can, but not to extend too much so that such actions would become politically risky at home. The key to all of this is a very risk-averse group of politicians in Canberra.

## SUMMARY

Our contention, then, is that NATO membership, or lack thereof, had little effect on Australian behavior except at the margins. Australian leaders were more concerned with walking the fine line between pleasing their important U.S. ally and minimizing military and political risks through contingent delegation, a moderate amount of oversight, and incentives to avoid casualties. On the one hand, Australia provided more troops than many NATO countries and allowed for relatively assertive SOF units. It was more willing to serve in one of the more dangerous parts of Afghanistan. Restrictions on its troops were much less obvious than those of Germany, Italy, or other countries, though restrictions still existed. It thus stood out as a forward-leaning country when compared to many in NATO. On the other hand, Australia's balancing act ruled out Australia itself taking a more visible leadership role in Uruzgan. To be asked to do more than many members of the alliance produced the natural and somewhat legitimate reply to look to the organization's membership first. In short, Australian behavior demonstrates yet again that a majority parliament political system allows the prime minister and minister of defense to set defense policy in response to domestic and international pressures.

---

34 This was mentioned by several people interviewed, including senior officers in the chain of command, Canberra, March 2010.
35 This was repeated in several interviews in Canberra in March 2010, and criticized by those outside of government.
36 Bubalo, "Obama's Surge," 7.
37 Interview with a senior member of the Department of the Prime Minister and Cabinet, Canberra, March 2010.

# Being Small: New Zealand's Experience in Afghanistan

On the surface, New Zealand would seem to be very similar to its Australian and Canadian cousins: a tradition of working with the British and Americans, similar institutions, few intrinsic interests in Afghanistan, a small but well-regarded special operations unit, and so on.[38] However, a few key differences stand out. New Zealand, unlike NATO and unlike Australia, did not invoke existing alliance commitments in the aftermath of 9/11. More important, two related aspects of the New Zealand deployment make caveats and other restrictions much less relevant: the size of the deployment and its location.

New Zealand's deployment to Afghanistan was much smaller than those of other English-speaking contributors. It committed 220 soldiers and no civilians during the period of our study. This troop size did much of the work that caveats did in other countries for reducing the risks of the mission, the discretion of the officers, and the political impact back home. So too did the location of much of New Zealand's commitment, as Bamyan, just to the west of Kabul, was a relatively unique part of Afghanistan, again reducing risks. So before we address how decisions are made in Wellington, New Zealand, we consider the location and size of the deployment.

## SMALL AND OUT OF THE WAY

The New Zealand contingent was the lead nation for the PRT in Bamyan, a small province in both size and population. Bamyan is a compact, remote, and high-elevation province, with a small population that is largely Hazara who have little sympathy for the Taliban. As a result, the New Zealanders were based in one of the quietest and safest locations in all of Afghanistan, even though the province is in the otherwise turbulent RC-East.[39]

New Zealand had around 140 officers and enlisted personnel in the PRT (with an additional 70- to 80-person SAS contingent). This small delegation meant that New Zealand could not be asked by ISAF to do too much. The New Zealanders actively patrolled the province and occasionally patrolled into Baghlan,

---

38 This section is based on interviews with members of Parliament, academics, and two roundtables, one with foreign affairs and New Zealand aid officials and the other with several highly placed colonels in the New Zealand Defense Force [NZDF], Wellington, March 17–19, 2010. The latter was most informative, and involved officers from Joint Operations, Strategic Commitments, International Defence Relations, and the chief of staff's office.

39 Indeed, it became one of the first to be transitioned from NATO to Afghan authorities in 2011. Neil Shea, "Afghanistan's Most Peaceful Province Is Now a Test Case for the Security Handoff." *Stars and Stripes,* September 18, 2011, http://www.stripes.com/news/afghanistan-s-most-peaceful-province-is-now-a-test-case-for-the-security-handoff-1.155476?localLinksEnabled=false, accessed September 20, 2011.

the neighboring province to the north where the Hungarians, burdened with caveats, had responsibility.[40] However, the New Zealanders could not do much more than patrols and run the PRT since they were essentially only one company of soldiers; anything larger required another force to do the work. Consequently, there were few opportunities, if any, for New Zealand to exercise caveats or play its red card since it simply was not asked to do any heavy lifting, such as participation in major combat operations in the province or beyond.[41] This is somewhat ironic given that New Zealand is the sole ISAF contributor that we have discovered thus far that explicitly discussed the red card procedure on its Internet site, noting, "Deployed personnel will only be employed in those locations and on those specific tasks and duties that have been agreed between the government and the international coalition. The SNO [senior national officer] would be authorised to *withhold the services of NZDF personnel if any task or proposed action is considered outside the scope of the PRT mandate, compromises New Zealand's national position, or may adversely affect New Zealand's national interests.*"[42] Again, these explicit procedures have largely been irrelevant since the New Zealand contingent was simply too small to be asked to do much.

However, there was another New Zealand contingent that had operational flexibility and got into harm's way. New Zealand had a small, seventy-person contingent of SOF on the ground in Afghanistan on and off since 2002. They were able to operate throughout Afghanistan, even beyond the reach of quick medical evacuation.[43] The New Zealand SOF were viewed as being quite flexible, but had to go back home to ask for permission on occasion. The chief of the defense force usually made such decisions, but some were made by the prime minister. The turnaround time for this process seemed to be much faster than for other countries—less than two hours.[44]

For most of its work, the New Zealand SAS in Afghanistan was largely invisible to politicians and the public back home, like special operators from other countries. This changed in January of 2010 after a Taliban assault in Kabul was repelled by the SAS and Afghan special forces, when a picture was taken of Willie Apiata, who had previously earned a Victoria's Cross for acts of bravery in 2004.[45] The publication of this picture in the *New York Times* revealed that the SAS was no

---

40 Interview with senior New Zealand army officer, Wellington, March 18, 2010.
41 This was the consensus of the senior military officers at the roundtable, Wellington, March 2010.
42 New Zealand Defence Force, "Afghanistan Deployment: Frequently Asked Questions," http://www.nzdf .mil.nz/operations/deployments/afghanistan/nz-prt/faq.htm, accessed May 12, 2010; emphasis added.
43 This was the consensus at NZDF roundtable, March 2010.
44 Again, the Colonels at the NZDF roundtable, March 2010, agreed that the decision process was quite quick.
45 This became a big story in the New Zealand newspapers. See, e.g., "Government to Reveal Details of SAS Deployments," *New Zealand Herald*, January 26, 2010, http://www.nzherald.co.nz/nz/news/article .cfm?c_id=1&objectid=10622392, accessed May 13, 2010.

longer used for disrupting terrorists and insurgents around the country,[46] but was working in and near Kabul to train Afghan special forces.[47] This happened again during the summer of 2011 when insurgents attacked the Intercontinental Hotel and photos of the SAS were published around the world.

The key here was that the combination of a flexible SAS and a limited (by size more than by caveats) conventional force paralleled the deployments of other countries, including Australia and France. This allowed New Zealand, like Australia, to be seen providing a meaningful contribution. In interviews, the SAS were seen as providing a "big strategic effect."[48] Yet this contribution was made with minimal risk. No New Zealanders were killed in Afghanistan until August 2010.

## EMPOWERED MINORITY AND COALITION GOVERNMENTS

The constant theme through the New Zealand interviews was the small size of the New Zealand population, its military, and its political class.[49] Officials in the Ministry of Defense numbered less than one hundred, and the total number of regulars in the New Zealand Defence Force was less than ten thousand. The army had nearly five thousand regular personnel, about one-fifth the size of Australia's army and one-fourth that of Canada's army. This clearly limited how large a force New Zealand could deploy and sustain. In theory, New Zealand could have deployed a larger force, but that force could not be sustained for the long term, nor could it be asked to go into harm's way frequently.

As in the other inheritors of British institutions, New Zealand has a governor general who is technically the commander in chief, but the prime minister makes all of the important decisions about the size, location, and duration of deployments and incorporates those decisions into the annual appropriations process. The chief of the defense force works with his staff to develop operational instructions to the commander on the ground. The joint forces commander, a position similar to that of the head of Canada's Expeditionary Forces Command and Australia's commander of Joint Operations Command, provides direction and oversight to the commanders on the ground, communicating frequently each week.

---

46 Dexter Filkins, "Kabul Attack Shows Resilience of Afghan Militants," *New York Times*, January 18, 2010, http://www.nytimes.com/2010/01/19/world/asia/19afghan.html?scp=1&sq=dexter%20zealand&st=cse, accessed May 13, 2010.
47 Actually, word of the location of the SAS deployment was first leaked by Norway's defense chief when the Norwegian equivalent was being rotated out of Kabul. David Pugliese, "David Pugliese's Defence Watch," October 13, 2010, http://communities.canada.com/ottawacitizen/blogs/defencewatch/archive /2009/10/13/new-zealand-sas-deploy-to-kabul.aspx, accessed May 13, 2010.
48 Interview with senior military officer, Wellington, March 18, 2010.
49 We are indebted to Matthew Shugart for his comments on this section.

One difference between New Zealand and its Anglo kin is the mixed member proportional electoral system in New Zealand, in which minority and coalition governments are the norm. The Labour Party formed coalitions with a series of much smaller parties, allowing Helen Clark to serve as prime minister from 1999 until 2008.[50] John Key then led a minority National Party government after the 2008 elections.

We would normally expect New Zealand's coalition governments to impose significant caveats on its troops in the field, especially given the larger societal trend toward pacifism in New Zealand, as exemplified by its nuclear-free stance.[51] Yet the New Zealand system provided the principal governing party with substantial power to set the governing coalition's agenda. Smaller coalition partners in New Zealand had little leverage over government policy due to their small size and their abundance. While the two big parties normally held between forty-three and fifty-eight seats each during the period of our study, smaller parties held no more than nine seats each in the 120-seat General Assembly. In 2002, there were four different parties with eight or nine seats, giving the Labour Party significant choice of its coalition partners. In 2005, all of the smaller parties lost seats except the Maori Party, so again Labour could dictate terms to its potential junior partners. In 2008, the National Party fell only a few votes short of a majority, and, other than the Greens (nine seats), no party won more than five seats. Again, the two larger parties had their choice of partners, greatly decreasing the negotiating leverage of any one of those potential partners.

As important is the fact that the smaller parties were quite fragile. Consider that the Progressive Coalition and United Future, both coalition members in 2002, ended the decade with one seat each. New Zealand First, which had a support agreement with the 2005 Labour government, collapsed and lost all of its seats. The leadership of the ACT New Zealand Party apparently had to rely on Prime Minister Key's threat to call an election to prevent an intraparty coup. The Green Party was the only stable smaller party, and it was the only one with a significant foreign policy stance, which was of nonviolence, yet its influence was muted since it was kept out of the governing cabinet for the entire decade.[52] In short, weak coalition partners meant that decisions about discretion and other aspects of New Zealand's deployment to Afghanistan were in the hands of the prime minister.

The two governments in question, Helen Clark's Labour Party and then John Key's National Party, took relatively predictable policies given their ideologies. A left-leaning coalition government under Clark deployed contingents to

---

50 From 1999 until 2002, Clark relied on the alliance and on help from the Greens.
51 This was reported in most of our interviews.
52 Interview with Keith Locke, Green Party, member of parliament, who served on the Foreign Affairs, Defence and Trade committee, Wellington, March 17, 2010.

Afghanistan to uphold UN resolutions, which fit into the larger New Zealand identity as responsible global citizen.[53] The Labour Party could act with the knowledge that the more conservative National Party would not oppose the deployment.
The National Party was focused on improving the U.S.–New Zealand relationship
after the bitterness that ensued following the declaration of a nuclear-free zone
and Clark's comments on the Iraq War under the administration of U.S. president
George W. Bush. Helping out in Afghanistan was part of the National Party's effort to repair U.S.–New Zealand defense ties.[54] Both parties supported deploying
a PRT. The only real point of controversy between the two major parties was the
2005 withdrawal of the SAS contingent and its redeployment back to Afghanistan in 2009. Labour pulled out the SAS in 2005 because it believed the Afghan
government was corrupt and the civil war was not winnable.[55] The National Party
redeployed the SAS as part of the larger effort to repair relations with the United
States. The government did not need to impose caveats in either case because the
deployment faced few risks (and no casualties) due to its size and location, and the
domestic situation provided each government with significant latitude.

## SUMMARY

This case, like that of the Canadians discussed in chapter 5, suggests that minority
governments have more room to maneuver than do coalition governments, at
least if opposition parties do not have a viable alternative governing coalition with
which to challenge the minority government. Minority governments are such for
a reason—the other parties have a hard time coalescing into a viable opposition,
providing those in power with some discretion. At no point, however, did NATO
membership or the lack thereof seem to affect New Zealand's behavior. Its participation was based on the UN backing the ISAF mission, and due to its ties with
the United States. Finally, the behavior of its troops on the ground was based on
their capabilities and size, not on NATO membership, and decisions on size and
composition were determined by domestic calculations.

# Concluding Nonmembership

Partner countries did not engage in fundamentally different behavior compared
to their NATO member-state counterparts. The choices made by Australia and
New Zealand to participate in the ISAF effort, to deploy in Uruzgan and Bamyan

---

53 This was mentioned in several of our interviews, March 2010.
54 This was reported in several of our interviews.
55 Interview with Chris Carter, Labour Party spokesperson for foreign affairs and member of parliament,
   Wellington, March 17, 2010.

with the combinations of assertive special forces and limited conventional forces, were entirely up to the politicians in Canberra and Wellington. Political dynamics and institutions within each country, along with the larger national interests involved, to include maintaining good relations with the United States and playing a role in multilateral efforts drove decisions. Certainly, Australia could have done more if it had chosen to. It could have led in Uruzgan despite its lack of NATO membership. New Zealand could have had a PRT somewhere else or contributed more troops. Both countries could have done more. But so too could many NATO alliance members who chose not to do so. The alliance allowed NATO leaders to put marginally more pressure on NATO members to contribute more, but alliance pressure was not determinative in any of these cases. Previous chapters have shown that the alliance facilitated interoperability between members, but the alliance took a backseat to national decisions. The same held true for alliance partners. The alliance itself did little to directly affect either Australia's or New Zealand's decisions. Those decisions were made in the same place for non-members as for members—namely, their respective national capitals.

# 8 Extending the Argument
## Libya and Operation United Protector

Up to this point we have focused on the issues associated with NATO coordination during International Security Assistance Force (ISAF) operations in Afghanistan. To assess the generalizability of our arguments, we extend our analysis to the 2011 intervention in Libya. In brief, the Libyan conflict was sparked by protests against the regime of Muammar al-Gaddafi in mid-February 2011, with the heart of the protest movement centered on the northeastern city of Benghazi. Rebels and government forces engaged in a series of often one-sided battles, with government troops engaged in alleged atrocities against the civilian population in areas sympathetic to the rebellion. On February 26, the UN Security Council (UNSC) passed Resolution 1970, which imposed an arms embargo and other sanctions on Libya. The rebels formed the National Transitional Council (NTC) in early March, and were recognized by the French government as the legitimate representatives of the Libyan people on March 10, 2011. Despite this diplomatic gain, the rebels lost significant ground to government forces in the first half of that month.

On the international front, the Arab League asked the UN Security Council to impose a no-fly zone over Libya. Things came to a head when Gaddafi threatened essentially to raze Benghazi. On March 17, the Security Council passed Resolution 1973, which enacted the requested no-fly zone as well as authorizing UN member states to use *all necessary means to protect civilians and civilian-populated areas in Libya*. The resolution, however, specifically ruled out regime change as a UN goal or the occupation of Libyan territory by foreign troops.

France, the United States, the United Kingdom, and other members of a coalition of the willing began a bombing campaign on March 19 against government forces threatening Benghazi. NATO's first formal involvement in the conflict came when the alliance took over the enforcement of the arms embargo on March 23 and the no-fly zone a day later. The alliance began Operation Unified Protector on March 31, an ironic name given the uneven participation in that operation. The conflict continued through the summer, during which time the International Criminal Court indicted Gaddafi and other senior Libyan officials in late June.

Tripoli eventually fell to rebel forces on August 22. On September 16, the UN Security Council passed Resolution 2009, establishing a UN mission in Libya, and the UN General Assembly recognized the NTC as holding Libya's General Assembly seat. Gaddafi was captured and killed by NTC forces on October 20, 2011. The NATO operation ended at the end of that month.

Two points are evident with regard to the Libyan conflict. The first point reflects the discussion from chapter 2 on forum shopping when choosing to intervene militarily. The main participants cycled through two forums during this intervention: a coalition of the willing and the NATO alliance. The second point builds on the discussion in chapter 3. The Libyan intervention was largely consistent with our ISAF findings on the relations between the domestic circumstances of each intervening nation and their conflict behavior. The next sections discuss both points in turn.

## Principal-Agent Relations and Forum Shopping

Recall from chapter 2 that one's choice of unilateral, coalition-of-the-willing, or alliance interventions highlight different forms of principal-agent relations between governments and their deployed military contingents. For the moment, we will ignore differences within each state (the subject of chapter 3 and the next section) and simply focus on the multilateral dynamics taking place on the international stage when contemplating an intervention. Figure 2.4 graphically depicts various principal-agent relationships that could be employed during a military intervention. Unilateral interventions reflect a relatively simple, single-principal contract between a principal and their military agent. Interventions by coalitions of the willing usually take the form of either collective or multiple principal relationships. Alliance interventions are best represented by hybrid PA models.

The Libyan intervention was a textbook example of intervention forum shopping. The intervention began as a coalition of the willing involving the French, British, and Americans. The coalition was motivated to protect Libyan civilians in the besieged city of Benghazi, the key remaining rebel stronghold in March 2011. The French in particular believed that Libyan leader Gaddafi would implement his threat to level the city in an effort to crush the rebellion. Authorization came from UNSC Resolution 1973, which called for member states "acting nationally or through regional organizations or arrangements, to take all necessary measures to protect civilians under threat of attack in the country, including Benghazi, while excluding a foreign occupation force of any form on any part of Libyan territory." Note, however, that the eventual intervention was not an UN-sponsored blue helmet mission. Instead, it involved three individual action plans, known as Operation Harmattan by the French, Operation Ellamy by the British, and Operation Odyssey Dawn by the United States (UK House of Commons 2012: 20). U.S.

Africa Command (AFRICOM) loosely coordinated these plans, but each country maintained operational control over its own military forces (Anrig 2011: 91; Cameron 2012: 18), and each country reported individually to the UN secretary general as to its actions in the region.

The NATO alliance was not viewed as a viable alternative in the lead-up to the initial intervention. A coalition of the willing was more attractive to the French given that it could take immediate action and help the French assert leadership in Europe and North Africa without the difficulties and compromises associated with reaching consensus within the North Atlantic Council (Clarke 2012: 9). On the latter point, the Germans and the Turks, among others, opposed taking action in North Africa without an Article V threat to the alliance, to say nothing of taking action under French leadership. From the U.S. perspective, a coalition of the willing was attractive because the British and the French were willing to take the lead (albeit with significant initial U.S. assistance). The British were the lone outliers, wanting the operation to take place under NATO auspices and utilizing NATO command and control systems (Quintana 2012: 33).

Problems arose immediately. Initial plans were for a coordinated attack on Libyan air defenses and select ground targets. The French, British, and Americans had agreed that U.S. and British missile strikes would destroy the Libyan air defense system, clearing the way for French and British air strikes on Libyan ground forces in and around Benghazi (Anrig 2011: 89; Cameron 2012: 20; Quintana 2012: 33). The French, however, began their attacks on Libyan ground forces on March 19, even before Franco-British-U.S. consultations were completed. The French claimed to be motivated by the perils facing Benghazi's population. The British appeared blindsided by French actions, which created Anglo-French tension that would remain in place for the duration of the operation (UK House of Commons 2012: 7, 35–36; Cameron 2012: 20).

As the operation unfolded, the international coalition quickly realized the limits of operating outside of NATO's command, control, logistics, and force generation capabilities. Under a coalition of the willing, the three allies could not use NATO command and control facilities. Instead, they operated through their national chains of command and coordinated through U.S. AFRICOM. The trouble here was that AFRICOM did not have dedicated forces or an internal command and control capability for major military actions. Nor did it have the key combat assets or enablers necessary for a sustained air operation or the ability to generate forces from participatory nations or other potential partner states (Quartararo, Rovenolt, and White 2012; Quintana 2012, 33).[1] The United States had to cobble together a convoluted chain of command, with AFRICOM in the lead on the

---

1 Quartararo, Rovenolt, and White (2012) detail these and other problems associated with the initial effort in Operation Odyssey Dawn, such as the inability to share intelligence with partner nations and the lack of bandwidth for communications.

overall operation and the U.S. European Command and Central Command providing forces and logistical capabilities as supporting commands.

U.S. officials quickly realized that a coalition of the willing was inappropriate to the circumstances, and NATO was a better intervention forum. By the end of March, the coalition had evolved into a NATO operation, dubbed Operation Unified Protector, at U.S. insistence and over French objections. The change in venue was possible only via a compromise demanded by the Turks and Italians. They agreed not to block the North Atlantic Council's approval of the Libyan mission on the condition that NATO not provide close air support for the rebels (UK House of Commons 2012).[2] This resulted in NATO's stated position being that alliance forces would attack anyone harming or threatening to harm civilians, whether attacks on civilians were instigated by Libyan government forces or the rebels. More important, the alliance ruled out an occupation force on Libyan territory, something that was anathema to many members of the alliance in the wake of their Afghanistan experience.

In sum, the intervention in Libya evolved over time as the main participants experimented with different multilateral mechanisms to coordinate their actions. They settled on the NATO alliance forum. Senior U.S. officials argued in the prelude to the 2012 NATO Chicago Summit that "Unlike an ad hoc coalition, NATO can respond rapidly and achieve its military goals by sharing burdens. In particular, NATO benefits from integrated structures and uses common funding to develop common capabilities."[3] The experience in Libya belies the former point while supporting the latter point. The British, French, and Americans initially tried a coalition of the willing precisely because it allowed for quick action without the compromises that would have been required for NATO action. The intervention became an alliance effort when the ad hoc coalition proved unable to sustain the logistics, command and control, and force generation requirements of an extended intervention. The forum shifted to the more efficient and sustainable alliance mechanism, but only after alliance members agreed on a series of political compromises (that at least the French had hoped to avoid).

## The Domestic Dynamics of Participating in the Libya Campaign

The second general point is that the patterns we observed in Afghanistan were largely repeated in the Libyan intervention. Presidential and majority parliamentary governments were less constrained than were other NATO governments. The

---

2 Turkey also demanded that the French not lead the mission, which led to NATO picking Canadian Lt. General Charles Bouchard as operational commander.
3 Tina Kaidanow, "The Chicago Summit and U.S. Policy," testimony of the principal deputy assistant secretary of state, Bureau of European and Eurasian Affairs, April 26, 2012, http://www.state.gov/p/eur/rls/rm/2012/188580.htm, accessed June 4, 2013.

historical experiences of their leaders were largely correlated with their observed behavior. Coalition governments, particularly left-leaning or broad coalitions, were often hesitant to commit forces to combat. In short, events in Libya demonstrated that the dynamics we found in Afghanistan are applicable to other multilateral efforts. NATO's experience in Afghanistan was hardly atypical.

But before unpacking who did what in Libya, we need to distinguish various types of participation in the Libyan intervention, from least to most risky in terms of the physical danger involved in the activity. We do so because mission design became the primary way countries controlled their forces in this effort. While agent selection, oversight, and incentives also may have been used, this particular mission provided a variety of ways for countries to be involved, so discretion stood out as the key mechanism. On the least risky side of the spectrum, there were those countries that did not participate in the intervention in any capacity. Most notably, Germany and Poland opted out of the entire campaign, while Turkey switched its stance over the course of the operation. Next were those countries that participated in enforcing the Libyan arms embargo: Bulgaria, Greece, and Romania (International Institute for Strategic Studies 2011). This naval embargo had very little risk, and was not that different from ongoing NATO counterterrorism operations already patrolling the Mediterranean and counterpiracy efforts off Somalia's shores. Patrolling the no-fly zone was slightly more dangerous because a plane could fail over Libyan territory. Several countries, including the Netherlands and Spain, contributed to the no-fly-zone but would not drop bombs. These countries faced minimal risk in that Libya did not have any real capability to threaten allied aircraft after the United States and British took out its air defense system in the initial days of the intervention. More risky were missions by countries willing to commit aircraft to attack ground assets. France, the United Kingdom, the United States, Belgium, Canada, Denmark, Italy, and Norway were willing to engage in such air strikes.[4]

The most important distinction was between those countries that participated in more dangerous missions, such as air strikes, and those that refused to participate or were only willing to engage in less risky behavior associated with the no-fly-zone or the sea embargo.[5] Where a country came down on this divide partially depended on its military capabilities. Some countries simply did not

---

4 Without access to classified information, we were not able to distinguish reliably between countries that participated in attacks against stationary ground targets in preplanned missions (so-called deliberate missions), and those countries willing to commit aircraft to the more risky missions, where aircraft would attack mobile ground assets on an as-needed basis (i.e., dynamic missions). Off-the-record conversations made it clear that countries varied rather systematically in their willingness to do the latter. We were also not able to verify which countries, if any, sent special operations forces into Libya, either to act as liaisons with the rebels or for other purposes. For one take on the role of advisors, see Alan Cowell and Ravi Somaiya, "France and Italy Will Also Send Advisers to Libya Rebels," *New York Times*, April 20, 2011, http://www.nytimes.com/2011/04/21/world/africa/21libya.html?pagewanted=all, accessed February 15, 2012.

5 A small number of ships enforcing the arms embargo close to Libyan shores came under fire from shore batteries, and there was some threat from Libyan mines. For a discussion, see Willett 2012.

have capabilities useful for attacks on mobile ground targets (Quintana 2012). But a significant factor in the decision as to who would do what depended on the political will of each individual country. Only a minority of the alliance's members participated in a substantial way, along with a few partners (Sweden, United Arab Emirates, and Qatar).[6] Thus, less than half of NATO members participated even in the least controversial aspects of the mission, and less than a third were willing to drop bombs (Jankowski and Kowalik 2011).[7] And it is here that the domestic political dynamics that we discussed in earlier chapters enter into the calculus.

Table 8.1 lists the behavior of the main participants in the Libyan operation, as well as the influential members of NATO who chose not to participate.[8] Two of the eight participant countries were presidential (U.S.) or premier-presidential (France) governments, systems that afford their leaders significant leeway to use force in whatever manner they so choose. Six of the eight participants in the air strikes were minority or coalition governments in parliamentary systems. At first blush, our discussion in earlier chapters would seem to rule out their participation; after all, these are the types of governments that tend to impose very restricted delegation contracts on their deployed militaries. As such we would expect them only to participate in enforcement of the arms embargo or in support roles.

Yet, when examined closely, their participation should not be completely surprising. Five of the six participatory countries were led by ideologically right-of-center governments, which tend to be relatively hawkish (Norway being the exception). Both the Canadians and the British have a history of security policy being run by the largest party in the government, whether that be a majority government or a parliamentary coalition. As discussed in more detail below, the government of David Cameron in England acted very much like it was a Conservative Party majority government, and its parliamentary rivals were effectively powerless to do anything about it. For all practical purposes then, the British system during the Libyan intervention acted like a majority party government, and the delegation contracts in those systems, as in their presidential counterparts, tend to depend on the proclivities of the head of government. Canada

---

6 For a discussion of Sweden's involvement, see Wagnsson 2011.
7 NATO quickly became sensitive about distributing information as to which countries were making what efforts in the Libyan conflict. It initially released a combat placemat for Libya (a set of maps and documents detailing which countries were contributing how many troops to specific locations), just as it had during the Afghan operation, but then quickly stopped doing so. Indeed, our requests for information about Libyan deployments were rebuffed despite our relatively good contacts at NATO headquarters. The final mission statistics fact sheet is notable for its omission of which countries did what. See *Operation Unified Protector Final Mission Stats*, November 2, 2011, http://www.nato.int/nato_static/assets/pdf/pdf_2011_11/20111108_111107-factsheet_up_factsfigures_en.pdf, accessed February 15, 2012.
8 For details on which countries contributed specific military assets, see MacKowski 2012.

**Table 8.1.** NATO Member Efforts in Libya

| Country | Institutions | Ideology | Maximum Effort |
|---|---|---|---|
| **Collective-Principal Countries** | | | |
| Belgium | Caretaker Government | NA | *Air Strikes* |
| Germany | Majority Coalition | Right-Center | None |
| Greece | Majority Coalition | Left | Naval Embargo |
| Italy | Majority Coalition | Right-Center | *Air Strikes* |
| Norway | Majority Coalition | Left-Center | *Air Strikes* |
| United Kingdom | Majority Coalition | Right-Center | *Air Strikes* |
| Canada | Minority → Majority Parliament | Right | *Air Strikes* |
| Denmark | Minority Coalition | Right-Center | *Air Strikes* |
| Netherlands | Minority Coalition | Right-Center | No Fly Zone |
| Sweden | Minority Coalition | Right-Center | No Fly Zone |
| Spain | Minority Parliament | Left-Center | No Fly Zone |
| **Single-Principal Countries** | | | |
| Turkey | Majority Parliament | Right-Center | Naval Embargo |
| France | Premier-Presidential | Right-Center | *Air Strikes* |
| Bulgaria | Premier-Presidential | Right | Naval Embargo |
| Romania | Premier-Presidential | Right-Center | Naval Embargo |
| Poland | Premier-Presidential | Right-Center | None |
| Portugal | Premier-Presidential | Left → Broad | None |
| United States | Presidential | Left-Center | *Air Strikes* |

Note: We used Shugart 2005 to code those countries not included in the tables in chapter 1. Characterizations of government ideology come from Döring and Manow 2012. Entries in italics indicate active participation in the more kinetic aspects of the intervention.

became a majority government midway through the intervention. Finally, the Italians only began conducting air strikes in late April, roughly six weeks after the operation had begun and when the risks of such strikes were proven not to be that severe. Even then they demonstrated extreme ambivalence through the summer of 2011.

## COUNTRIES WITH SINGLE PRINCIPALS

By and large, those countries where conflict decision making authority was guided by a single principal behaved consistent with expectations. We begin with reviews of French and American actions, followed by short discussions of other notable single-principal countries.

## France

France's behavior during the Libyan intervention reinforces the conclusions from chapter 4 that presidents have significant latitude to craft whatever delegation contract they wish with regard to their military agents. The determining factor in such government systems is the preference of the president and whether he values military behavior more than military outcomes. Leaders who value behavior are more likely to enact contingent delegation contracts vis-à-vis their military agents, making them less likely to engage in robust military actions in all but the most unlikely circumstances. Presidents who value outcomes are more likely to craft unrestricted delegation contracts with their military agents, allowing those agents to take more aggressive actions if that is what will achieve said outcome. Translated to the Libyan campaign, we would expect that a French president who valued behavior would be less action oriented compared to a leader who valued military outcomes.

The Libyan intervention was very clearly Nicolas Sarkozy's war, and Sarkozy seemed motivated first and foremost by preventing the fall of Benghazi and ensuring that the Libyan rebels were not defeated. His alleged motivations in pushing for this outcome vary depending on which source one chooses to believe, to include the assertion of French leadership in European security policy, the affirmation of the recent Franco-British defense cooperation treaty, an overcompensation for French inaction in earlier Arab Awakening movements in Tunisia and Egypt, retaliation for Gaddafi's general interference in France's Africa policies and specifically as a legacy of the 1983 conflict between French and Libyan forces in Operation Manta, the influence of French intellectuals such as Bernard-Henri Lévy, the desire to divert domestic audiences from French economic problems and Sarkozy's own declining fortunes, or the desire to outflank more right-wing xenophobic parties.[9] Regardless of the true motivation behind his actions, the French president seemed determined to achieve specific outcomes in Libya.

The result was that Sarkozy was the first leader to recognize the Libyan rebels as the rightful government of Libya (on March 10, 2011). He pushed for the allied intervention and made sure that France was the first country to launch air strikes. During military hostilities, French aircraft began the intervention with strikes against Libyan government tanks surrounding Benghazi, even before the planned start of the campaign. French aircraft participated in the greatest number of air strikes of any partner in the intervention.[10] France, along with the United

---

9 See Cameron 2012: 17–18; "Sarkozy's Libyan Surprise," *Economist*, March 14, 2011, http://www
.economist.com/blogs/newsbook/2011/03/france_and_libya, accessed February 15, 2012. Sarkozy's
intervention seemed to have worked on the domestic front in that the intervention was reauthorized by
a supermajority vote of the National Assembly on July 12, 2011 (Anrig 2011: 96).
10 For specifics on the number and targets of French sorties, see Anrig 2011: 97–98.

Kingdom, used sea-based helicopters to attack Gaddafi's forces, a riskier move than just relying on traditional fixed-wing airpower. Finally, France is said to have deployed special operations units to Libya. All this is consistent with an outcome-oriented leader who controls the national decision-making apparatus. In sum, French actions are consistent with our expectations.

## The United States

As we discussed in chapter 4, the U.S. presidential system represents a single-principal model when it comes to decisions to use force internationally. That was certainly the case in the Libyan intervention. While the administration of President Barack Obama consulted regularly with members of Congress, the decision to intervene was not generated on Capitol Hill.[11] The summary of a March 18, 2011, meeting between the president and Congress's bipartisan, bicameral leadership on the subject of Libya is instructive. The president briefed members of Congress "on the limited, discrete and well-defined participation that he envisioned for the United States to help implement the UN Resolution 1973" (White House 2011: 29). He did not ask for congressional authorization to intervene, and, indeed, was rebuked by the House of Representatives for failing to get prior congressional authorization before using force.[12]

President Obama's advisers were of two minds with regard to Libya. Supporting intervention were Secretary of State Hillary Rodham Clinton, Susan Rice, the U.S. Ambassador to the UN, and Samantha Power, a member of the president's national security staff.[13] Opposing intervention were a variety of senior military officers and Secretary of Defense Robert Gates. Before coalition operations began, for example, Defense Secretary Gates expressed his reluctance to begin a large-scale U.S. intervention when he said, "All of the options beyond humanitarian assistance and evacuations are complex. We also have to think about, frankly, the use of the U.S. military in another country in the Middle East."[14]

The result was that President Obama was a reluctant intervener. He eventually settled on a fourfold rationale for military intervention in Libya, to include limiting regional instability, preventing a humanitarian catastrophe, demonstrating that the United States cared about the North African people, and maintaining

---

11 For a list of the administration's consultations with Congress over Libya, see White House 2011: 26–31.

12 The rebuke came on a 268–145 House vote on June 3, 2011. See Foley 2011.

13 Joby Warrick, "Clinton Credited with Key Role in Success of NATO Airstrikes, Libyan Rebels," *Washington Post*, October 30, 2011, http://www.washingtonpost.com/world/national-security/hillarys-war-how-conviction-replaced-skepticism-in-libya-intervention/2011/10/28/gIQAhGS7WM_story.html, accessed May 1, 2012; Michael Crowley, "Susan Rice, Samantha Power, Rwanda and Libya," *Time*, March 24, 2011, http://swampland.time.com/2011/03/24/susan-rice-samantha-power-rwanda-and-libya/, accessed May 1, 2012.

14 Defense Secretary Robert Gates, quoted in Anrig 2011: 90, from a press conference on March 1, 2010.

the credibility of the UN Security Council in the aftermath of its Resolution 1973 (White House 2011: 2–3). All this sounds familiar when we compare the U.S. position to that of the French. The difference between the two countries was the American emphasis on preventing full U.S. involvement in a war with another Muslim state. In the context of our earlier discussion on presidential systems, the United States wanted to avoid specific types of behavior.

Behavioral constraints on U.S. actions were embodied in the headline-grabbing (and much derided) phrase claiming the United States was "leading from behind." The United States took an active role at the beginning of the Libyan conflict, destroying the Libyan air defense system with a combination of cruise missiles and precision air strikes.[15] The U.S. role quickly changed as Operation Odyssey Dawn became Operation Unified Protector. By the end of March, just as the transfer was about to occur, President Obama made clear that he was putting constraints on U.S. military actions: "I said that America's role would be limited; that we would not put ground troops into Libya; that we would focus our unique capabilities on the front end of the operation and that we would transfer responsibility to our allies and partners. Tonight, we are fulfilling that pledge."[16] In the words of the official White House progress report that came once the operation transferred to NATO control in early April, "U.S. military involvement has been limited to a supporting role" (White House 2011: 5), with the U.S. withdrawal of its combat aircraft from action after that point (Anrig 2011: 92).

By mid-June 2011, European nations plus Canada had conducted three-fourths of all air sorties over Libya, and most strike sorties, and were providing all of the ships enforcing the arms embargo. The United States focused on providing combat "enablers" such as intelligence capabilities and refueling aircraft, and on providing precision munitions to countries that were running low, among other things.[17] In short, the U.S. government behaved consistent with our predictions, with the president having relative freedom of action from a domestic institutional perspective, allowing him to delegate authority consistent with his underlying preference on the outcome versus behavior spectrum.

## Poland

The Poles decided not to participate in the Libyan campaign. As noted in chapter 4, Poland has a premier-presidential system that provides the president with significant discretion over security policy. Bronislaw Komorowski, of the Civic Platform

---

15 For specifics on U.S. aircraft participation in the Libyan campaign, see Anrig 2011: 97–98.
16 Barack Obama, "Remarks by the President in Address to the Nation on Libya, 28 March 2011," http://www.whitehouse.gov/the-press-office/2011/03/28/remarks-president-address-nation-libya, accessed May 1, 2012.
17 For a more complete list, see White House 2011: 11.

party, held the presidency on an acting basis following the April 2010 plane crash that killed President Lech Kaczynski, and assumed the presidency on a more permanent basis after winning the August 2010 presidential election in his own right. The Polish system allows the president to choose the prime minister, and Komorowski chose Donald Tusk, also of the Civic Platform party, for that office. Civic Platform formed a governing coalition in parliament with the Polish People's Party.

These political dynamics were important for Poland's decisions regarding Libya. At the time of the Libyan intervention there were Polish parliamentary elections scheduled for early October 2011. Senior officials in the Civic Platform party were not about to get involved in a potentially costly and endless North African war even though they had roughly thirty advanced F-16s that could have been used in the campaign. They were not going to risk their chances at reelection over a NATO action that made no reference to Article V threats.[18] Their bet seems to have paid off, in that Civic Platform won a plurality of seats in the 2011 election and Donald Tusk won a second term as prime minister.

## Turkey

Turkey illustrates how a prime minister with a solid majority can have a great deal of flexibility, as we would expect from a single-principal country. Prime Minister Erdoğan was initially critical of the use of force against Libya, calling it "absurd" ("Erdogan's Lament" 2011). As leader of a moderate Muslim party, Erdoğan was averse to the Western use of force against yet another Muslim country. Once presented with a series of fait accompli however, to include UNSC Resolution 1973, the start of air strikes, and the likely end of the Gaddafi regime, he recognized the inevitable and agreed to participate in the embargo. In exchange, Turkey was able to push for a NATO lead to the alliance effort instead of a French-British effort,[19] and to insist that the NATO commander was not French.

## COUNTRIES WITH COLLECTIVE PRINCIPALS

At first glance, countries where conflict decision making authority was guided by a collective principal (i.e., coalition governments) had more variable behavior that appeared to diverge from our expectations. Upon closer examination, and when we factor in the ideological positions of the various political parties within each coalition, however, patterns of behavior conform more closely to what we would expect.

---

18 Interview with senior Polish defense official, Washington, D.C., February 27, 2012.
19 Charles A. Kupchan, "Libya's Strains on NATO," interview with Bernard Gwertzman, April 4, 2011, http://www.cfr.org/libya/libyas-strains-nato/p24582, accessed June 4, 2013.

## Canada

Canada was a surprisingly robust contributor to the early stages of the intervention, despite having a minority government. Prime Minister Stephen Harper faced little resistance in March when deploying six fighter planes and two air-refueling tankers to the skies over Libya, even though his government's minority status had led to an early withdrawal from Afghanistan (Anrig 2011: 92–93). Here is where political ideology becomes important. Harper had the flexibility to participate in the early stages of the air campaign because all major parties in parliament supported the intervention. The plight of Libyan civilians fit the *responsibility to protect* norm that the Liberals had promoted when they had been in power. Similarly, the other two major parties in parliament, the New Democratic Party and the Bloc Québécois, found it difficult politically to oppose a humanitarian mission. So while the Libyan mission fit the Conservative Party's desire to be seen as a muscular leader in the world, Harper's government faced no real opposition from parliament because the parliament as a whole supported the mission. Minority government ended in May 2011 when Prime Minister Harper gained a majority of seats in the parliament, providing him the flexibility to sustain the mission without reliance on opposition party support.[20]

## The United Kingdom

Given that the United Kingdom was led by a coalition government of Conservatives and Liberal Democrats, we would expect it to engage in highly contingent delegation contracts with its military. That should have translated into more limited participation in the operation than we observed. Yet the British government acted very much like a majority party government when it came to Libya policy. The reasons were twofold. First, the Liberal Democrats had little influence over the government's foreign policy because the Conservatives held the prime minister, defense minister, and foreign minister posts. Second, the Liberal Democrats had few incentives to defect from the government coalition and force elections. Calling for a new election might provide Labour with an absolute majority, which would freeze out the Liberal Democrats from their current government

---

20 The New Democratic Party leader, Jack Layton, had pushed the left-wing party toward the center of the Canadian political system, jettisoning old ideology that was anti-NATO, as he wanted the party to be seen as serious and suitable for governing. After his death that summer, the NDP's more pacifist members were able to push the party into opposition when the mission was extended a second time in September (the parliamentary vote for the first extension having been 294–1). By then, however, the Harper government did not need the NDP's support to sustain a governing coalition. See Chantal Hebert, "NDP Retreats from Layton's Position," *Guelph Mercury*, September 27, 2011, http://www.guelphmercury.com/opinion /columns/article/600356--ndp-retreats-from-layton-s-libya-position, accessed February 17, 2012.

ministries. Absent elections, there was no viable opposition coalition that could unseat the Conservatives and form a new government, in that the Liberal Democrat and Labour parties did not have the combined seats to form a parliamentary majority of their own.[21] Players can only be seen as having a veto if they can credibly threaten to exit. Thus, the center-right parliamentary coalition and the lack of viable alternative domestic coalitions provided Prime Minister David Cameron with significant freedom of action during this crisis.[22]

It seems clear that the British decision to participate in the Libyan intervention was taken by Cameron. According to one influential report, "The impetus for the UK to intervene came very much from the top, with a hawkish prime minister pushing the operation despite private military warnings of the risks" (Johnson and Mueen 2012: 2). Prime Minister Cameron's main motivation appeared to be to avoid a Srebrenica-like massacre during his tenure in office.[23] He also very much wanted to avoid the loss of civilian life, whether due to Libyan government actions or collateral damage from British aircraft (UK House of Commons 2012: 27). Cameron asked the military to draft plans for a no fly zone in late February 2011 (Anrig 2011: 89), and warned Parliament one day after UNSC Resolution 1973 passed that he would order the British military into action to implement the resolution. He argued that intervention was in the British national interest and was made legitimate by Resolution 1973.

Cameron's decision on Libya contravened both the process by which security decisions were supposed to be made in the United Kingdom and the advice of his senior military and civilian advisers (UK House of Commons 2012: 32). The British 2010 Strategic Defense and Security Review (SDSR) established fairly stringent prerequisites before the British would use force internationally. Those criteria specified that British national interests must be at stake, that there were clear benefits to the nation from intervention, that there were clear goals to the operation, that there was a viable exit strategy, and that the intervention be supported by international law (UK House of Commons 2012: 31). In May 2010, the British government also created a new National Security Council, modeled roughly on the U.S. example, to vet decisions according to the priorities in the SDSR and to ensure coordinated interagency consultations and implementation of national security decisions. Prime Minister Cameron appeared to violate the terms of the SDSR when it came to the Libyan decision (Clarke 2012: 7). Moreover, he seems to have ignored the advice of the National Security Council and

---

21 The Conservatives held 306 seats, with 326 needed for a majority in the House of Commons. The Liberal Democrats held 57 seats, while the Labour Party had 255 seats.

22 The House of Commons acquiesced to the prime minister's decision with an overwhelming 557–13 vote on March 21, 2011.

23 See Clarke 2012: 8, citing "David Cameron's Libyan War: Why the Prime Minister felt Qadhafi had to be Stopped," *Guardian*, October 2, 2011.

specifically his senior political and military advisers from across the government. For example, General Sir David Richards, the uniformed chief of the defense staff, was against the intervention, as was Defense Minister Liam Fox (Cameron 2012: 16; Clarke 2012: 8).[24]

The result was that the British were very active participants in the Libyan intervention and were willing to take significant risks. They launched Tomahawk cruise missiles during the first day of the fighting; their aircraft engaged ground targets; they sent Apache attack helicopters into combat, launched from ships in the Mediterranean. The British even sent in special forces to act as liaisons with the Libyan rebels and to monitor sensitive sites on the ground.[25] In sum, the British behaved very much consistent with the government's conservative leanings and their tradition of security policy being run out of 10 Downing Street.

## Belgium

Perhaps the most interesting and underrated part of the Libyan campaign was the role played by Belgium. As we saw in chapter 6, the Belgian military faced significant restrictions in Afghanistan. Yet Belgium was one of the few countries willing to engage in air strikes in Libya. What explains the change? Part of it is likely due to the humanitarian nature of the intervention, consistent with the *responsibility to protect* and a UN authorization.[26] We cannot help but notice, however, that a caretaker government was making the decisions in Belgium during 2011. So, Belgium went from a multiple-veto-player, fragile coalition government in 2009 with correspondingly high restrictions on its troops in Afghanistan to essentially no veto-players and a much more flexible mission in Libya. That lack of accountability allowed the government cabinet more freedom of action than it would otherwise have in a standard coalition government. Given how popular the mission was in the Parliament, the government had few restraints.

## Denmark

Like Canada's, Denmark's coalition politics were simplified by the consensus shared across the political spectrum in support of the mission. The parliament supported the Libyan mission unanimously, with the exception that the

---

24 Prime Minister Cameron clearly believed the intervention was in Britain's national interest when he argued in the House of Commons on March 21, "The UN has reached a conclusion and I think that we should back it. As I said the other day, just because we cannot do the right thing everywhere does not mean we should not do it when we have clear permission for and a national interest in doing so." See UK House of Commons 2012: 20.

25 For specifics of the British contribution to the air campaign, see Anrig 2011: 99–100; and UK House of Commons 2012: 45–46. For allusions to British special forces operating in Libya, see UK House of Commons 2012: 30, 40.

26 Interview, senior Belgian air force officer, Washington, D.C., 2012.

ex-communists dropped out of the governing coalition after a week of the bombing campaign. Denmark stayed in the fight until the end, even though it encountered ammunition shortages along the way. The combination of the *responsibility to protect* with a UN mandate and a NATO effort appealed across the political spectrum, so that coalition politics did not get in the way of the deployment.

## Germany

The Germans did not participate in the Libyan operation, which is somewhat surprising given that they could very well have done so in a limited fashion and still been consistent with our model. Chancellor Angela Merkel chose to abstain when the United Nations Security Council voted on Resolution 1973, and refused to participate in any NATO effort near and over Libya. Merkel seems to have wanted to avoid a repeat of the criticism she received from across the political spectrum for German participation in Afghanistan by refraining from all Libyan operations.[27] Germany's decision made NATO's effort in Libya more challenging both because the alliance could have used German advanced fighter bombers and because Germans staffed NATO Airborne Warning and Control Systems planes.[28] Merkel also pulled German ships out of the fleet that was enforcing the arms embargo.

These decisions were quite unpopular in Germany. Chancellor Merkel and her foreign minister Guido Westerwelle appeared to overreact to German war exhaustion. Merkel and Westerwelle underestimated the desire of Germans, including parliamentarians, not to be that far out of step with their NATO allies. "The decision is a serious mistake of historic dimensions," argued Volker Rühe, a member of Merkel's own party and a former defense minister.[29] While dropping bombs on Libya might have gone too far, participating in less risky aspects of the mission such as the arms embargo would likely have been supported in the parliament. The irony is that Merkel received much more criticism for Germany's stance than would have occurred had they participated in the relatively passive no-fly zone or arms embargo.

## Italy

Italy played an interesting, evolving, and inconsistent role in this conflict. It first demanded a UN resolution in exchange for the use of Italian bases. It then supported the no-fly zone with eight Italian aircraft. Eventually it took part in air

---

27 Some speculate that Merkel was trying to improve her domestic standing by imitating Gerhard Schroeder's stand against the Iraq war in 2002–03. See Kupchan, "Libya's Strains on NATO."

28 Germany sent AWACS crews to Afghanistan so that non-German AWACS operators could staff the NATO planes for the Libyan mission. See UK House of Commons 2012: 41.

29 "Libya Crisis Leaves Berlin Isolated," *Der Spiegel Online*, March 28, 2011, http://www.spiegel.de /international/germany/0,1518,753498,00.html, accessed February 15, 2012.

strikes while also calling for a cease-fire and withdrawing naval and air assets.[30] As Ben Lombardi notes, "Italian policy during the first weeks of the uprising in Libya was characterized by hesitancy and hedging" (2011: 35).

There were proximate causes for Italy's indecision, such as Italy's close commercial relationships with Gaddafi, its fear of being overwhelmed with Libyan refugees, and the fact that Prime Minister Silvio Berlusconi was in the midst of a series of controversies (Lombardi 2011). Underlying all this, however, was the fact that the Italian system of fragile coalition governments biases their conflict decisions. Italy tends to be cautious when it comes to using force, as an international misstep can lead to the collapse of a governing coalition. Even when it began to participate in NATO air strikes in late April, it subsequently asked for a cease-fire in mid-June and then withdrew its aircraft carrier from the conflict in July (Anrig 2011). Italian leaders may have realized that ending the Libyan crisis as quickly as possible was good for domestic politics, particularly if the anti-immigrant Northern League was going to remain in the Italian governing coalition.[31] After all, a long-lasting civil war in Libya would produce even more refugees on Italian shores, and the hope that Gaddafi could contain the crisis was dashed by the second month of the NATO effort. At the same time, the Italians did not appear to want to take ownership of the conflict, consistent with the behavior of a fragile coalition government.[32]

## The Netherlands

Dutch behavior was consistent with our expectations for a right-leaning coalition government. The Dutch sent a military contingent consisting of an F-16 squadron and a naval vessel, a contribution similar to that of Canada, Denmark, and Norway. The Dutch, however, only monitored the no-fly zone and helped to enforce the arms embargo (Anrig 2011). They would not participate in air strikes. Given that differences among Dutch parties led to the 2010 collapse of the government and Dutch withdrawal from Afghanistan, these limitations made sense from a domestic political perspective. The desire to be a good member of NATO

---

30 See Anrig 2011: 93; and "Rome Joins the War in Libya," *PressEurope*, April 26, 2011, http://www.press europ.eu/en/content/news-brief-cover/617231-rome-joins-war-libya, accessed February 15, 2012.

31 The Northern League, a party often accused of borderline xenophobia, was concerned that Gaddafi's collapse would have undesired implications for immigration. Given the increasing power of far-right parties in Italy, and with the Northern League in the governing coalition, conflicting impulses of isolationism and anti-immigration were evident in Italian decisions. Italy tried to pass the buck on the immigrants by giving them visas that would allow them to leave and move on to other member countries within the European Union. This provoked France at first, but then produced an agreement on pushing the EU to fight illegal immigration. It is notable that this agreement was reached just as Italy began to participate meaningfully in the Libyan operation. See "Rome Joins the War in Libya"; see also Lombardi 2011.

32 The Italian case provides additional evidence reinforcing the idea that the combination of xenophobia and coalition politics can produce contradictory pressures to do both less and more, as we saw in chapter 6.

meant participation in the Libyan operation, but not in a particularly risky or assertive stance.

## Norway

Norway defied our expectations, as it participated in the air strikes despite being governed by a left-center coalition government. We would have expected the country to restrict its effort to either the less risky no-fly zone or the even less visible naval embargo. Instead, Norway was one of the most forward-leaning of countries.[33] The combination of the *responsibility to protect*, the UN resolution authorizing the mission, and a desire to support NATO gained enough traction among the left-wing to support the mission (Riste 2005). The air campaign was sufficiently taxing on Norwegian resources, however, that the government withdrew before Gaddafi and Tripoli fell, making Norway the first NATO member to reduce its commitment, from six F-16s to four (in June 2011), and to then drop out of the mission entirely (by the end of July).[34]

## Comparisons

In general, we expected left-of-center governments to opt out of the Libyan operation entirely, with more centrist and center-right coalition governments to agree at least to participate in the naval embargo and perhaps the no-fly zone. We expected center-right coalitions where there was not a viable domestic political alternative, majority parliamentary governments, and presidential systems would have the discretion to participate in the air strikes. Actual behavior in the Libyan operation contained some surprises. While many coalition governments abstained from participating, we found some left-center parties were more supportive of this effort than we initially expected, largely because of the humanitarian and multilateral dimensions of the mission (Rathbun 2004). The decisions in Belgium, Denmark, and Norway all appear at least partially motivated by these beliefs. Other governments, like those of Canada or the United Kingdom, had no viable opposition to constrain their prime ministers' decisions. Countries with presidents or prime ministers leading single-party parliamentary majority governments had more freedom of action to base conflict decisions on the beliefs of the head of government. French president Sarkozy stood out, pushing the United

---

33 Norway actually got its F-16s to the Mediterranean quickly, but paused until the command and control arrangements of the air effort could be ironed out (Anrig 2011).

34 These conclusions were reinforced by conversations with Per Marius Frost-Nielsen, who served as an operations officer of the Royal Norwegian Air Force, based in Crete in 2011, and who is now a PhD student at the University of Trondheim in Norway.

States into the engagement and being the first to begin air strikes. President Obama was able to tailor the U.S. military effort depending on what was needed to facilitate NATO's success while minimizing the visibility of American contribution. Turkey's Prime Minister Erdoğan was able to adjust to changing events, moving from opposing the effort to guarded participation.

# Alternative Accounts

The main alternative arguments we addressed in chapter 1 do not explain national behavior during the Libyan intervention. Realism yields either contradictory or indeterminate predictions in this case. Public opinion is not correlated with overall country participation. Strategic culture is not a particularly useful explanation either.

## REALISM

Realism is difficult to apply here since the Gaddafi regime posed little direct threat to Europe or the United States. Indeed, the military threat from Libya had appeared minimal ever since the Gaddafi regime denounced the September 11, 2001, terrorist attacks and agreed in late 2003 to give up its nuclear weapons program. The only security threat posed by Libya in 2011 was indirect in nature—namely, refugee flows to southern Europe (Greenhill 2010). Countries that did not face this threat should not have cared about events in Libya, to say nothing of using force, yet Norway, the United Kingdom, the United States, and others were willing to do just that. More generally, there were two diametrically opposed ways for NATO countries to address the refugee threat, both of which are consistent with realist theory. They could support Gaddafi, ending the rebellion quickly and thus stemming the flow of emigrants, or they could oppose Gaddafi in an all-out offensive aimed at regime change so that the proximate cause of flight would end quickly. But again, either action is a stretch from a realist perspective. But even putting aside that objection, realist theory provides little guidance as to which alternative makes the most sense from the lens of power politics. Italy's ambivalence at the outset of the conflict, for example, reflects its confusion over how best to prevent Africans from reaching Italian shores. If anything, realists should argue that nations should have supported Qaddafi, in that this would have been the less costly expenditure of state resources.[35]

---

35 Indeed, see Stephen Walt, "What if Realists Were in Charge of U.S. Foreign Policy," *Foreign Policy*, April 30, 2012, http://walt.foreignpolicy.com/posts/2012/04/30/what_if_realists_ran_us_foreign_policy _a_top_ten_list accessed May 4, 2012.

## PUBLIC OPINION

Just as public opinion did not correlate with patterns of participation and agency control in Afghanistan, public support for the Libyan effort did not covary with what countries were willing to do. Table 8.2 lists public approval of the Libyan intervention by country, with corresponding levels of effort.[36]

We see no clear pattern in the data. Some countries whose populations strongly approved of the mission limited themselves to only the no-fly zone, or simply did nothing at all (Portugal). Countries with relatively less-supportive publics varied in their contributions, with Italy participating in air strikes, Turkey participating in the naval embargo, and Germany and Poland opting out entirely. While low public support did seem to matter here, variations in public opinion do not help account for the variation among the rest of the NATO countries.

## STRATEGIC CULTURE

The remaining alternative explanation of NATO behavior in Libya focuses on strategic culture. Discussions of German participation in ISAF or refusal in Libya almost always turn to strategic culture, despite the argument that German pacifism is overrated (Rathbun 2006). The problem when using strategic culture to explain German behavior, or any state behavior for that matter, involves knowing what aspects of national culture are determining such behavior. One could argue that Germany's abstention in Libya was due to its reluctance to use force except in self-defense, a legacy of World War II. The trouble here is that this explanation runs up against another German core belief. Chancellor Angela Merkel, by opting out of the operation entirely, ran directly against the norms and expectations that Germany traditionally seeks to build and reinforce transatlantic unity. This latter view would see a deviation from multilateralism as anathema.[37] So, to use a historic example of these conflicting cultural beliefs, German participation in the Kosovo air campaign was controversial because it was the first major deployment of German forces since World War II, but had public support precisely because it was a humanitarian campaign conducted by NATO. At the same time, one might also argue that U.S. behavior in Libya was contrary to American strategic culture. Taking a backseat to the French and British is outside the norm for Americans.

---

36 Entries in table 8.2 do not include countries from which we were not able to get reliable public opinion data for the Libyan campaign.

37 This, of course, is not the first time Germany was reluctant to go along with the multinational consensus. Germany recognized Croatia and Slovenia during the disintegration of Yugoslavia, despite the preferences of others (Crawford 1996), but, in that case, German politicians still tried to work through European institutions.

**Table 8.2.** Libya and Public Opinion

| Country | Percent Approval[a] | Maximum Effort |
|---|---|---|
| Sweden | 69% | No-Fly Zone |
| Netherlands | 65% | No-Fly Zone |
| United States | 59% | Air Strikes |
| France | 58% | Air Strikes |
| Portugal | 57% | None |
| Spain | 54% | No-Fly Zone |
| United Kingdom | 53% | Air Strikes |
| Italy | 47% | Air Strikes |
| Bulgaria | 46% | Naval Embargo |
| Romania | 39% | Naval Embargo |
| Germany | 37% | None |
| Poland | 35% | None |
| Slovakia | 30% | None |
| Turkey | 23% | Naval Embargo |

[a] Percent approving Libyan intervention by international forces (Nyiri and Veater-Fuchs 2011). A different survey (Unver 2011) had Belgian and Canadian support at or over 70 percent.

Indeed, the United States almost always insisted in leading NATO operations, a caveat of sorts.

None of the alternative accounts appear to provide as strong an explanation as does our two-stage institutional and political model of state behavior. There is a strong relationship among domestic institutions, parties in power, political beliefs, and participation in Operation Unified Protector. These dynamics help to account for the recurring problem of a two-tiered (at least) NATO, with some countries doing far more and others doing far less in Afghanistan and beyond.

## Summary

In thinking about the lessons learned from Afghanistan, one question always arises: Were the dynamics there unique? In 2011 we observed a demonstration of the dynamics we found in NATO's efforts in Afghanistan at work when the "Arab Awakening" came to Libya. NATO once again revealed its strengths and its limitations. Countries will shop for the most advantageous forum for their military efforts, and the move from a coalition of the willing to an alliance effort proves that NATO has added value. France sought a coalition of the willing. Most of the actors found the Atlantic alliance to be the better form of multilateral military operation. Yet the resulting NATO operation occurred within key constraints. The missions over Libya and in the seas nearby only involved a subset of the organization. At the same time, the cooperation and interoperability required for Operation Unified Protector took almost a month to achieve.

In terms of domestic dynamics, what was relevant in Operation Medusa in Kandahar in 2006 was again important over Libya in 2011. Countries varied in what they were willing to risk and to contribute, and those differences produced political friction. The United States faced criticism at home and abroad for doing both more and less than people expected, but institutions empowered President Obama to make all of the big decisions even if his secretary of defense disagreed. Other countries were able to support the mission because their domestic opponents could not cooperate enough to block the effort. Minority governments, as in the cases of Canada and Denmark, had a degree of latitude in the Libyan effort. The application of the *responsibility to protect* norm enabled right-wing and centrist parties to gain enough support from the left to pursue the mission even in coalition governments. Still, Italy's vacillations demonstrated that multilateral warfare, even when it involves no boots on the ground, can be very problematic for coalition governments.

As chapter 1 demonstrated, these problems are not new to NATO or to multilateral warfare. This chapter illustrates that, whatever other lessons are produced by the Afghanistan experience, the realities of civilian control of militaries in coalition warfare are enduring. In chapter 9 we conclude by considering our findings' implications for future operations and research.

# 9 Implications for Policy and Theory

*We will never establish unity of command. It is unachievable. We can try to get unity of effort through common understandings.*
—Senior official, Allied Joint Forces Command, Brunssum, Belgium, 2011

We began this book by arguing that war is an inherently dangerous endeavor for countries, for soldiers, and for politicians. Fighting as part of a coalition or alliance may be seen as a way to reduce risks by sharing responsibilities, but as we have demonstrated throughout this study, multilateral warfare is quite risky indeed. Countries may join military coalitions or an alliance effort because they share common interests, but shared interests do not always equate to agreement as to the best ways to pursue those interests. Too often, individual countries engage in efforts that either distract from or undermine the overall coalition effort. Complicating the picture still further is when one's troops are under the command of individuals from other countries.

NATO operations in Afghanistan are no exception to this rule. This book has documented how the NATO experience in Afghanistan has been complicated by different national commands operating under a variety of civil-military dynamics and with different conceptions of the International Security Assistance Force (ISAF) mission. To be sure, as of early 2013, NATO had made significant progress in the Afghan campaign. Yet ISAF operations have been plagued by inefficiencies despite NATO being the most powerful, institutionalized, interoperable, and practiced security institution in existence today—and perhaps ever. In the preceding chapters we have sought to explain the behavior of specific NATO members in Afghanistan and, in so doing, tease out the broader dynamics involved whenever countries seek to cooperate in combat. Our penultimate chapter, on Libya, along with our introduction, demonstrates that these processes are not unique to Afghanistan but are inherent in multilateral warfare.

In this concluding chapter we will first summarize what we have found—the consistencies and the contradictions across the contingents that operated in

Afghanistan with some comparisons to the Libyan experience. We will then develop the implications of this book for both future research and policy makers.

For scholars, we consider the book's contribution to research on alliances, civil-military relations, and the impact of domestic politics upon foreign policy. With regard to alliances, we consider how domestic political debates affect the search for the appropriate venue by which to conduct a multilateral military intervention, the so-called forum shopping we discussed in earlier chapters. We discuss how our understanding of the principal-agent delegation contract inherent in any military deployment should consider all four means of controlling military agents, to include agent selection, contingent delegation, oversight, and incentives and how future research can apply our model to other cases and categories of agents. And finally, we come back to how democracies vary in their use of these control mechanisms in systematic ways depending on their domestic political institutions and the preferences of their leaders.

For policy makers, the lesson from Afghanistan is that caveats and other differences in national control of military contingents are not going to go away. Those differences are inherent in modern democracies' attempts to control their militaries and will affect multilateral operations now and into the future. We consider the impact of national perspectives on NATO's effectiveness, taking seriously the complexity of Afghanistan and the reality that any multilateral effort, on the part of NATO or another entity, will face similar challenges. We review some of the tactics NATO and its members used to mitigate the challenges associated with multilateral interventions. We conclude by reviewing recent efforts to specialize within the alliance given financial constraints on defense budgets and NATO's response in the Smart Defence Initiative.

## Comparisons and Contradictions

Our argument is that most of the NATO story in Afghanistan resided not in Brussels nor in Kabul but in the national capitals of the participating countries. There was simply too much behavioral variation among allies and over time to focus on the secretary general, the supreme allied commander for Europe, or the North Atlantic Council as the key driver of NATO member decisions. While these alliance actors certainly mattered in shaping what ISAF did, events revealed that behavior on the ground and in the air were largely driven by dynamics within the national capitals.

We demonstrated that there are systematic differences among the advanced democracies participating in ISAF operations. Those differences depend on the structures of each country's political institutions and on the beliefs of key decision makers empowered by those institutions. We examined four mechanisms used by civilian officials to direct their deployed militaries, to include the selection of specific military officers, restricted delegation of authority given to those officers (i.e., caveats), oversight of those officers, and incentives to reward or sanction particular officer behavior or military outcomes. We found patterns in the use of these mechanisms, depending on whether a country was led by a parliamentary coalition or a single key decision maker such as in a presidential or majority parliamentary government. The size of the governing coalition and its ideology mattered, exacerbating or ameliorating the challenges inherent in coalition governments. For presidential and parliamentary majority governments, the previous experiences of key decision makers affected whether they prioritized military outcomes or appropriate behavior, with implications for all four civilian control mechanisms.

Because caveats were the most visible and easily comparable means by which countries could and did influence their contingents, we can show the impact of institutions on discretion with table 9.1. By and large, our expectations were largely realized when it came to discretion.

**Table 9.1.** Government Institutions and Caveats in Afghanistan

| Country | Institutional Type | Caveats[a] |
|---|---|---|
| Belgium | Coalition Parliament | Tight → Less Tight |
| *Denmark* | *Coalition Parliament* | *Loose* |
| Germany | Coalition Parliament | Tight → Less Tight |
| Italy | Coalition Parliament | Tight |
| Netherlands | Coalition Parliament | Medium |
| Norway | Coalition Parliament | *Loose* → Medium |
| Sweden | Coalition Parliament | Medium |
| Australia | Coalition Parliament until 2007, Majority Parliament | Medium |
| *Canada* | *Minority Parliament* | *Medium* → *Loose* |
| France | Premier-Presidential | Medium → Loose |
| Poland | Premier-Presidential | Loose |
| Romania | Premier-Presidential | Tight |
| Spain | Majority Parliament | Tight |
| Turkey | Majority Parliament until 2007, Premier-Presidential | Tight |
| United Kingdom | Majority Parliament | Loose |
| United States | Presidential | Loose |

*Note*: Italics indicate cases that are exceptions at first glance.
[a] Caveats range from loose to tight, focusing mostly on geographic restrictions and limits on offensive operations.

A most revealing contrast in democracies is what happens when change occurs. Coalition governments shifted positions mostly when the composition of the coalition changed—becoming broader or narrower, shifting left or right—as in the cases of Germany and Norway. Changes in key decision makers mattered most in presidential and single-party parliamentary systems. Canada, France, and the United States shifted stances in Afghanistan when key principals (respectively, chief of defense staff, president, secretary of defense) were replaced. American and Turkish stances during the Libyan mission also demonstrate that significant change can happen when one person is the key decision maker and he changes his mind. Coalition governments simply cannot "change their mind" that easily and may be biased toward inaction (as Italy proved in Libya).

We developed hypotheses that addressed the four aspects of the delegation contract because civilian control of contingents abroad is more than just about caveats, despite the attention they received in the media and by politicians. In general, we found that our expectations held up across the board. Domestic institutions helped us identify who key principals were in each country and established broad expectations for those principals' behavior. We supplemented that information with considerations of preferences, both at the individual and government coalition levels, with individuals' views on prioritizing outcomes or behavior based on their past experiences, and political parties' stances determined by where they stood on the left-right ideological spectrum. Combined, these variables helped us develop specific hypotheses on how principals would craft their delegation contracts with military agents.

In chapters 4 and 5, we found that presidents and prime ministers in single-party systems acted as individuals rather than groups. They focused on selecting agents and manipulating agent incentives much more so than did coalition governments. In the course of research, we found that minority governments were a bit more complex, as the leaders of such governments faced varying constraints and pressures depending on how much cooperation they needed from outside parties and how well the opposition parties could get along. For instance, in the Canadian case, the minority government acted more like a single-party majority government because the opposition could not agree upon anything besides the time limit of July 2011. In chapter 6, we found that coalition governments tended to have relatively tight restrictions on their deployed troops, although some of those with right-leaning governments, such as Denmark, were less willing to impose strict caveats. Coalition governments tended to have strict oversight, as demonstrated by the Germans and the Dutch. Again, the Danes proved that their exceptional behavior fit the larger logic of this book, since their narrower coalition provided less incentive to do strict oversight.

Despite its shortcoming as a democracy, Afghanistan is starting to develop civilian control over the military, with domestic politics playing a role in what the

Afghan National Army (ANA) is willing to do. As the Afghans began taking more responsibility, they acted more as an ally with areas of responsibility and less like trainees to be moved and ordered as NATO saw fit. Even as early as the spring of 2012, Afghan units played their red cards, refusing to engage in nighttime raids.[1] Kevin Sieff notes that "'[i]n the last two months, 14 to 16 [night] operations have been rejected by the Afghans,' said Gen. Sher Mohammad Karimi, the top Afghan army officer. 'The U.S. has said, "This operation better be conducted. It's a high-value target." Then my people said, "It's a high-value target. I agree with you. But there are so many civilian children and women [in the area].""'[2]

While this may be seen as "defiance," the reality is that empowering the ANA means giving the former students the ability to say no. Given how controversial these raids have been, it should not be surprising that the first times the ANA wields the red card, it is over these operations. The more Afghanistan becomes an ordinary country, democratic or not, the more it will use a variety of means to control how its forces are used. Building the ANA is not just about training more kandaks but also developing civilian control of the military. These red cards signify that NATO will have to view the Afghans as an allied contingent with similar constraints. That may not eliminate all frustration, but it could allow ISAF commanders to apply the mitigation strategies that they have developed over ten years of war in Afghanistan and from prior experiences in the Balkans.

## Implications for Future Research

As we noted in chapter 1, there has been relatively little work done on how alliances operate during wartime, with more study focused on why countries form alliances and how long they endure. As a consequence, how multilateral warfare actually works (or does not work) is poorly understood. We chose to study NATO because it not only has been involved in a particularly long and controversial mission in Afghanistan but because it is the most capable, most institutionalized, and most practiced alliance or coalition of this or perhaps any era. NATO has arguably succeeded in out-of-area interventions as long as one keeps the standards relatively low. That success, however, has not come without internal friction whenever burdens are not shared evenly or optimally across the alliance.

One implication of our work is the shedding of light on the forum-shopping process associated with military interventions. Recall from chapter 2 that forum shopping occurs when countries have more than one option from which to choose when deciding whether and how to intervene. The experiences of Afghanistan

---

1  Kevin Sieff, "Afghan Commanders Show New Defiance in Dealings with Americans," *Washington Post*, May 11, 2012, http://www.washingtonpost.com/world/asia_pacific/afghan-commanders-show-new -defiance-in-dealings-with-americans/2012/05/11/gIQAMdNTHU_story.html, accessed May 15, 2012.
2  Ibid.

and Libya remind us that while there may be other outlets for multilateral military operations, NATO, despite its limitations (or perhaps because of them), is almost always the preferred intervention forum for its member states. A key distinction between NATO and the United Nations, for instance, is that NATO tends to set relatively broad parameters within which countries can choose to operate while the UN tends to set restrictive rules of engagement. As a result, NATO actually gives countries more useful flexibility. In addition, NATO countries are far more interoperable than are the militaries in most UN operations, and NATO has a ready-made force generation process. These advantages make NATO a preferred choice in most recent interventions.

In the interventions of the recent past and the near future, some have viewed coalitions of the willing as an attractive alternative to NATO and its relatively burdensome decision processes in Brussels (Kreps 2011; Weitsman 2013). What is often underappreciated is that coalitions of the willing have many of the problems that formal alliances have but come with fewer benefits. The United States learned in Iraq that countries can still have caveats and play red cards in a coalition of the willing. The "willing" really only refers to countries willing to participate in the effort. It does not refer to "willing to do everything one is asked to do," as the tales in chapter 1 illustrated. Still, more research is required to assess how less formalized, multilateral military efforts compensate for the challenges with which NATO has become quite familiar and even relatively adept.

There is another, more subtle, distinction between NATO and alternatives that we found in the course of research that could use more systematic exploration. NATO appears to put pressure on left-wing parties in ways that other multilateral endeavors, such as coalitions of the willing, do not. In several countries, including Canada in regard to Libya and in the Netherlands throughout the Afghanistan effort, weaker (smaller, or younger, or both) left-wing parties faced a dilemma. To be seen as a mainstream party suitable for being a coalition partner or leading party, these left-wing parties, with pacifist backgrounds, had to be seen as supportive of or compatible with NATO. This has meant supporting some NATO efforts, such as Libya for Canada's New Democratic Party (for the first few months at least) and the Dutch training mission Afghanistan in 2011 for the GreenLeft and Democrats-66 parties. This was not something we were looking for, so we did not engage in a systematic comparison of left-wing parties across Europe to determine what conditions require such parties to need to appear to be NATO-supportive. Moreover, in our cases, it is hard to determine the relative impact of this dynamic compared to the effects of UN and *responsibility to protect* norms. In future work, scholars should consider under what conditions left-wing parties are constrained by this dynamic and when they can ignore such pressures. Parties might be driven by public opinion or intraparty dynamics, or by clever agenda-setting on the part of other parties. On this last point, supporters of interventions could choose an intervention forum precisely to trap left-wing parties into supporting the intervention. The point here is that future work should explore how NATO may matter in a variety of ways, including shaping domestic political debates.

The second set of implications deals with the use of principal agency (PA) theory in civil-military relations. This book is hardly the first effort to apply principal-agent logic to understanding civilian control of the military. It is, however, the only work that we know of that combines two different uses of PA models. The first use was at the international level. Here we categorized military interventions according to which type of PA model most closely represents the command relationship between deployed military units and the multilateral entity guiding those units. That categorization allowed us to determine where deployed military units were likely to look for guidance. In the NATO case, the command relationships represented a hybrid PA model, which meant that deployed units had to decide which delegation path was more influential: the national chain of command or the ISAF chain. We demonstrated in chapter 2 and in the case study chapters that the national chain trumped the NATO chain. The second use of PA models was at the subnational level. Here we explicitly distinguished four control mechanisms used by civilian principals—agent selection, contingent delegation, oversight, and incentives—to control their deployed military contingents, and linked their use to different types of democratic governments during military conflicts. In this way our approach went beyond many treatments of PA relations in the civil-military relations literature. We focused on all four mechanisms of control in a cross-national study, rather than on a single mechanism used across countries or the use of multiple mechanisms in a single country. Our study showed not only that there are multiple ways to control military agents but that countries vary systematically in which means they use.

The next step is to consider this full toolbox of control mechanisms in other contexts. We explored their use by different types of democracies. Our cases suggested, however, a possible correlation between the size of a country and its reliance on particular control mechanisms. For example, smaller countries with smaller militaries may not be able to rely upon agent selection if there are very few qualified officers for key posts. Conversely, agent selection is an especially useful tool in countries with large forces, such as the United States, particularly if it demands that coalition forces must be commanded by Americans. Other possible questions might include the use of control mechanisms across a wider range of coalition-of-the-willing interventions, across time, or by authoritarian states rather than democracies.

Another potentially fruitful research agenda involves the evolution of caveats, a key aspect of any delegation contract. As caveats gained greater attention and opprobrium at a series of NATO summits, countries promised to reduce them. An interesting question is whether countries react to these criticisms in the same way that they reacted to reductions in tariffs (by creating nontariff barriers). Instead of formal restrictions that are listed in the transfer of authority paperwork, countries in the future might rely on other means to restrict their forces, such as limiting the capabilities available to deployed commanders. We saw that some ISAF countries sent very few helicopters to Afghanistan, greatly constraining what their contingents could do. For the Germans, this shortage of lift capacity combined with their various standard operating procedures to constrain greatly the reach of German forces. Future research could explore whether such capability limits are intended to reduce risk or are simply due to shortages.

Finally, there are implications in our work for the control of civilian agencies deployed in war. There was a very important civilian side to the conflict in Afghanistan, as counterinsurgency and stabilization efforts involve more than just combat but also governance and development. The alliance supported a "comprehensive approach" that was to coordinate all three major efforts: defense, democracy, and development. Just as countries need to influence how their militaries act abroad, they also need to control their diplomats and aid officials (and the police and wardens doing security sector reform and the like). But while the various militaries coordinated via NATO, there was no NATO apparatus aimed at command and control on the civilian side. Each provincial reconstruction team was run by a country or a partnership of countries, with nearly all instructions coming from the respective national capitals. Future scholarship on the civilian side should take quite seriously the arguments we have made here, as they apply fully to control of deployed civilians. There are multiple means to control civilian aid workers, diplomats, and the like, including agent selection, discretion, oversight, and incentives. We know of no source that discusses how those mechanisms are used on the civilian side during military conflicts, and indeed if control mechanisms used for civilians lead to civilian behavior that works at cross-purposes to military efforts. In short, analysts should consider whether countries use similar means to control their military and civilian contingents, what the consequences may be for "whole of government" efforts if the civilians and military are managed differently, and whether there is systematic variation among democracies.

The remaining set of implications for new research focuses on domestic politics and foreign policy. Our work is another in a line of analysis focusing on domestic institutional differences. Our contribution on this front is threefold. First, we specifically incorporated a consideration of actor preferences into our domestic institutional analysis. Our combined approach may be slightly less parsimonious than other models, but it provided us with interesting and well-supported hypotheses. Second, we gathered new insights into the workings of coalition governments. While some scholars, particularly Juliet Kaarbo (2008, 2012), have considered how coalition government influences decision making, this work was previously not connected to how countries engage in war. By adopting and adapting George Tsebelis's (2002) veto-player arguments and Brian Rathbun's (2004) linkage between ideology and foreign policy stances, we can understand not only why coalition governments would tend to impose more restrictions on their troops in the field but also why they may not use other means to control their troops. Also, we could anticipate *which* coalition governments might manage to give greater discretion. Third, our evidence demonstrated an important distinction between coalition governments and their presidential and majoritarian counterparts. We found that the distinctions between presidential systems and British-style parliamentary systems are not as significant as Deborah Avant (1994) has argued, at least in comparison with coalition governments. Future research may suggest whether the distinctions drawn between these different types of democracies hold up in other realms besides alliance warfare—such as defense procurements, doctrine, and decisions to go to war. Along the way, we learned of key differences in how legislatures oversee their militaries. More work is required to understand the variation within key types—within Westminster systems and among other parliamentary systems.

The Afghanistan mission was an ideal case for comparative analysis—dozens of countries participated in both Operation Enduring Freedom and ISAF, with governments and leaders back home changing over time. While countries faced similarly difficult challenges in the field, they did not react identically. The effort in Libya demonstrated that the dynamics we found in Afghanistan were not unique to that particular conflict. Future work should consider these and other cases, as they are fruitful for comparing and contrasting how countries react to various domestic and international pressures. Likewise, policy makers would be wise to look to the lessons from ISAF as they consider new multilateral military operations.

## Lessons Learned for Policy Makers

The first lesson that policy makers should draw from this experience is that caveats and other "inconvenient" mechanisms of national control are not going to go away and are inherent in any multilateral military effort. Article V of the NATO

Treaty has opt-out language precisely because it would be difficult to get countries to agree to the treaty and certainly agree to a military effort if the article obligated countries to give up any and all control over their militaries when deployed under a NATO banner. This is not just about countries unwilling to give up sovereignty; it is more critically an issue of civilian control of the military. For many countries, every war they fight, every use of force, is part of a multilateral effort. If these countries always just turned over their forces to an alliance with no means to influence how they operate, they would be surrendering civilian control of their militaries, an often overlooked but critically important feature of democratic governance. Organizations such as NATO cannot get rid of caveats and their ilk. The best NATO can do is to mitigate their impact. In this section of the conclusion, we first review how these challenges impact the effectiveness of operations. We consider how such obstacles could be surmounted or ameliorated. We then evaluate the policy initiative that NATO has deployed to address the fiscal crisis—the Smart Defence Initiative—since our study has significant implications for this effort.

## EFFECTIVENESS

The tales we told in chapter 1 as well as in the case studies indicate that national control often gets in the way of military operations. Red cards, caveats, phone calls home, frequent changes in leadership, and very specific incentives can all add friction to a war effort, making it harder for an alliance or a coalition to achieve its aims. Evaluating the impact of these mechanisms of control upon NATO's effectiveness in Afghanistan is quite difficult. First, NATO officials have expressed frustration about how to measure success.[3] Without clear "metrics" of success it is hard to measure whether any particular strategy or tactic is effective. That is, without a good measure of the outcome, it is hard to ascertain the impact of different causal factors. Second, failure in Afghanistan will have many mothers and fathers. National control may have an impact, but it is hard to disentangle the relevance of these limitations from other forces at work: Pakistan's support for various insurgents; President Hamid Karzai's tactics, which have often undermined the alliance's effort; and the role of poppy cultivation and corruption across the Afghan government and population. Third, the war is more than just about the battlefield, and NATO is mostly a military organization. It got involved in the civilian side, but has much less capacity there. Instead, NATO members and partners followed

---

3 This was observed by the authors while attending roundtables that included senior NATO leadership.

their preferred governance and development efforts in their sectors, which had the potential to work at cross-purposes among regions and over time.

Despite these disclaimers, it is clear that the mixture of caveats, phone leashes, restricted capabilities, and all the rest did reduce NATO's effectiveness. The Germans had very little visibility over their sectors due to the combination of helicopter shortages, restrictive rules of engagement, and standard operating procedures. The same is true for the western part of Afghanistan, with the more quietly restricted Italians. The Dutch and Australians relied on different strategies (phones and reliance on special operations, respectively) to reduce risks, causing their forces to be less effective than otherwise would have been the case. Still, because NATO's more flexible members could not deploy more troops with the United States distracted by Iraq, with the Canadians and Danes having small armies, with the British overstretched, and so on, the forces with more caveats and restrictions were making contributions, holding some territory that would otherwise have lacked any presence by outside forces.

The key, ultimately, is this: any effort by more than one country is arguably less efficient than if one country can handle the operation alone. But with the United States constrained and unable to dedicate more troops to Afghanistan throughout most of the decade, NATO troops filled that gap, perhaps underperforming when compared to the United States, but being more effective than the alternative of having no forces at work in the north, west, and south of Afghanistan. As we learned from the Libyan experience, coalitions of the willing may be fast but they lack the capacity that NATO has developed over the decades, not to mention the added legitimacy.

## MITIGATING RESTRICTIONS

As we documented in chapter 1 and then in the case study chapters, the various mechanisms that democracies use to manage their troops are not new, and they are certainly not novel to the commanders of NATO operations.[4] These officers may not always know all of the restrictions, nor will they know when the phone calls home will produce nos rather than yesses, but they have learned some tactics to anticipate these problems and reduce their impact. Here, we address three different methods that have been used when confronting challenges posed by national control of contingents: creative force allocation, scenario scheming, and reliance upon special operations forces (SOF).

---

4   Yet many military officers remain unaware of how NATO interacts with its members. See Stephen Saideman, "Shield and the US: How Realistic Is the Avengers Movie?" *Duck of Minerva* (blog), May 27, 2012, http://duckofminerva.blogspot.ca/2012/05/shield-and-us-how-realistic-is-avengers.html, accessed June 21, 2012.

First, if countries vary in what they can do, NATO commanders can try to deploy the various contingents in ways that maximize each contingent's effectiveness. During the Balkan wars, NATO enforced an embargo that limited the goods reaching the rump Yugoslavia.[5] In any embargo there are concentric circles around the targeted ports. The ships in the outer ring have the responsibility of detecting ships that might violate the embargo and signaling to them so that the potential violators turn around. The second ring of ships engages in similar activity with more strident warnings. If a ship continues past, the NATO vessels in the inner ring may then use force, firing across the bow, boarding the ship, or even firing upon the ship if need be. The problem, of course, is that not all countries participating in the embargo have the same comfort level in using force. Those with more restrictive rules of engagement due to caveats or capabilities limitations can be placed on the outer ring where the risks and requirements are much lower. In the case of the Balkan embargo, German ships were placed on the outer ring and the U.S. and British ships were the last line of enforcement.

In Afghanistan, the deployment of contingents around the country largely matched what countries could do—the Americans, Brits, Danes, and Canadians were in the more "kinetic" south and east not only because they did not have geographic restrictions but because they also had few limits on their ability to use force. The Germans, Italians, and Spaniards would have been less than effective if they had moved south or east because of their restrictions on the use of force. Former ISAF commander and head of the Canadian military General Rick Hillier said in such a circumstance, "They would have zero effect and be a disaster for their own contingent."[6]

This strategic deployment of troops obviously has political consequences—some countries bear more risk and responsibility than others. This uneven burden sharing creates resentment on all sides, felt by publics and by leaders. However, the alternative, to put troops who have their hands tied into harm's way, is a very dangerous and counterproductive way to operate.

Second, NATO leaders can learn as much as they can to fine-tune their expectations. The commander of NATO forces in Kabul in 2004, Brigadier General Jocelyn Lacroix, brought together the commanders of all of the ISAF contingents in the area at the time.[7] He gave each officer three standard scenarios covering the range of potential operations, and asked each commander to call home and work out what his nation could and could not contribute to each of these scenarios.

---

5  Retired Canadian vice admiral Greg Maddison, who had served in this NATO effort and later as Deputy Chief of the Defence Staff, shared this strategy in an interview, Montreal, June 19, 2007.

6  General Rick Hillier indicated that a unit burdened with caveats that was moving to RC-S (not identifying the Germans specifically) would sacrifice lives without achieving much; interview, Ottawa, March 11, 2008.

7  Interview with Brigadier General Jocelyn Lacroix, former commander of Kabul Multinational Brigade, Kingston, Ontario, February 6, 2007.

Lacroix then had each national commander brief the rest of the contingent commanders on what they would and would not do in each of the three situations. This allowed not only Lacroix as the NATO commander but all of the senior officers of all of the contingents to reset expectations. As a result, commanders would not be asked to do things that they would have to decline, avoiding embarrassment. Instead of nagging countries to do what they cannot do, NATO leaders learned to encourage them in less embarrassing ways.[8] This tactic is good for reducing embarrassment and increasing predictability, but it does not produce radically more flexible partners.

The third tactic is to rely on unconventional forces to avoid the restrictions imposed by caveats, red cards, phone calls, and the like. Special operations forces are cloaked in secrecy, which limits public scrutiny and in many situations legislative oversight. The result is that these units operate in places that conventional forces are not allowed to tread and with different rules of engagement. SOF essentially allow countries to do more than they might otherwise do. The Australian story in chapter 7 was largely about risk mitigation and limiting oversight. The Special Air Service and commandos were doing nearly all of the combat because they were better at war, with lower likelihood of incurring casualties, and reduced oversight might have been advantageous as well to those in power. Any student of the NATO war in Afghanistan will have heard of rumors of German special operations forces operating outside of Regional Command–North.

There are two problems with reliance on SOF. Most obviously, they undermine democratic control of the military if there are different rules for SOF, especially if those rules are designed to evade legal restrictions on conventional forces. The other problem is that the S in SOF stands for *special*, which logically means that these are smaller units. SOF cannot occupy large swathes of territory, and because they are so few, they can be overextended over the course of a long mission. Using SOF may be the most appealing way to try to address caveats, but the easiest choice often has the greatest consequences. It is not clear that the stakes in any operation are worth subverting civilian control of the military.

## THE SMART DEFENCE INITIATIVE AND BURDEN SHARING

The Smart Defence Initiative is the NATO alliance's most recent attempt to reconcile shrinking defense budgets with the security needs of the alliance. To put Smart Defence into context, consider that fully half of NATO members regularly

---

8  To be clear, we also had interviews with officers who preferred to use shame to try to persuade reluctant allies.

do not meet the alliance's stated defense spending goal of 2 percent of national gross domestic product. Many members of the alliance do not have the political will and/or public support to increase defense spending. Absent a significant threat to national survival, states usually face the opposite pressure: to cut defense spending in favor of domestic priorities. This is particularly true during periods of fiscal austerity, such as during the 2008–13 global downturn and the corresponding European debt crises.

One solution to insufficient investments in defense is to specialize. Rather than trying to field a complete military force with very limited defense budgets, it would, in theory, be more efficient and cost-effective for alliance members to focus on select niche capabilities. Individual states would spend their limited dollars on one advanced military capability, and do it well, rather than spreading themselves thin trying to buy a little bit of everything. For example, a country could focus on air defense, light infantry, or chemical weapons response teams— just to name a few possibilities—rather than trying to field a complete air force, army, and navy, all with the most advanced equipment and all at the same time. In theory, the alliance as a whole would still maintain a complete spectrum of military capabilities and could aggregate those capabilities whenever needed for alliance operations. The benefits of Smart Defence would include better integration of European military forces and less demand on the United States to provide the required equipment and personnel to fill out hollow European military capabilities.

The debate over Smart Defence seems to ignore the dynamics identified in this book. Will countries that specialize in niche capabilities procure them in adequate amounts for alliance needs? Might not countries with critical capabilities refuse to participate in an alliance intervention, impeding that intervention? Will countries participating in interventions have so many caveats that they cannot be relied upon? In short, is the NATO alliance capable of providing complementary, rather than redundant, equipment and forces?

NATO tried to foster specialization in the early years of the twenty-first century with the Prague Summit.[9] Lord George Robertson, NATO secretary general at the time, said that the goal was for "role specialization for smaller countries, joint procurement projects, or pooling of assets."[10] And indeed, new NATO members did just that.[11] The push for niche capabilities was met with skepticism, however,

---

9  North Atlantic Treaty Organization, "Prague Summit Declaration," Press Release (2002) 127, November 21, 2002, http://www.nato.int/docu/pr/2002/p02-127e.htm, accessed April 24, 2013.

10 Lord George Robertson, quoted in Christina Mackenzie, "NATO Aims to Create New Niche," November 19, 2002, http://www.flightglobal.com/news/articles/nato-aims-to-create-new-niche-158077/, accessed June 3, 2013.

11 The Prague Seven were the seven members—Bulgaria, Estonia, Latvia, Lithuania, Romania, Slovakia, and Slovenia—invited to join NATO at the Prague Summit.

from countries that were reluctant to give up their defense autonomy, even if that autonomy relied on outdated weapons systems.[12] French Defense Ministry officials were quoted at the time as saying that "No government is going to agree to be limited to one area of specialty."[13] Another concern was that this initiative would actually make the alliance *less* interoperable. Specialization would further speed the ongoing trend toward creating a two-tiered NATO. One tier would include members with more complete forces—such as the United States, the United Kingdom, France, and perhaps Germany—each capable of global power projection, either individually or in small partnerships. These members would maintain more complete and advanced military capabilities. The second tier would include the rest of the alliance, the vast majority of whom could not operate successfully either alone or in partnership with other second-tier nations. As important for our purposes, specialization in the early years of the new century never moved beyond the smaller and less powerful NATO countries. Perhaps this was because, in the view of many transatlantic security specialists, "Past initiatives within NATO or the EU to promote role specialization *have all foundered on the question of trust, namely the fear that other countries will not bring missing capabilities into play when needed.*"[14]

Specialization was not evident to a significant degree with regard to ISAF deployments among countries making significant contributions of more than five hundred soldiers. Indeed, specialization was rejected by major ISAF members. For example, the United States refused to rely on any other country for critical military needs or capabilities. The Netherlands refused to deploy ground forces without its own F-16s for close air support. Specialization, when it did occur, was occasionally the cause of resentment or misunderstanding among ISAF members. Major ISAF contributors sometimes did not trust the specialized capabilities provided by their allies.

Resentment over specialization would also occur in the opposite direction, when units from one country would have to assist or even rescue units from another because that second country did not have the inherent capabilities to accomplish the mission on its own. A classic example occurred in Regional Command–South (RC-South) between the Canadian and British contingents in the first years after NATO assumed responsibility for the region. The Canadians had not brought significant logistical and transportation capabilities with them, instead relying on allied capabilities when they needed to travel overland. The

---

12 Stanley Sloan, *Re-engineering the Transatlantic Security and Defense Relationship*. Wilton Park Conference Report 1129, September 23, 2011, https://www.wiltonpark.org.uk/wp-content/uploads/wp1129-report.pdf, accessed October 1, 2011.
13 Mackenzie, "NATO Aims to Create a New Niche."
14 Sloan, *Re-engineering the Transatlantic Security and Defense Relationship*, 6; emphasis added.

British, who operated in a neighboring sector and had transportation capabilities, grew to resent this. In the words of one British brigadier general who served in RC-South, "Every time the Canadians wanted to move somewhere, we would have to move them. We took casualties every single time. Their movements were getting my soldiers shot."[15] Specialization, then, often did not occur or sometimes led to alliance inefficiencies and resentment among ISAF members.

These dynamics will become increasingly problematic over the next several years, as most NATO countries and partner nations face pressure to cut their defense budgets. The more specialization that is attempted as a result, the more vulnerable will be the alliance to the vagaries of the domestic political processes within each alliance member. As countries cut or tailor their defense capabilities, alliance members will be forced to rely on allies to provide the various capabilities that the country will no longer be able to provide on its own. Again, this makes a great deal of sense in theory. But in alliance warfare, allies sometimes do not always show up when needed or they show up but are not able to do what is needed.

Consider that specialization worked in the 2011 Libyan intervention, but only just barely and only because the United States, the United Kingdom, and France—three countries that still had relatively complete militaries—did the lion's share of the work. The Americans and the British largely neutralized the Libyan air defense system to start the intervention. The British and French conducted the majority of the subsequent air strikes on Libyan ground targets, while five other (non-U.S.) countries took part in air strikes to a lesser degree. The United States provided roughly 70 percent of the intelligence, refueling, strategic lift, and unmanned aerial vehicle capabilities during Operation Unified Protector. A variety of other nations enforced the no-fly-zone and the sea-based embargo. That said, precision munitions were in short supply as the conflict dragged out, and the operation could not have lasted long without U.S. munitions and support capabilities (Quintana 2012).[16] Once again there were denunciations of a two-tiered NATO and frustrations at dramatically uneven burden sharing (Bandow 2012; Barry 2011; Etzioni 2012; Noetzel and Schreer 2012). In the words of one observer, "The campaign has also shown the limits of force specialization within Europe. With countries such as Germany opting out or others, such as Italy, offering only hesitant support, the campaign kicked off without vital European capabilities" (Anrig 2011: 105).

The domestically inspired restrictions on some countries will mean that their allies, who also have specialized militaries, could be at great risk when conflicts

---

15 Interview with senior British military officer, Washington, D.C., February 2009.
16 "If the United States military were to cease its participation in the NATO operation, it would seriously degrade the coalition's ability to execute and sustain its operation designed to protect Libyan civilians and to enforce the no-fly zone and the arms embargo." White House 2011: 13.

start. A specialized cast of NATO characters will have to hope that political restrictions do not impede the support they expect and need from their alliance
partners who have critically needed, specialized capabilities. What, then, are supporters of the NATO alliance to do when Smart Defence may founder on the
question of trust—trust in whether an ally with a promised critical capability will
participate fully in a future conflict or will have actually spent the money on the
required capability? An assessment of each country's domestic circumstances can
help identify when allies might fall short on both measures. That same assessment
holds a key to a possible solution.

The goal in any NATO strategy should be to take advantage of both the domestic political makeup and national military capabilities of each member state. One
could tailor NATO strategy depending on whether or not Article V was invoked
for a military operation. For non–Article V missions that occur outside of NATO
territory, like Libya, one solution would be to negotiate a formal alliance operation to take advantage of NATO's coordination and force generation mechanisms.
Participation in the mission would be asked of member states that had the specialized tools/capabilities necessary for the operation and the domestic political
leeway to participate. In most circumstances that would rule out member states
that had parliamentary coalition governments or minimal military assets. Participation would essentially have to come from moderately powerful countries with
presidential or majority parliamentary governments—that is, Canada, England,
France, Poland, and Turkey. Even here, though, there would be no guarantee of
participation or of unconstrained participation, as witnessed by Turkish behavior
in ISAF and Libya or Polish abstention in Libya. To sweeten the pot, the alliance
could reward contributors with "flags to posts" in exchange for unconstrained
contributions, an idea that the British parliament has already advocated (UK
House of Commons 2012: 63). This would be particularly germane for postings in
deployed commands or NATO operational headquarters. Essentially, the alliance
would trade influence for participation.

A different recruitment strategy could be used for Article V missions. Here, all
alliance members would be expected to participate in traditional Article V missions aimed at the territorial defense of NATO territory. Participation would be
mandatory, which is a change from the current alliance rules. The rationale here
would be that ignoring a military attack on a NATO member state's territory calls
into question the alliance's overall purpose and certainly that particular state's alliance membership. Those members who failed to agree to this requirement could
leave the alliance. With full participation, one could utilize the specialization
afforded by the Smart Defence Initiative with less concern that one or another
country would fail to come to the aid of its neighbor, and minimize the fear that
currently exists in the minds of some officials in central European member states.

# Conclusion

We began this book with two conflicting views on the value of military coalitions and alliances. Napoleon Bonaparte's view was that coalitions were more trouble than they were worth. Winston Churchill took the opposite view, believing that alliances were crucial for military success. In the current era, proponents of each argument have used NATO's war in Afghanistan as an example that proves their point. On the one hand are those who believe the alliance has been more trouble than it is worth; that the alliance's outdated equipment, persistent caveats, and co-ordination problems have forced the United States to do most of the heavy lifting in the conflict. The ISAF mission, from this perspective, has exposed the inherent weaknesses in the alliance, and Libya has simply reinforced that impression. On the other hand are those who argue that the NATO alliance has been instrumental to the successes we have seen in Afghanistan; that allies have fought valiantly in dangerous regions, provided international legitimacy to the effort, and eased the burden on the United States, which consequently allowed it to focus on other conflicts and hot spots. The alliance has been strengthened as a result, as proven by the military success in Libya.

This book has demonstrated that the NATO alliance is alive and well, but that no one should be complacent and assume that the alliance will always be this way. We argued that the NATO alliance establishes a hybrid principal-agent relationship that has advantages over alternative coalition-of-the-willing arrangements, particularly from the perspective of the leading members of the alliance. Most important, the alliance allows countries to maintain control over their individual militaries while providing alliance-wide coordinated command and control, interoperability standards, force generation procedures, and international legitimacy. At the same time, the alliance's decision-making mechanisms allow for national control over military contingents, a prerequisite for military interventions by advanced democracies and something those countries do not seem prepared to forgo. The NATO alliance's procedures allow countries to maintain such country-specific control mechanisms, and that freedom ensures that member states are willing even to consider contributing to alliance efforts.

Domestic politics is a double-edged sword for the alliance, however. For all the good that domestic variability provides in terms of civil-military relations, there are negative effects associated with different domestic perspectives on NATO missions. Indeed, there is cause for concern on behalf of the alliance as we factor in the domestic level of analysis into alliance debates. Different countries will use different control mechanisms—whether agent selection, contingent delegation, oversight, or incentives—depending on their domestic institutional structure and the political dynamics within that structure.

As we saw in several cases in this book, differences in those control mechanisms have led to inefficient use of alliance resources and political friction between alliance members. A recent U.S. progress report on Afghanistan made this very point with regard to national caveats, noting, "National caveats are invoked by individual coalition partners to ensure forces operate in accordance with their respective national laws and policies. Regardless of national caveats, all ISAF coalition partners in Afghanistan operate according to the ISAF Rules of Engagement, which govern the use of force. Although some allies and partners have reduced these caveats, national caveats continue to constrain ISAF operations by limiting the types of missions a given country's forces are authorized to undertake. Senior U.S. leadership consistently emphasizes the need to reduce national caveats in order to allow for the greatest operational effect."[17]

Combine caveats with ever-tightening budgets caused by sovereign debt crises—on both sides of the Atlantic—and we could eventually reach a point at which the Europeans believe that non–Article V overseas contingency operations are simply too expensive and risky, and the United States believes that the benefits of securing European interests are just not worth the cost. At that point the alliance will be finished. Secretary of Defense Robert Gates noted in a June 2011 speech in Brussels that "if current trends in the decline of European defense capabilities are not halted and reversed, future U.S. political leaders—those for whom the Cold War was not the formative experience that it was for me—may not consider the return on America's investment in NATO worth the cost" (quoted in Sloan 2011: 4).

We believe that NATO has not yet reached that point and is not going away anytime soon. It is the most interoperable and powerful alliance on the planet, helping to coordinate the efforts of many of the world's advanced democracies. For some countries, any multinational effort has to be a NATO operation or they will not participate. There are times when a great power like the United States might feel that it is easier to operate alone. With NATO, however, the United States has allies that bring international legitimacy, assets that the United States does not possess, and capabilities that are in short supply. The United States relied heavily on the allies in Afghanistan when the administration of President George W. Bush was focused on Iraq. With China and other challenges in Asia, the United States will have to rely on NATO to help out in Europe, the Middle East, and North Africa. Going it alone is less desirable than warring as a coalition, even with all of the restrictions and problems presented in this book.

---

17 U.S. Department of Defense, *Report on Progress Toward Security and Stability in Afghanistan*, April 2012, p. 12, http://www.defense.gov/pubs/pdfs/Report_Final_SecDef_04_27_12.pdf, accessed May 1, 2012.

The major lesson here is that countries planning to use force in the world today must enter collaborative arrangements with their eyes wide open. There are challenges associated with multilateral warfare. Each country may be a burden bearer or a rations consumer, depending on the situation, the personalities of the leaders, and the imperatives of coalition politics at home. Successfully engaging in multilateral, military operations requires managing the risks involved. This book identifies one set of difficulties—how other countries control their contingents—and how they vary. By doing so, we hope that the next set of leaders to deploy troops are aware of the inevitable trade-offs when allies go to war.

# References

Aldrich, John H., Christopher Gelpi, Peter Feaver, Jason Reifler, and Kristin Thompson Sharp. 2006. "Foreign Policy and the Electoral Connection." *Annual Review of Political Science* 9(1): 477–502.

Alter, Karen J., and Sophie Meunier. 2009. "The Politics of International Regime Complexity." *Perspectives on Politics* 7(1): 13–24.

Altfeld, Michael F. 1984. "The Decision to Ally—A Theory and Test." *Western Political Quarterly* 37(4): 523–44.

Ambinder, Marc, and D. B. Grady. 2012. "The Story of How U.S. Special Forces Infiltrated Pakistan." *Atlantic*, February 15.

Anderson, Terry H. 2011. *Bush's Wars.* New York: Oxford University Press.

Anrig, Christian F. 2011. "Views and Analyses—Allied Air Power over Libya: A Preliminary Assessment." *Air and Space Power Journal* 25(4): 89–109.

Auerswald, David. P. 1999. "Inward Bound: Domestic Institutions and Military Conflicts." *International Organization* 53(3), 469–504.

———. 2000. *Disarmed Democracies: Domestic Institutions and the Use of Force.* Ann Arbor: University of Michigan Press.

———. 2004. "Explaining Wars of Choice: An Integrated Decision Model of NATO Policy in Kosovo." *International Studies Quarterly* 48(3): 631–62.

Auerswald, Philip E., and David P. Auerswald. 2000. *The Kosovo Conflict: A Diplomatic History through Documents.* Cambridge: Kluwer Law International.

Avant, Deborah D. 1994. *Political Institutions and Military Change: Lessons from Peripheral Wars.* Ithaca, NY: Cornell University Press.

Baltrusaitis, Daniel F. 2010. *Coalition Politics and the Iraq War: Determinants of Choice.* Boulder, CO: First Forum.

Bandow, Doug. 2012. "NATO and Libya: It's Time to Retire a Fading Alliance." *Forbes*, January 2.

Barnett, Michael N., and Martha Finnemore. 2004. *Rules for the World: International Organizations in Global Politics.* Ithaca, NY: Cornell University Press.

Barno, David W. 2007. "Fighting 'The Other War': Counterinsurgency Strategy in Afghanistan, 2003–2005." *Military Review* 87(5): 32–44.

Barry, Ben. 2011. "Libya's Lessons." *Survival* 53(5): 5–14.

Beasley, Ryan K., Juliet Kaarbo, Charles F. Hermann, and Margaret G. Hermann. 2001. "People and Processes in Foreign Policymaking: Insights from Comparative Case Studies." *International Studies Review* 3(2): 217–50.

Beer, Francis A. 1969. *Integration and Disintegration in NATO*. Columbus: Ohio State University Press.

Bennett, D. Scott. 1997. "Testing Alternative Models of Alliance Duration, 1816–1984." *American Journal of Political Science* 41(3): 846–78.

Bensahel, Nora. 1999. The Coalition Paradox: The Politics of Military Cooperation. PhD diss., Department of Political Science, Stanford University, Stanford, CA.

———. 2003. *The Counterterror Coalitions: Cooperation with Europe, NATO, and the European Union*. Santa Monica, CA: RAND.

———. 2006. "A Coalition of Coalitions: International Cooperation against Terrorism." *Studies in Conflict and Terrorism* 29(1): 35–49.

Bercuson, David Jay. 1996. *Significant Incident: Canada's Army, the Airborne, and the Murder in Somalia*. Toronto: M&S.

Bergen, Peter. 2011. *The Longest War: The Enduring Conflict between America and Al-Qaeda*. New York: Free Press.

Berger, Thomas U. 1998. *Cultures of Antimilitarism: National Security in Germany and Japan*. Baltimore: Johns Hopkins University Press.

Bergman, Torbjörn, Wolfgang C. Müller, and Kaare Strøm. 2000. "Introduction: Parliamentary Democracy and the Chain of Delegation." *European Journal of Political Research* 37(3): 255–60.

Blanchard, Christopher M. 2009. *Afghanistan: Narcotics and US Policy*. New York: Nova Science.

Brewster, Murray, ed. 2011. *The Savage War: The Untold Battles of Afghanistan*. Mississauga, ON: Wiley.

Brooks, Risa. 2008. *Shaping Strategy: The Civil-Military Politics of Strategic Assessment*. Princeton, NJ: Princeton University Press.

Brooks, Risa, and E. A. Stanley. 2007. *Creating Military Power: The Sources of Military Effectiveness*: Stanford, CA: Stanford University Press.

Brzezinski, Zbigniew. 2009. "A Tale of Two Wars: The Right War in Iraq, and the Wrong One." *Foreign Affairs* 88(3): 148–52.

Bueno de Mesquita, Bruce, and Rudolph M. Siverson. 1995. "War and the Survival of Political Leaders: A Comparative Study of Regime Types and Political Accountability." *American Political Science Review* 89(4): 841–55.

Bueno de Mesquita, Bruce, Alistair Smith, Rudolph M. Siverson, and James D. Morrow. 2005. *The Logic of Political Survival*. Cambridge, MA: MIT Press.

Busch, Marc L. 2007. "Overlapping Institutions, Forum Shopping, and Dispute Settlement in International Trade." *International Organization* 61(4): 735–61.

Calvert, Randall L., Matthew Daniel McCubbins, and Barry R. Weingast. 1989. "A Theory of Political Control and Agency Discretion." *American Journal of Political Science* 33(3): 588–611.

Cameron, Alistair. 2012. "The Channel Axis: France, the UK and NATO." In *Short War, Long Shadow: The Political and Military Legacies of the 2011 Libya Campaign*, ed. Adrian Johnson and Saqeb Mueen, 15–24. London: Royal United Services Institute.

Camyar, Isa. 2011. "Party Politics and International Trade: Mainstream Parties, Niche Parties, and Trade Openness." *International Studies Quarterly* 56(2): 397–404.

Chan, Steve, and William Safran. 2006. "Public Opinion as a Constraint against War: Democracies' Responses to Operation Iraqi Freedom." *Foreign Policy Analysis* 2(2): 137–56.

Chiozza, Giacomo, and H. E. Goemans. 2004. "International Conflict and the Tenure of Leaders: Is War Still Ex-Post Inefficient?" *American Journal of Political Science* 48(3): 604–19.

Chryssogelos, Angelos-Stylianos. 2010. "Undermining the West from Within: European Populists, the US and Russia." *European View* 9(2): 267–77.

Clark, Wesley K. 2001. *Waging Modern War: Bosnia, Kosovo, and the Future of Combat*. New York: Public Affairs.

Clarke, Michael. 2012. "The Making of Britain's Libya Strategy." In *Short War, Long Shadow: The Political and Military Legacies of the 2011 Libya Campaign*, ed. Adrian Johnson and Saqeb Mueen, 7–14. London: Royal United Services Institute.

Cogan, Charles. 2010. "Washington, Sarkozy, and the Defence of Europe." *European Political Science* 9(2): 165–75.

Cohen, Eliot A. 2002. *Supreme Command: Soldiers, Statesmen, and Leadership in Wartime*. New York: Free Press.

Cooley, Alexander, and James Ron. 2002. "The NGO Scramble: Organizational Insecurity and the Political Economy of Transnational Action." *International Security* 27(1): 5–39.

Crawford, Beverly. 1996. "Explaining Defection from International Cooperation: Germany's Unilateral Recognition of Croatia." *World Politics* 48(4): 482–521.

Cross, Major T. 1985. "Forward Defence—A Time for Change?" *RUSI Journal* 130(2): 19–24.

Daalder, Ivo H., and James Goldgeier. 2006. "Global NATO." *Foreign Affairs* 85(5): 105–13.

Daalder, Ivo H., and Michael E. O'Hanlon. 2000. *Winning Ugly: NATO's War to Save Kosovo*. Washington, DC: Brookings Institution Press.

Davidson, Jason W. 2006. "The Prodi Government and Italy-US Relations: The Case for Optimism." *International Spectator* 41(3): 91–98.

———. 2011. *America's Allies and War: Kosovo, Afghanistan, and Iraq*. New York: Palgrave Macmillan.

Dawson, Grant. 2007. *"Here is Hell": Canada's Engagement in Somalia*. Vancouver: University of British Columbia Press.

Desch, Michael C. 1999. *Civilian Control of the Military: The Changing Security Environment*. Baltimore: Johns Hopkins University Press.

Diamond, Larry Jay, and Marc F. Plattner. 1996. *Civil-Military Relations and Democracy*. Baltimore: Johns Hopkins University Press.

Dieterich, Sandra, Hartwig Hummel, and Stefan Marschall. 2010. *Parliamentary War Powers: A Survey of 25 European Parliaments*. Geneva: Geneva Centre for the Democratic Control of Armed Forces.

Dimitriu, George, and Beatrice de Graaf. 2010. "The Dutch COIN Approach: Three Years in Uruzgan, 2006–2009." *Small Wars and Insurgencies* 21(3): 429–58.

Döring, Holger, and Philip Manow. 2012. "Parliament and Government Composition Database (ParlGov)." *An Infrastructure for Empirical Information on Parties, Elections and Governments in Modern Democracies* 12(10): 1–8.

Drezner, Daniel W. 2007. *All Politics Is Global*. Cambridge: Cambridge University Press.

Duffield, John. 1995. *Power Rules: The Evolution of NATO's Conventional Force Posture*. Stanford, CA: Stanford University Press.

Elgie, Robert. 1999. *Semi-Presidentialism in Europe*. Oxford: Oxford University Press.

———. 2009. "Duverger, Semi-Presidentialism and the Supposed French Archetype." *West European Politics* 32(2): 248–67.

"Erdogan's Lament." 2011. "Erdogan's Lament: What Lies behind Turkey's Ambivalence over NATO's Operation in Libya." *Economist*, April 7.

Etzioni, Amitai. 2012. "The Lessons of Libya." *Military Review* 92(1): 45–54.

Eyre, Dana P., and Marc C. Suchman. 1996. "Status, Norms, and the Proliferation of Conventional Weapons: An Institutional Theory Approach." In *The Culture of National Security: Norms and Identity in World Politics*, ed. Peter J. Katzenstein, 79–113. New York: Columbia University Press.

Farrell, Theo. 1998. "Cultural Realism: Strategic Culture and Grand Strategy in Chinese History." *Review of International Studies* 24 (3): 407–16.

———. 2001. "Transnational Norms and Military Development: Constructing Ireland's Professional Army." *European Journal of International Relations* 7(1): 63–102.

———. 2005. "World Culture and Military Power." *Security Studies* 14(3): 448–88.

———. 2010. "Improving in War: Military Adaptation and the British in Helmand Province, Afghanistan, 2006–2009." *Journal of Strategic Studies* 33(4): 567–94.

Farrell, Theo, and Stuart Gordon. 2009. "COIN Machine: The British Military in Afghanistan." *Orbis* 53(4): 665–83.

Fassina, Neil E. 2004. "Constraining a Principal's Choice: Outcome versus Behavior Contingent Agency Contracts in Representative Negotiations." *Negotiation Journal* 20(3): 435–59.

Feaver, Peter D. 1998. "Modeling Civil-Military Relations: A Reply to Burk and Bacevich." *Armed Forces and Society* 24(4): 595–602.

———. 1999. "Civil-Military Relations." *Annual Review of Political Science* 2(1): 211–41.

———. 2003. "The Civil-Military Gap in Comparative Perspective." *Journal of Strategic Studies* 26(2): 1–5.

Feaver, Peter D., and Christopher Gelpi. 2004. *Choosing Your Battles: American Civil-Military Relations and the Use of Force.* Princeton, NJ: Princeton University Press.

Felbab-Brown, Vanda. 2009. "Peacekeepers among Poppies: Afghanistan, Illicit Economies and Intervention." *International Peacekeeping* 16(1): 100–114.

Foley, Elise. 2011. "House Rebukes Obama Administration on Libya." *Huffington Post*, June 3, 2011.

Foreign Affairs Committee of the House of Commons. 2009. *Global Security: Afghanistan and Pakistan (HC 302).* London: Stationery Office.

Franks, Tommy R. 2005. *American Soldier.* New York: HarperCollins.

Gallis, Paul. 2003. *NATO's Decision-Making Procedure.* Washington, DC: Congressional Research Service.

Gartzke, Erik, and Kristian Skrede Gleditsch. 2004. "Why Democracies May Actually Be Less Reliable Allies." *American Journal of Political Science* 48(4): 775–95.

Gaubatz, Kurt Taylor. 1999. *Elections and War: The Electoral Incentive in the Democratic Politics of War and Peace.* Stanford, CA: Stanford University Press.

Ghez, Jeremy, and F. Stephen Larrabee. 2009. "France and NATO." *Survival: Global Politics and Strategy* 51(2): 77–90.

Glenn, John. 2009. "Realism versus Strategic Culture: Competition and Collaboration?" *International Studies Review* 11(3): 523–51.

Goodwin, Doris Kearns. 2005. *Team of Rivals.* New York: Simon and Schuster.

Gordon, Michael R., and Bernard E. Trainor. 2006. *Cobra Two.* New York: Pantheon Books.

Gourevitch, Philip, and Errol Morris. 2009. *The Ballad of Abu Ghraib.* Toronto: Penguin.

Greenhill, Kelly M. 2010. *Weapons of Mass Migration: Forced Displacement, Coercion, and Foreign Policy*. Ithaca, NY: Cornell University Press.

Grossman, Sandford J., and Oliver D. Hart. 1983. "An Analysis of the Principal-Agent Problem." *Econometrica* 51(1): 7–45.

Haass, Richard. 2009. *War of Necessity, War of Choice: A Memoir of Two Wars*. New York: Simon and Schuster.

———. 2010. "We're Not Winning. It's Not Worth It: Here's How to Draw Down in Afghanistan." *Newsweek*, July 18.

Hagan, Joe D., Philip P. Everts, Haruhiro Fukui, and John D. Stempel. 2001. "Foreign Policy by Coalition: Deadlock, Compromise, and Anarchy." *International Studies Review* 3(2): 169–216.

Hale, Julian. 2009. "Continuing Restrictions Likely on Some NATO Forces in Afghanistan." *Defense News*, September 21.

Hartley, Keith, and Todd Sandler. 1999. "NATO Burden-Sharing: Past and Future." *Journal of Peace Research* 36(6): 665–80.

Hawkins, Darren G. 2006. *Delegation and Agency in International Organizations*. Cambridge: Cambridge University Press.

Hazelbag, Lenny. 2009. "Political Decision Making of the Mission in Uruzgan, a Reconstruction." In *Complex Operations: Studies on Lebanon (2006) and Afghanistan (2006–present)*, ed. Michiel Weger, Frans Osinga, and Harry Kirkels, 251–76. Breda, Netherlands: Netherlands Defence Academy.

Hermann, Margaret G., and Charles F. Hermann. 1989. "Who Makes Foreign Policy Decisions and How: An Empirical Inquiry." *International Studies Quarterly* 33(4): 361–87.

Herspring, Dale. 2009. "Civil-Military Relations in the United States and Russia." *Armed Forces and Society* 35(4): 667–87.

Hillier, Rick. 2010. *A Soldier First: Bullets, Bureaucrats and the Politics of War*. Toronto: HarperCollins.

Hodge, Amanda. 2012. "Afghan Spies to Protect Diggers." *Australian*, February 22.

Hodge, Nathan. 2011. *Armed Humanitarians: The Rise of the Nation Builders*. New York: Bloomsbury.

Holsti, Ole R. 2004. *Public Opinion and American Foreign Policy*. Rev. ed. Ann Arbor: University of Michigan Press.

Horn, Bernd. 2010. *No Lack of Courage: Operation Medusa, Afghanistan*. Toronto: Dundurn.

Hoyle, Craig. 2008. "UK Cancels Typhoon's Icelandic Air Policing Duty." *Flightglobal*, November 25.

Huntington, Samuel P. 1957. *The Soldier and the State: The Theory and Politics of Civil-Military Relations*. Cambridge, MA: Harvard University Press.

Hutton, John. 2009. "The Future of NATO." Speech at the Center for Strategic and International Studies, Washington, DC, March 19.

International Institute for Strategic Studies. 2011. *Operation Unified Protector—Allied Assets Deployed to Libya*. Washington, DC: International Institute for Strategic Studies.

Jankowski, Dominik P., and Col. Tomasz K. Kowalik. 2011. "NATO after Libya." *Armed Forces Journal*, November.

Janowitz, Morris. 1961. *The Professional Soldier*. New York: Free Press.

Jervis, Robert. 1976. *Perception and Misperception in International Politics*. Princeton, NJ: Princeton University Press.

Johnson, Adrian, and Saqeb Mueen, eds. 2012. *Short War, Long Shadow: The Political and Military Legacies of the 2011 Libya Campaign*. London: Royal United Services Institute.

Johnston, Alastair Iain. 1995. *Cultural Realism: Strategic Culture and Grand Strategy in Chinese History*. Princeton, NJ: Princeton University Press.

Johnston, Karin Lynn. 2010. "Germany, Afghanistan, and the Process of Decision Making in German Foreign Policy: Constructing a Framework for Analysis." DPhil diss., University of Maryland.

Jones, Seth G. 2009. *In the Graveyard of Empires: America's War in Afghanistan*. New York: Norton.

Kaarbo, Juliet. 1997. "Prime Minister Leadership Styles in Foreign Policy Decision-Making: A Framework for Research." *Political Psychology* 18(3): 553–81.

———. 2008. "Coalition Cabinet Decision Making: Institutional and Psychological Factors." *International Studies Review* 10(1): 57–86.

———. 2012. *Coalition Politics and Cabinet Decision Making: A Comparative Analysis of Foreign Policy Choices*. Ann Arbor: University of Michigan Press.

Kaarbo, Juliet, and Ryan K. Beasley. 2008. "Taking It to the Extreme: The Effect of Coalition Cabinets on Foreign Policy." *Foreign Policy Analysis* 4(1): 67–81.

Kaarbo, Juliet, and Margaret G. Hermann. 1998. "Leadership Styles of Prime Ministers: How Individual Differences Affect the Foreign Policymaking Process." *Leadership Quarterly* 9(3): 243–63.

Kaarbo, Juliet, and Jeffrey S. Lantis. 2003. "The 'Greening' of German Foreign Policy in the Iraq Case: Conditions of Junior Party Influence in Governing Coalitions." *Acta Politica* 38(3): 201–30.

Katzenstein, Peter J. 1996. *The Culture of National Security: Norms and Identity in World Politics*. New York: Columbia University Press.

Keeler, John T. S. 1993. "Executive Power and Policy-Making Patterns in France: Gauging the Impact of Fifth Republic Institutions." *West European Politics* 16(4): 518–44.

Khong, Yuen Foong. 1992. *Analogies at War: Korea, Munich, Dien Bien Phu, and the Vietnam Decisions of 1965*. Princeton, NJ: Princeton University Press.

Kier, Elizabeth. 1997. *Imagining War: French and British Military Doctrine between the Wars*. Princeton, NJ: Princeton University Press.

Kiewiet, D. Roderick, and Mathew D. McCubbins. 1991. *The Logic of Delegation: Congressional Parties and the Appropriations Process*. Chicago: University of Chicago Press.

Krebs, Ronald R. 2004. "A School for the Nation? How Military Service Does Not Build Nations, and How It Might." *International Security* 28(4): 85–124.

Kreps, Sarah. 2010. "Elite Consensus as a Determinant of Alliance Cohesion: Why Public Opinion Hardly Matters for NATO-Led Operations in Afghanistan." *Foreign Policy Analysis* 6(3): 191–215.

———. 2011. *Coalitions of Convenience: United States Military Interventions after the Cold War*. Oxford: Oxford University Press.

Lafraie, Najibullah. 2009. "NATO in Afghanistan: Perilous Mission, Dire Ramifications." *International Politics* 46(5): 550–72.

Lagassé, Philippe. 2010. *Accountability for National Defence: Ministerial Responsibility, Military Command and Parliamentary Oversight*. Montreal: Institute for Research on Public Policy.

Lagassé, Philippe, and Joel J. Sokolsky. 2009. "A Larger 'Footprint' in Ottawa: General Hillier and Canada's Shifting Civil–Military Relationship, 2005–2008." *Canadian Foreign Policy Journal* 15(2): 16–40.

Leeds, Brett Ashley. 2003. "Alliance Reliability in Times of War: Explaining State Decisions to Violate Treaties." *International Organization* 57(4): 801–27.

Leeds, Brett Ashley, and Burcu Savun. 2007. "Terminating Alliances: Why Do States Abrogate Agreements?" *Journal of Politics* 69(4): 1118–32.

Legro, Jeffrey. 1995. *Cooperation under Fire: Anglo-German Restraint during World War II*. Ithaca, NY: Cornell University Press.

Lepgold, Joseph. 1998. "NATO's Post–Cold War Collective Action Problem." *International Security* 23(1): 78–106.

Levy, Jack S. 1997. "Prospect Theory, Rational Choice, and International Relations." *International Studies Quarterly* 41(1): 87–112.

Lijphart, Arend. 1999. *Patterns of Democracy: Government Forms and Performance in Thirty-Six Countries*. New Haven, CT: Yale University Press.

Lindstrom, Aaron D. 2003. "Consensus Decision Making in NATO: French Unilateralism and the Decision to Defend Turkey." *Chicago Journal of International Law* 4: 579–86.

Lombardi, Ben. 2011. "The Berlusconi Government and Intervention in Libya." *International Spectator* 46(4): 31–44.

Lyne, Mona, and Michael J. Tierney. 2003. "The Politics of Common Agency: Implications for Agent Control with Complex Principals." Paper presented at the American Political Science Meeting, Philadelphia, August.

Mackay, Andrew, and Steve Tatham. 2009. *Behavioural Conflict. From General to Strategic Corporal: Complexity, Adaptation and Influence.* Shrivenham Papers Number 9. Shrivenham, England: Defence Academy of the United Kingdom.

MacKowski, Joanne. 2012. "Table of Military Assets." In *Short War, Long Shadow: The Political and Military Legacies of the 2011 Libya Campaign,* ed. Adrian Johnson and Saqeb Mueen, ix–xii. London: Royal United Services Institute.

Mahnken, Thomas G., and James R. FitzSimonds. 2003. "Revolutionary Ambivalence: Understanding Officer Attitudes toward Transformation." *International Security* 28(2): 112–48.

Maley, William, ed. Forthcoming. *Afghanistan: Civil-Military Lessons Learned—A Comparative Study.* Sydney: Australian Civil-Military Centre.

Maloney, Sean M. 2009. *Confronting the Chaos: A Rogue Military Historian Returns to Afghanistan.* Annapolis, MD: Naval Institute Press.

Maltzman, F. 1998. *Competing Principals: Committees, Parties, and the Organization of Congress.* Ann Arbor: University of Michigan Press.

McCowan, David B. 1987. *The Senate Investigation into the Removal of General of the Army Douglas MacArthur.* PhD diss., Department of History, Mississippi State University.

McCubbins, Mathew D., and Thomas Schwartz. "Congressional Oversight Overlooked: Police Patrols versus Fire Alarms," *American Journal of Political Science* 28: 16–79.

Mearsheimer, John J. 1981. "Maneuver, Mobile Defense, and the NATO Central Front." *International Security* 6(3): 104–22.

———. 1983. *Conventional Deterrence.* Ithaca, NY: Cornell University Press.

Medcalf, Jennifer. 2008. *Going Global or Going Nowhere? NATO's Role in Contemporary International Security.* Oxford: Peter Lang.

Meyer, Christoph. 2006. *The Question for a European Strategic Culture: Changing Norms on Security and Defence in the European Union.* New York: Palgrave-Macmillan.

Michel, Leo G. 2003. *NATO Decisionmaking: Au Revoir to the Consensus Rule?* Strategic Forum 202. Washington, DC: National Defense University Press.

Miller, Gary J. 2005. "The Political Evolution of Principal-Agent Models." *Annual Review of Political Science* 8(1), 203–25.

Miller, Gary J., and Andrew B. Whitford. 2002. "Trust and Incentives in Principal-Agent Negotiations." *Journal of Theoretical Politics* 14(2): 231–67.

Miller, Gary J., and Andrew B. Whitford. 2007. "The Principal's Moral Hazard: Constraints on the Use of Incentives in Hierarchy." *Journal of Public Administration Research and Theory* 17(2): 213–33.

Mirrlees, James. 1976. "The Optimal Structure of Incentives and Authority within an Organization." *Bell Journal of Economic and Management Sciences* 7: 105–31.

Moe, Terry M. 1984. "The New Economics of Organization." *American Journal of Political Science* 28(4): 739–77.

Mueller, John. 2006. *Overblown: How Politicians and the Terrorism Industry Inflate National Security Threats, and Why We Believe Them.* New York: Simon and Schuster.

———. 2009. "Inflating Terrorism." In *American Foreign Policy and the Politics of Fear: Threat Inflation Since 9/11,* ed. A. Trevor Thrall and Jane K. Cramer, 192–209. New York: Routledge.

Mueller, John, and Mark Stewart. 2010. "Hardly Existential: Terrorism as a Hazard to Human Life." Paper presented at the Annual Convention of the International Studies Association, New Orleans.

Murdoch, James C., and Todd Sandler. 1991. "NATO Burden Sharing and the Forces of Change—Further Observations." *International Studies Quarterly* 35(1): 109–14.

Netherlands, Government of. 2005. *Bestrijding internationaal terrorisme: Brief Van De Ministers Van Buitenlandse Zaken, Van Defensie En Voor Ontwikkelingssamenwerking.* The Hague: Government of Netherlands.

———. 2007. *Bestrijding internationaal terrorisme: Brief Van De Ministers Van Buitenlandse Zaken, Van Defensie En Voor Ontwikkelingssamenwerking.* The Hague: Government of Netherlands.

Noetzel, Timo, and Benjamin Schreer. 2012. "More Flexible, Less Coherent: NATO after Lisbon." *Australian Journal of International Affairs* 66(1): 20–33.

Noetzel, Timo, and Benjamin Schreer. 2009. "Does a Multi-Tier NATO Matter? The Atlantic Alliance and the Process of Strategic Change." *International Affairs* 85(2): 211–26.

Nyiri, Zsolt, and Ben Veater-Fuchs. 2011. *Transatlantic Trends 2011.* Washington, DC: German Marshall Fund of the United States.

O'Donnell, Clara Marina. 2012. "Poland's U-Turn on European Defense: A Missed Opportunity?" *Brookings Institution U.S.-Europe Analysis Series* 53(6): 1–7.

Olson, Mancur, and Richard Zeckhauser. 1966. "Economic Theory of Alliances." *Review of Economics and Statistics* 48(3): 266–79.

Oneal, John R., and Mark A. Elrod. 1989. "NATO Burden Sharing and the Forces of Change." *International Studies Quarterly* 33(4): 435–56.

Palazzo, Albert. 2008. "No Casualties Please, We're Soldiers." *Australian Army Journal* 5(3): 65–78.

Palmer, Glenn. 1990. "Corralling the Free Rider: Deterrence and the Western Alliance." *International Studies Quarterly* 34(2): 147–64.

Pearlman, Michael D. 2008. *Truman and MacArthur: Policy, Politics, and the Hunger for Honor and Renown*. Bloomington: Indiana University Press.

Peterson, Susan. 1996. *Crisis Bargaining and the State: The Domestic Politics of International Conflict*. Ann Arbor, MI: University of Michigan Press.

Posen, Barry. 1984. *The Sources of Military Doctrine: France, Britain, and Germany between the World Wars*. Ithaca, NY: Cornell University Press.

Pressman, Jeremy. 2008. *Warring Friends: Alliance Restraint in International Politics*. Ithaca, NY: Cornell University Press.

Public Accounts Committee of the House of Commons. 2009. *Ministry of Defence: Support to High Intensity Operations (HC 895)*. London: Stationery Office.

Qazi, Shehzad H. 2010. "The 'Neo-Taliban' and Counterinsurgency in Afghanistan." *Third World Quarterly* 31(3): 485–99.

Quartararo, Joe, Sr., Michael Rovenolt, and Randy White. 2012. *Libya's Operation Odyssey Dawn: Command and Control*. Washington, DC: National Defense University.

Quintana, Elizabeth. 2012. "The War from the Air." In *Short War, Long Shadow: The Political and Military Legacies of the 2011 Libya Campaign*, ed. Adrian Johnson and Saqeb Mueen, 31–40. London: Royal United Services Institute.

Rashid, Ahmed 2009. *Descent into Chaos: The US and the Disaster in Pakistan, Afghanistan, and Central Asia*. New York: Penguin.

Rathbun, Brian C. 2004. *Partisan Interventions: European Party Politics and Peace Enforcement in the Balkans*. Ithaca, NY: Cornell University Press.

———. 2006. "The Myth of German Pacifism." *German Politics and Society* 24(2): 68–81.

Republic of France. 2008. *The French White Paper on Defence and National Security*. New York: Odile Jacob.

Ricks, Thomas E. 2006. *Fiasco: The American Military Adventure in Iraq*. New York: Penguin.

Rietjens, Sebastiaan J. H. 2008. "Managing Civil-Military Cooperation: Experiences from the Dutch Provincial Reconstruction Team in Afghanistan." *Armed Forces and Society* 34(2): 173–207.

Riste, Olav. 2005. *Norway's Foreign Relations: A History*. 2nd ed. Oslo: Universitetsforlaget.

Roets, Arne, and Alain Van Hiel. 2009. "The Ideal Politician: Impact of Voters' Ideology." *Personality and Individual Differences* 46(1): 60–65.

Roper, Steven D. 2002. "Are All Semipresidential Regimes the Same? A Comparison of Premier-Presidential Regimes." *Comparative Politics* 34(3): 253–72.

Rubin, Barnett R., and Ahmed Rashid. 2008. "From Great Game to Grand Bargain: Ending Chaos in Afghanistan and Pakistan." *Foreign Affairs* 87(6): 30–44.

Rubin, Barnett R., Amin Saikal, and Julian Lindley-French. 2009. "The Way Forward in Afghanistan: Three Views." *Survival* 51(1): 83–96.

Rumsfeld, Donald. 2011. *Known and Unknown: A Memoir.* New York: Sentinel.

Ryjáček, Jan. 2009. "Losing the Power of Parliament? Participation of the Bundestag in the Decision-Making Process Concerning Out-of-Area Military Operations." *German Politics* 18(4): 485–500.

Saideman, Stephen M. 2012. "You Can Check Out Anytime You'd Like: Comparing the Dutch and Canadian 'New' Missions in Afghanistan." Paper presented at the Annual International Studies Association Conference, San Diego, April 1–4.

Saideman, Stephen M., and R. William Ayres. 2008. *For Kin or Country: Xenophobia, Nationalism, and War.* New York: Columbia University Press.

Samuels, David, and Matthew Soberg Shugart. 2010. *Presidents, Parties, and Prime Ministers: How the Separation of Powers Affects Party Organization and Behavior.* Cambridge: Cambridge University Press.

Sanchez, Ricardo S., and Don T. Phillips. 2008. *Wiser in Battle: A Soldier's Story.* New York: HarperCollins.

Sandler, Todd, and John F. Forbes. 1980. "Burden Sharing, Strategy, and the Design of NATO." *Economic Inquiry* 18(3) : 425–44.

Schafer, Mark. 2000. "Issues in Assessing Psychological Characteristics at a Distance: An Introduction to the Symposium." *Political Psychology* 21(3): 511–27.

Shimizu, Hirofumi, and Todd Sandler. 2002. "Peacekeeping and Burden-Sharing, 1994–2000." *Journal of Peace Research* 39(6): 651–68.

Shugart, Matthew Sogberg. 2005. "Semi-Presidential Systems: Dual Executive and Mixed Authority Patterns." *French Politics* 3(3): 323–51.

Shugart, Matthew Sogberg, and John M. Carey. 1992. *Presidents and Assemblies: Constitutional Design and Electoral Dynamics.* Cambridge: Cambridge University Press.

Sloan, Stanley. 2011. "Re-engineering the Transatlantic Security and Defense Relationship." Wilton Park Conference, Report 1129, September 28, 2011. https://www.wiltonpark.org.uk/wp-content/uploads/wp1129-report.pdf, accessed September 15, 2013.

Snyder, Glenn. 2007. *Alliance Politics.* Ithaca, NY: Cornell University Press.

Snyder, Jack L. 1984. *The Ideology of the Offensive: Military Decision Making and the Disasters of 1914.* Ithaca, NY: Cornell University Press.

Stein, Janice Gross, and J. Eugene Lang. 2007. *The Unexpected War: Canada in Kandahar.* Toronto, ON: Viking Canada.

Strasser, Steven. 2004. *The Abu Ghraib Investigations: The Official Reports of the Independent Panel and Pentagon on the Shocking Prisoner Abuse in Iraq*. New York: Public Affairs.

Strøm-Erichsen, Anne-Grete. 2005. *Militære bidrag til operasjoner I Afghanistan og Irak*. Redegjørelse i Stortinget. Oslo: Forsvarsdepartementet.

Stulberg, Adam N. 2005. "Managing Military Transformations: Agency, Culture, and the US Carrier Revolution." *Security Studies* 14(3): 489–528.

Szarka, Joseph. 2009. "Nicolas Sarkozy as Political Strategist: *Rupture Tranquille* or Policy Continuity?" *Modern and Contemporary France* 17(4): 407–22.

Tatham, Steve. 2009. "Tactical Strategic Communication: Placing Informational Effect at the Centre of Command." *British Army Review* 147: 58–66.

Terriff, Terry, Frans Osinga, and Theo Farrell, eds. 2010. *A Tranformation Gap: American Innovations and European Military Change*. Stanford, CA: Stanford University Press.

Thies, Wallace J. 2009. *Why NATO Endures*. Cambridge: Cambridge University Press.

Thruelsen, Peter Dahl. 2008. "Counterinsurgency and a Comprehensive Approach: Helmand Province, Afghanistan." *Small Wars Journal* 19(2): 201–20.

Trønnes, Otto. 2012. "Norwegian Caveats in Afghanistan from 2001–2008." Trondheim: Department of Sociology and Political Science, Norwegian University of Science and Technology.

Tsebelis, George. 2002. *Veto Players: How Political Institutions Work*. Princeton, NJ: Princeton University Press.

UK House of Commons. 2012. *Operations in Libya: Ninth Report of Session 2010-12*. London: Stationery Office.

Unver, Akin. 2011. "NATO's Libya Operation Unpopular in Turkey." *Foreign Policy Association*, May 12.

U.S. Department of Defense. 2005. *The Schlesinger Report: An Investigation of Abu Ghraib*. New York: Cosimo Reports.

Vennesson, Pascal. 2003. "Civil–Military Relations in France: Is There a Gap?" *Journal of Strategic Studies* 26(2): 29–42.

Vogelaar, Ad L. W., and Eric-Hans Kramer. 2004. "Mission Command in Dutch Peace Support Missions." *Armed Forces and Society* 30(3): 409–31.

Wagnsson, Charlotte. 2011. "A Security Community in the Making? Sweden and NATO Post-Libya." *European Security* 20(4): 585–603.

Walt, Stephen M. 1987. *The Origins of Alliances*. Ithaca, NY: Cornell University Press.

Waltz, Kenneth. 1979. *Theory of International Politics*. Reading, MA: Addison-Wesley.

Weitsman, Patricia A. 2004. *Dangerous Alliances: Proponents of Peace, Weapons of War*. Stanford, CA: Stanford University Press.

———. 2013. *Waging War: Alliances, Coalitions, and Institutions of Interstate Violence*. Stanford, CA: Stanford University Press.

Wessel, Ramses A. 2008. "The Netherlands and NATO." In *Legal Implications of NATO Membership: Focus on Finland and Five Allied States*, ed. Juha Rainne, 137–61. Helsinki: Erik Castrén Institute of International Law and Human Rights.

White House. 2011. *United States Activities in Libya*. Washington, DC: White House.

Willett, Lee. 2012. "Don't Forget about the Ships." In *Short War, Long Shadow: The Political and Military Legacies of the 2011 Libya Campaign*, ed. Adrian Johnson and Saqeb Mueen, 41–51. London: Royal United Services Institute.

Williamson, O. E. 1975. *Markets and Hierarchies: Analysis and Antitrust Implications, A Study in the Economics of Internal Organization*. New York: Free Press.

Woodward, Bob. 2002. *Bush at War*. New York: Simon and Schuster.

———. 2004. *Plan of Attack*. New York: Simon and Schuster.

———. 2006. *State of Denial*. New York: Simon and Schuster.

———. 2011. *Obama's Wars*. New York: Simon and Schuster.

Zegart, Amy B. 1999. *Flawed by Design: The Evolution of the C.I.A., J.C.S., and N.S.C.* Stanford, CA: Stanford University Press.

———. 2007. *Spying Blind: The CIA, the FBI, and the Origins of 9/11*. Princeton, NJ: Princeton University Press.

# Index

Page numbers in *italics* indicate a figure or a table.